Evelyn Jacks'

ESSENTIAL TAX FACTS

Secrets and Strategies
for Take-Charge People

2013 EDITION

KNOWLEDGE BUREAU
NEWSBOOKS

WINNIPEG, MANITOBA, CANADA

ISBN No. 978-1-897526-98-9

Printed and bound in Canada

Canadian Cataloguing in Publication Data

Jacks, Evelyn

Evelyn Jacks' Essential tax facts: Secrets and Strategies for Take-Charge People – 2013 ed.

Includes Index

1. Income tax – Canada – Popular works. 2. Tax planning – Canada – Popular works. I. Title. II. Title: Essential tax facts

HJ4661.J212 2006   343.7105'2   C2006-904910-6

Published by: Knowledge Bureau, Inc.
187 St. Mary's Road, Winnipeg, Manitoba R2H 1J2
204-953-4769 Email: reception@knowledgebureau.com

Research and Editorial Assistance: Walter Harder and Associates
Cover and Page Design: Typeworks

MIX
Paper from
responsible sources
FSC® C016245

Table of Contents

Introduction

B ack in 1972, 50 years ago, Canada underwent a major tax reform under the direction of Finance Minister Edgar Benson. Coincidently, this is my 50th book about taxes and tax-efficient wealth management; a subject I started writing about 32 years ago when I was pregnant with my first child.

When you get to know a subject so deeply, over a long period of time, some insights are bound to emerge. I'd like to share some of them with you, because I am passionate about helping you keep more of your hard earned income and capital, in the aftermath of the most significant financial upheaval the modern world has seen.

The first insight is this: Knowing more about your tax system is going to pay off. It will make you richer immediately and give you more control over your financial future. For millions of people this becomes real when they file their tax returns each spring. They become richer because when they are sure they have used all the tax deductions and credits they're entitled to, and they get the biggest tax refund possible, they can focus on building tax-efficient wealth, because they get to work with more of their own money.

When you learn to do that, you'll be *comparatively richer, too.*

That's because the majority of taxpayers are so complacent about their tax affairs that they are willing to prepay and overpay them every two weeks all year long, without earning a cent for it! They happily provide the government with an interest-free loan of their gross wages, and then rejoice at the size of their tax refund in the spring.

Some call that "*intaxication*"... the euphoria of getting a tax refund, which lasts until you realize it was your own money to start with. (Look it up—it's in the Urban Dictionary.) Intaxicated people give up control of the first dollars they earn.

Take charge people, on the other hand, make it their business to initiate sound tax strategies to create bigger dollars to work with *every day*... they "detax" if you will. *"Detaxication"* is important to your financial health, because everyone wants more of your dollars these days, including debt-burdened governments.

A second insight begins there. In response to difficult times, governments are once again adding "super taxes" on six figure taxable incomes, which is an easy thing to shrug off at first glance, if your income is nowhere near that. Most people have no trouble with the concept of increasing taxes on the rich.

But here's the big secret no one is talking about: in the absence of the general averaging provisions Finance Minister Benson introduced with his tax hikes of 50 years ago, today's "super taxes" are an immediate tax on your inheritances. There are millions of dollars in unspent pension accumulations and accrued capital gains. Last surviving spouses—widows and widowers who have frugally saved and worried about having enough for their entire lifetimes—will now leave close to 50% (or more in some cases) to their biggest beneficiary—government—upon their deaths.

If this concerns you, and it should, because it can well be that your financial future is at risk, it's time to take charge. This book will help you unlock the essential tax facts you need to know to pay only the correct amount of tax on your income. At the same time, it will teach you a few simple strategies for the tax-efficient accumulation, growth, preservation and transitioning of your savings, to keep more of them in the family, so future generations can build on your financial legacy.

Tax secrets, strategies and essential tax facts: knowing more about them will help you reward yourself with self-reliance: that is, the peace of mind of knowing there is enough for you and your loved ones to live your life with both dignity and fun! That's what motivated me to learn more about tax 32 years ago and it's been an interesting and rewarding journey I hope you too will embark on and benefit from in this new financial world filled with new tax and pension reforms.

Evelyn Jacks

PART I

Tax Secrets and Strategies

CHAPTER 1

What Governments Know

If you ever want to know what governments know, read the federal and provincial budget papers. They are fascinating documents (really!) and they are compiled by really smart people.

They tell you, for example, what interest rates are projected to be over the next five years on treasury bills and government bonds; and how that compares to growth in the economy, the risk factors to growth, and what inflation rates might be, too. This information can help you make important decisions about your money, like whether you should retreat to the "safety" of bonds where principal is guaranteed, purchase a rental property or pay off a mortgage instead.

The budget forecasts tell us how economic factors and tax changes will impact our investment decisions. For example, you'll find projected inflation rates over the next five year period there, together with the projected growth in tax revenues. When you consider a common decision like whether to buy a Canada Savings Bond, this information can be very valuable.

For example, with interest rates of less than one percent on your CSBs and inflation rates projected at an average of 2% in the time you hold your CSB investment, no matter how you do the math, your principal, though "guaranteed," is losing its purchasing power over time and producing a negative return after taxes.

This is what governments know and the information is yours to work with as you work hard to manage your money. While there is little you can do about the economic or political events that dominate our daily news channels, it is within your scope to understand what governments know and then work in collaboration with our your professional advisors to take charge of your financial future.

Particularly if you have lots of savings, or *will have soon*, perhaps because you will inherit wealth from someone else, earn a large bonus or sell a business, your goal in taking charge of your money today is to build and then preserve your *future wealth*. The tax planning you do will help you connect the dots between what the government knows about economic growth and taxation, and the growth and sustainability of your capital.

> **Here's the tax secret** > Taxes arise not just on *income* but also on *capital*—the money you have saved to create your future income. The growth of wealth in your lifetime will naturally occur if you do some of the right things, but it is also subject to attack from eroders like inflation and uncertain economic outcomes. To secure your own future, and that of your heirs, you can take charge and protect earnings and savings by controlling your taxes.

This is very important because, whether or not you see your financial affairs in this way, *you may be considered to be 'rich' for tax purposes* and in line for new "high income surtaxes" on withdrawal of savings as a pension or on the money that's left unspent. Fortunately, under our system of self-assessment, it is your legal right to arrange your affairs within the framework of the law to pay the least possible taxes. Please read on to learn more.

How Economics and Taxes are Linked to Your Future Income. In this book we will talk how to get better after-tax returns on your investments and the opportunities to make your public and private pension accumulations last longer.

For example, if you know the income level your Old Age Security will be clawed away at, you may better plan your withdrawals from pensions to stay clear of that income threshold. In another example, if you are building your net worth with real estate investments, you will likely be interested in understanding how your increasing property values will be taxed when the assets are eventually sold. It will be important to you that governments keep the capital gains inclusion rate at 50%.

In the past, when there has been too much public debt and not enough economic activity, Old Age Security clawbacks have increased, and so have capital gains inclusion rates. A future increase in interest rates, which are predicted, also boosts public debt charges. As today's longer term borrowing arrangements at low interest rates mature, refinancing debt at higher interest rates becomes very expensive for governments.

We had this scenario in the 80s and 90s, but today, unfortunately our deficits are higher still—over $600 billion for the federal government alone. Provincial debts, of course, add to this. Where does the new money come from to pay for all this debt? Hopefully, it will come from positive economic outcomes that raise taxes: growing economies, higher wages and bigger business profits.

And that's how economics and taxes are linked. If those positive outcomes don't happen, we look to the taxpayer. Recently, in provinces like Ontario and Nova Scotia, and by a new minority government in Quebec, new *high income surtaxes* on the rich have been introduced to pay for public services. This is a worrisome trend for your future wealth. Here's why:

The term "rich" requires definition: you might be surprised that it may apply to your family, too. Windfalls and one-time financial events occur at different times in a family's financial lifecycle and can push your income into a high surtax category. Even Grandpa, today a typical pensioner, will fit into the "rich" profile for tax purposes, if he sells his business or dies with a large accumulation in his unspent RRIF account.

According to a recent *CD Howe Institute* study[1], rich people do indeed pay their fair share. The 25,000 families who will be subject to the high income tax in Ontario for example, already pay 20% of all taxes. In fact, the top 1% of earners make about 12% of all income from taxable sources in Ontario but pay 27% of all income taxes. The top 10% of earners are responsible for 66% of all net income taxes, and the top 25% are responsible for 88% of all provincial income taxes. Meanwhile, the bottom 75% of all taxpayers pay only 12% of all taxes.

What happens when we overtax the top 25% of taxpayers? According to the CD Howe Institute 'rich' people respond to over-taxation in a variety of different ways, and the outcomes, not surprisingly, have the effect of reducing revenues to governments. In a nutshell, while some people will do nothing, many will do the things that make everything worse: reduce personal productivity by refusing overtime shifts, for example, or move to a lower taxed jurisdiction.

That's a particular challenge for indebted provinces. Because wealthier people have the resources to move, they will, especially if they also have skills that are in demand. In Canada, such moves tend to be inter-provincial, so those

---

[1] 2012 CD How Institute, "The Unexpected Impact of Ontario's 'Tax on the Rich'".

provinces that tax too aggressively may in fact find they will lose their top tax producers to other lower-taxed provincial jurisdictions.[2]

Other taxpayers will do the wrong things: they will enter the underground economy and become tax evaders, making it difficult for legitimate business owners to compete against those who don't pay taxes. Everyone else will need to cover the tax gap, and suffer the consequences of increased audit activities. Most people don't want to experience those negative outcomes.

A better strategy is to build tax-efficient wealth, to protect against difficult economic times.

Tax Strategy

Average Canadians who have accumulated wealth for their future will keep more of it if they can connect the dots between economic and tax policies. Most high income earners will respond to the possibility of rising tax brackets and rates by making it their priority to plan for tax-efficient income sources, manage the taxes on their appreciating assets, and be more vigilant about making sure all the tax deductions and credits they are entitled to are used.

---

[2] 2004, J.Rhys Kesselman and Ron Cheung, "Tax Incidence, Progressivity and Inequality in Canada," The Canadian Tax Journal, 52(3):709-789.

CHAPTER 2

What You Should Know

We have a "*self-assessment*" system in which we compute and pay our taxes. The onus is on each individual filer to compute taxable income, determine which deductions and credits to claim to arrive at income taxes payable and to show that the figures we have computed are right in case of a tax audit.

It is indeed the law, to pay your taxes. Every once in a while, someone believes they are a "natural person" not required to file tax returns or pay taxes in Canada. Just to be completely clear: that's not only nonsense, but CRA's successful convictions of tax delinquents is hard evidence of the reality. You can look that up for yourself on the CRA website.

You will see that the CRA can and will fine you if you owe money but don't file on time and pay. The late filing, gross negligence and tax evasion penalties are enormous, not to mention the interest compounding daily at the *prescribed interest rate* set by the government (based on the average rate for 90-day Treasury Bills during the first month of the last quarter) plus 4%.

The tax year for most tax filers is the "calendar year"—January to December. So, you'll want to plan carefully then, before you move to a province with higher tax rates. Do that in January rather than December, so that your income for the whole year is taxed at the lower rates.

Here's the tax secret > If you move around a lot, exactly how do you know what's your province of residence? Provincial residency (and the requirement to pay taxes to a specific provincial jurisdiction) is based on where you "ordinarily reside" on December 31.

Provincial tax rates and credits do vary from one province to the next and are computed using additional provincial schedules attached to the federal return (T1). In Quebec, the definition of taxable income differs; but all the other provinces use a common definition. The variations between the provinces come not only from the tax brackets and rates but also in the various refundable and non-refundable tax credits provinces extend to you. In the rest of our discussions throughout this book, we will refer to provisions relating specifically to the federal return, and the provinces that have a common definition of taxable income.

Your T-Slips. Most income earned is reported to you and to CRA by employers and financial institutions on an information slip. CRA does a "matching" of the slips and what you have entered on your return. You can expect to receive either a *Notice of Reassessment* if the amounts don't match. The most common information slips for those who aren't receiving pension income are: T3—*Statement of Trust Income Allocations and Designations,* T4—*Statement of Remuneration Paid, and the* T5—*Statement of Investment Income.*

Self-Reporting Income, Deductions and Credits. As a general rule, CRA will require you to keep documentation showing any income sources for which you did not receive a slip, as well as the amounts paid for any deductions or credits you will claim. Often CRA provides a form for the taxpayer to calculate the allowable deduction or credit. Even though you're not required to submit most paper documentation with the tax return, you must keep those records for at least seven years.

You'll receive a "high level" introduction to the elements of your tax return in this section of the book, so you can learn what's important from a tax planning perspective. But for a line-by-line tax preparation guide, please pick up a copy of *Jacks on Tax.*

Tax Strategy

Tax compliance is necessary so file a tax return every year. It's always best to keep documentation for 10 years, because you can adjust most federal tax provisions over a 10 year period, in case of errors or omissions. Voluntarily complying to correct errors and omissions will also help you to avoid expensive and unnecessary gross negligence and tax evasion penalties, plus compounding interest.

PART II

The Tax Return

CHAPTER 3

Your Most Significant Financial Document

Most people don't have a personal net worth statement or financial plan at their fingertips—although they should, to better gauge financial outcomes and make decisions. But over 26 million people do file a tax return because they are required by law to do so on time if they are taxable.

If you are not taxable, you'll be highly motivated to file because your T1 is your ticket to lucrative tax credits and social benefits that can supplement your income all year long in some cases. In fact, over six million or 25% of those who file a tax return in Canada, file a "nil return" largely for the purposes of claiming refundable tax credits from federal and provincial governments.

Here's the tax secret > For millions of people, the tax return is the most significant financial document and filing one is probably the most important financial transaction of the year. It's the key document used to redistribute wealth to lower and middle income families. Understanding your tax filing outcomes, therefore, is a great place for families of all income levels to be more proactive about their financial planning.

The tax return reports on history—last year's financial transactions. It adds the income you earned 'actively' from employment or self-employment, to the income you earned on 'passive' sources—pensions, investments and the gains or losses earned when you disposed of assets. Those terms are important ones to keep in mind as you think about leveraging your tax savings opportunities.

Balance Due Days. Your tax return "reconciles" what the correct amount of tax should have been for the *calendar year*—January to December. It then establishes whether you will receive a refund (if you overpaid your taxes), or if you must pay a balance due. For most people that balance due date is April 30. However, if you are a proprietor—the owner of an unincorporated small business—you and your spouse have until June 15 to file without incurring late filing penalties. But be aware that you'll pay interest on your balance due, as if your filing deadline was April 30, so it always pays to file by then if you are self-employed.

A refund is a bad thing. This tax filing outcome, unfortunately, is stacked in the government's favor, because, fully 60% of Canadians overpay their taxes during the year with the average tax refund clocking in at $1,580!

That's more than many people save for their retirement every year, and why you should take the time to discover some of the tax secrets and strategies in this book: the majority of people in Canada have the opportunity to take charge of more of their own hard earned money by arranging their affairs within the framework of the law to pay the least taxes possible. You can too.

For the approximately 15% of taxpayers who owe money to the government at the end of April (or June 15 in the case of unincorporated business owners), reducing the average amount they must pay (about $4,000), is the biggest concern.

A reduced cash flow is at stake at tax time and all year long in these cases. When you owe the government more than $3,000 this year or in either of the preceding two tax years, you'll fall into a *"quarterly instalment remittance"* profile. That means, you will be required to prepay your income taxes for next year starting on September 15, December 15, March 15 and June 15. This can cause significant financial hardship, as you can imagine, if you just finished paying $3,000 or more on April 30 or June 15. A few tax secrets and strategies can help you increase your cash flow.

Tax Strategy

Avoid owing more than $2,999 at your balance due date. Consider making your RRSP contribution, more charitable donations, splitting income between two tax years or with family members, deferring income to the future, or changing your income sources to "average down" the taxes you pay on your income overall. Filing as a tax savvy family helps, too.

CHAPTER 4

Who is Taxed in Canada?

Let's dig a little deeper now, into some of the essential tax facts you can use to formulate your own tax-savvy approach to putting more of your own money to work for you. Individuals resident in Canada must file a tax return if any of the following apply:

- They owe income taxes on their balance due date.
- CRA requests that they file a return.
- They have an amount outstanding under the RRSP Home Buyers' Plan (HBP) or Lifelong Learning Plan (LLP).
- They are required to contribute to the Canada Pension Plan (CPP) because of self-employment income.
- They are self-employed and opted to participate in the *Employment Insurance (EI)* program for self-employed taxpayers.
- They disposed of capital property or otherwise earned a capital gain.
- They elect jointly with their spouse to split *eligible pension income.*
- They received an advanced payment of the *Working Income Tax Benefit (WITB).*
- They are required to repay Old Age Security benefits.

The most common reasons taxpayers who are not required to file may wish to file one anyway are:

- To receive a refund of overpaid income taxes.
- To apply for federal refundable tax credits like the Canada Child Tax Benefit (CCTB), GST/HST Credit or the Working Income Tax Benefit.
- To report capital losses for the purposes of reducing capital gains in the prior three years or to carry those loss balances forward to offset capital gains in the future.
- To qualify for provincial tax credits and benefits.

What happens when you have income from foreign sources? In some countries, such as the United States, taxation is based on citizenship. In Canada, however, the government levies income taxes based on residency.

Here's the tax secret > As a general rule, residents of Canada are taxed on their *world income* in Canadian dollars. In addition, the government imposes income taxes on non-residents who earn income in Canada.

Where income is taxed in more than one jurisdiction, tax treaties have been worked out so that credit is given for taxes already paid to the foreign jurisdiction. If you were subject to withholding taxes in a foreign country, be sure to claim a *foreign tax credit*.[3]

Residency. For most individuals, the question residency is a straight-forward one. If you reside in Canada for 183 days or more, you're a resident for tax purposes, and you must file a tax return if the taxes due on your world income less deductions exceeds your credits. The question of residency gets trickier when you spend part of the year outside Canada.

Some people are considered "deemed residents." This includes those who visit Canada for 183 days or more in the year, students studying abroad temporarily or members of the Canadian Armed Forces, those working in a foreign country under a program of the Canadian International Development Agency or those who work as a high commissioner, ambassador, officer or servant of Canada, for example. Also included in the definition are spouses or children of those taxpayers.

"*Immigrants*" become residents once they establish their permanent residency in Canada. "*Emigrants*" become non-residents of Canada once they establish permanent residency in another country.

Immigrants and emigrants are often referred to as 'part-year residents' for tax purposes. Part-year residents are taxable on world income for the period in which they are resident in Canada. For the remainder of the year, they are taxed as non-residents.

In short, an immigrant will file a tax return in the year of immigration and report on that return world income earned after immigration. An emigrant will file a tax return for the year of emigration which includes world income earned prior to emigration.

---

[3] A foreign tax credit is credit against your Canadian taxes for income or profit taxes paid to a foreign jurisdiction with which Canada has a tax treaty.

Here's the tax secret > Emigrants from Canada must file a "final
return" to which a departure tax will be applied to capital gains
resulting in the increase in value of taxable assets as of the date
of departure.

Most people and their money belong to one taxing jurisdiction or another,
which depends on where their permanent residence is. While some board a
sailboat and start travelling around the world, hoping to avoid tax altogether,
governments tend to attach residency to your last taxing jurisdiction when
you don't take up residence in another jurisdiction. Knowing that will help
you comply and avoid costly penalties and interest for failure to file, when
you are compelled to do so, retroactively.

Non-Residents. In addition to taxing the world income of residents, the
government of Canada imposes income taxes on non-residents who earn
income in Canada. Except where there is an international tax agreement
restricting the collection of such taxes, anyone in Canada who pays income
to a non-resident is required to withhold income taxes from those payments.

In most cases, this is the only tax that the government will get on that income
as the non-resident will generally not be filing a Canadian income tax return.
In certain circumstances, non-residents may file a Canadian income tax
return and get a refund of some or all of the taxes withheld. For line-by-line
tax filing tips, please see my book for do-it-yourself filers, *Jacks on Tax*.

Tax Strategy

Remember that international tax treaties now make it more
difficult for mobile taxpayers around the world to shirk their
responsibilities to the tax department. Filing a tax return on time
in the right taxing jurisdiction and province will preserve your
rights to portability of income sources, pensions and savings,
especially if you plan to travel in your future.

CHAPTER 5

What's Your Tax Bracket?

To achieve long term financial success, you will want to understand how the tax system works to your best advantage. Every dollar saved in tax is another dollar that could be invested to create wealth: financial sustainability and peace of mind.

Here's the tax secret > There are only six things you need to know about the marginal tax rate system in Canada, which helps you understand how the next "like" dollar you earn will be taxed. You've learned a couple of them already and understood an important concept about how we are taxed in Canada.

Under our *"progressive system of taxation,"* you'll pay more the more you earn, but you may also receive less in income redistribution. Here are the six things to know:

1. **Canadian residents are taxed on world income in Canadian funds.**

2. **There are two levels of tax.** Canadians pay income taxes to both the Federal and Provincial Governments.

3. **Every individual has a Tax Free Zone:** the Basic Personal Amount.

    (a)   The BPA on the federal return is indexed annually with inflation.

    (b)   The BPA is different for each province, and may differ from the federal amount. Depending on the province, it may or may not be indexed.

    (c)   Other tax deductions and credits available to the individual may increase the Tax Free Zone.

4. **Federal Tax Brackets and Rates.** The tax system is based on a series of incremental income ranges (i.e.: tax brackets) to which tax rates are applied. The Federal Tax Brackets at the time of writing are shown in the table below:

Federal Tax Brackets

Bracket	Lower Level	Upper Level	Tax Rate
1	0	$10,822	0%
2	$10,823	$42,707	15%
3	$42,708	$85,414	22%
4	$85,415	$132,406	26%
5	$132,407+		29%

Accordingly, if you're single and earned $100,000 in taxable income:

- The first $10,822 would be taxed at a rate of zero.
- The amount earned in bracket 2 would be taxed at 15%.
- The amount earned in bracket 3 would be taxed at 22%.
- The amount earned between $85,415 and $100,000 would be taxed at 26%.
- The result is "Federal" tax payable.

It may make sense, that if your income situation may bump you into the next tax bracket (example: you are withdrawing taxable income from your RRIF or are going to receive a bonus at work), that you would try to avoid that extra bump in your tax rate by trying to time some of the income to arrive in the next tax year, do some income splitting with a family member if the income qualifies, or reduce income with an RRSP deduction, if you have the available contribution room.

5. **Different income sources attract different marginal tax rates.** A taxpayer's marginal tax rate is a measure of the rate of tax that they will pay on the next dollar of income earned (and therefore it is also a measure of the amount of income tax that would be saved by a deduction of one dollar). As you'll recall, there are four different rates of tax payable at the federal level—the higher the taxpayer's income, the higher the tax rate. Each province also levies taxes on its residents in a similar manner. Only one province—Alberta—has a flat tax rate.

Because preferential income tax treatment is given to dividends and capital gains, a taxpayer's marginal tax rate differs depending on the type of income as well as their province of residence.

Marginal tax rates can differ, depending on a variety of tax attributes attached to your income. For example, the highest marginal rates will apply to ordinary employment income, interest income, rental income as well as public and private pension sources, such as RRIF withdrawals.

Other income sources, such as: dividend income, and capital gains income resulting from increases in value of capital assets upon disposition, attract different marginal tax rates, due to the way tax is calculated on these sources.

Consider the example shown on the calculator image below:

- An Ontario resident has $100,000 in taxable income.
- You can see both i) the "average tax rate" and ii) the "marginal tax rate." The average tax rate is the total tax paid on taxable income, divided by the total income subject to tax. The marginal tax rate is the tax rate on the next dollar of income earned.
- The table shows the marginal tax rates for four types of income earned: i) ordinary income, ii) dividends from a privately owned small business corporation, iii) dividends from a publicly owned corporation and iv) capital gains income.

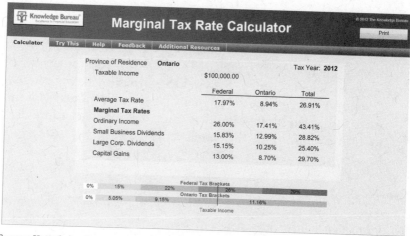

Source: Knowledge Bureau E-Tools available at knowledgebureau.com

Use this information to make important investment decisions that are tax efficient:

- **What is the type of income you are making today?** (ordinary income, dividends from small business corporations, public company dividend, or capital gains income)?

- What tax rate are you paying on that income source?
- How close is your income to the next tax bracket above this?
- How much additional income you can draw, from the same source, before your marginal tax rate changes?
- How close is your income to the next tax bracket below this income level? This will tell you how much tax you may save by re-allocating income from one source to another. Notice how both the federal and provincial tax bracket ranges are displayed at the bottom of the calculator.

6. **What tax bracket are other family members in?** While we are taxed as individuals, most Canadians make economic decisions as a family unit. In the case of some tax provisions, net family income is a factor as well. That's why family tax filing is more powerful. It's the subject of the next part of the book.

However, as an example, if a spouse is taxed at a lower tax rate today, or will be in the future, family income splitting may make sense. Whenever income can be shifted from a higher-income taxpayer to the income of a lower-income taxpayer, within the framework of the law so as to pay the least amount of tax, there is a significant tax benefit.

The tax department doesn't like this of course. For those reasons, the *Attribution Rules* must be observed. These rules, discussed in more depth later in the book, generally disallow the transfer of income or capital from a higher earner in the family to a lower, with certain exceptions. However, couples may get around these rules by drawing up a bona fide loan between them to transfer capital with commercial terms and prescribed interest rates. In other cases, one spouse can hire the other to earn income from the family business. The tax advantages can be significant.

Here's the tax secret > Consider that a single taxpayer earning $100,000 will pay approximately $27,000 in income tax. Alternatively, two $50,000 income earners will pay about $20,500 in tax. *This is an annual saving of close to $6,500; projected over 20 years, a total saving of over for the family of over $130,000.*

What income source should be earned next? If you were to receive another source of income, what would be the tax impact be? If you have a choice, for example, when both spouses have RRSP accumulations, who should withdraw the income? These are important questions because taking the time to consider them will in fact both increase your after-tax cash flow and preserve your capital.

Tax Strategy

By better understanding how your current and next dollars of income are taxed, you can, in consultation with your professional financial advisors, better plan to minimize tax, and keep more value in your capital accumulations. In fact, small changes in your taxable income structure create the after-tax income results you need, *helping you to avoid taking more risks in your investment selection strategies.* This is also a great hedge against inflation, because you'll keep more money invested and compounding in growth.

CHAPTER 6

How Income Sources are Taxed

You already know a lot about the taxation of income sources from our discussion of marginal tax rates. Let's dig a little deeper now and better explain the tax attributes attached to "active" and "passive" income, so you pay the least amount of taxes legally possible on all your earnings.

A. Active Income

There are two types of "active earnings": employment and self-employment.

Employment Income. Most Canadians will have employment income at some point in their careers. Employers must issue T4 slips by the end of February of the following year. On the T4 slip the employer will indicate the taxable amount of wages or salaries in Box 14, but also the taxable perks or benefits of employment which may not have been received in cash. An employer-provided vehicle is a common example.

The T4 slip also lists amounts that have been withheld from the employee's paycheque for which a tax deduction or credit is available. This can include Statutory Deductions the employer is required to make: CPP contributions, EI premiums and Income Taxes. Employer-sponsored pension plans (or Registered Pension Plans (RPP)), union dues and work-based charitable donations are examples of non-statutory deductions.

These amounts are claimed as non-refundable credits on the tax return:

- CPP contributions through employment
- Employment Insurance premiums paid
- Donations made through the employer

RPP contributions and union dues are claimed as deductions on the appropriate lines.

Here's the tax secret > Employment income is "qualifying" income for many lucrative tax deductions and credits on the tax return. This includes:

- Contributions to an RRSP.
- Child care expenses incurred to earn that employment income.
- The disability supports deduction if the tax filer is disabled and requires assistance to earn that employment income.
- Moving expenses if he or she moved at least 40 km closer to a new work location in Canada.
- Employment expenses if he or she was required to pay those expenses in order to earn that employment income.
- Clergy residence deduction and a deduction for Canadian Armed Forces and Police working in a high risk "war zone."
- A home relocation loan deduction if the employer accepted an employer-provided loan to take a job at a new location.
- The securities option deduction if the employee reports a taxable benefit as a result of exercising an option to purchase shares in the employer's company or a previously deferred benefit which has been added to income.
- A northern residents deduction if they live in a prescribed northern zone for at least six months beginning or ending in the taxation year.

Employees are also eligible to claim the Canada Employment Amount, a non-refundable credit of approximately $1,100 to acknowledge the costs of driving to and from work, lunches, clothing and other expenses of working for a living.

Self-Employment. Self-employment income is income from a business owned by a proprietor or the shareholders of a corporation. As a corporation is a separate legal entity, it must file a separate T2 tax return.

For the purposes of this book, we'll discuss proprietorships, which are unincorporated business entities. Net income or "profit" from the proprietorship must be reported on the T1 tax return. All reasonable expenses that were incurred to earn income from the business may be deducted in computing the "profit" from the business.

For the most part, business income is self-reported. That is, the individual prepares a statement of income and expenses for the business and adds the net business income to his or her other income for the year when they file their tax returns.

In addition, the most common amounts eligible for non-refundable tax credits on the T1 return include:

- CPP contributions on income from self-employment.
- Employment Insurance premiums paid if the taxpayer elects to participate in the EI program to be eligible for special benefits.

Net income from self-employment is qualifying income for the purposes of the following:

- Making and deducting contributions to an RRSP.
- Claiming child care expenses incurred to earn that self-employment income.
- Claiming the disability supports deduction if he or she is disabled and requires assistance to earn that self-employment income.
- Claiming moving expenses if he or she moved at least 40 km closer to a new business location in Canada.
- Claiming the "employer's portion" of CPP contributions payable on self-employment income as a deduction.

This topic is a large one and the subject of the book *Make Sure It's Deductible* by Evelyn Jacks, available from www.knowledgebureau.com.

B. Passive Income

The income that we will discuss most in this book is income from property. This is a specific type of income that is not actively earned by the taxpayer like employment or self-employment income, but is income that is earned on a capital asset. The most common types of income from property are:

- Interest income
- Dividends
- Rents
- Royalties

We will be discussing each of these in detail in the coming chapters. Note however, that capital gains, which may result from the sale or deemed disposition of a capital asset are not considered to be income from property and the rules that apply to income from property do not apply to capital gains.

In the *Income Tax Act,* income from property is defined as the "profit" from that property. Although the *Act* does not specifically define "profit" this is interpreted to mean that in calculating income from property (and also from a business), the taxpayer may deduct any reasonable expense that is incurred in earning that income.

This is quite different from employment income where any expense not specifically allowed by the *Act* may not be deducted from employment income. The most common expenses deducted from income from property are carrying charges such as:

- Safety deposit box fees
- Accounting fees
- Investment counsel fees
- Management and safe custody fees
- Interest paid on money borrowed to make the investment.

As noted above, capital gains are not income from property so carrying charges may not be claimed against capital gains income.

Special rules apply to certain types of income from property, specifically dividends from taxable Canadian corporations and rents. These rules will be discussed in detail later.

Capital Gains. A capital gain occurs when an asset whose value has increased over its cost base is sold or deemed to be sold. More specifically, a capital gain is calculated as:

Proceeds of Disposition – Adjusted Cost Base – Outlays and Expenses

Capital gains are given preferential income tax treatment in that the taxpayer is not required to include the full capital gain in income. The capital gain is multiplied by an inclusion rate (currently 50%) to determine the taxable capital gain. In later chapters, we'll go into detail about each of these terms as well as the special rules that apply to specific types of capital gains.

Other Types of Income. Other types of taxable income include:

- Old Age Security Benefits
- Canada Pension Plan Benefits
- Registered Pension Plan income
- Foreign pension income
- RRSP or RRIF income
- RDSP income
- RESP income and taxable portions of research grants or student awards

• Taxable support payments received (generally spousal support)

Please see the commentary on tax savvy retirements, investing and life events later in the book. For help with do-it-yourself tax filing, please see *Jacks on Tax*, available at www.knowledgebureau.com

Adventures and concerns in the nature of trade. Briefly, an "adventure or concern in the nature or trade" is a term used by CRA to describe a source of income that it considers to be business income even though a business has not been set up by the taxpayer. The activities generally involve a transaction or a series of transactions which may appear to be capital in nature (i.e. the taxpayer prefers to report income is a capital gain and only 50% taxable) but because of their relation to the taxpayer's other sources of income or because of the number of similar transactions, CRA considers them to be business income (100% taxable).

This can bring an unwelcome and expensive change on reassessment of taxes after a tax audit. You'll want to seek the help of an experienced tax professional to determine whether you have a good case for a reversal of CRA's opinion.

Tax Strategy

You will get the best after-tax results if you can arrange to earn a variety of different income sources, thereby "averaging down" taxes payable each year because different marginal tax rates apply to different income sources. Earning active income will also help you to fund future retirement income sources.

CHAPTER 7

Tax Exempt Income

If you can get it—and I know you can—a great tax efficiency strategy is to earn more tax exempt income. There are in fact, many sources, of which most people are unaware.

Here's the tax secret > As a general rule, exempt income sources are not entered on the Canadian tax return at all. If you reported these amounts in error, you may contact the tax department to have them removed.

The most common types of exempt income are the following:
- Capital gains on the sale of a home used as a principal residence
- Capital gains on publicly traded shares donated to a registered charity or private foundation
- TFSA income earnings and withdrawals
- Inheritances
- Income exempt by virtue of a statute including the *Indian Act*
- Canadian Service Pensions, *War Veterans Allowance Act* Allowances
- Certain employee benefits, like education required by the employer
- Lottery winnings
- Proceeds from accident, disability, sickness or income maintenance plans where the taxpayer has made all the (non-deductible) premiums
- Refundable provincial or federal tax credits
- Payments for Volunteer Emergency Services—up to $1,000 if the Volunteer Firefighter Tax Credit is not claimed
- Social Assistance Payments received for providing foster care

- Scholarships and Bursaries for students eligible to claim the full-time Tuition, Education and Textbook Amount or that relate to elementary or secondary programs
- RCMP Pension or Compensation received in respect of an injury, disability or death arising directly out of, or directly connected with, the service of a member in the RCMP
- MLA and Municipal Officers Expense Allowances
- Service Pensions from Other Countries on account of disability or death arising out of war service received from a foreign country that was an ally of Canada at the time of the war service

Tax Strategy

Most Canadians can significantly increase their wealth over their lifetimes by earning three tax exempt income sources: gains on the sale or disposition of their principal residence, investments in a TFSA and the private funding of wage loss replacement plans, which provide a tax exempt income should something happen to your ability to earn a living.

CHAPTER 8

Managing the Dreaded T1

A basic understanding of the elements of the T1 tax return is required to have a fruitful conversation about a successful and tax-efficient outcome for your income and capital. This is true even if it's your goal never to do your own tax return.

Here's the tax secret > There are only four five basic elements in the T1 return, which you'll need to become familiar with. It helps to print out a copy of your tax return from your tax software or CRA's website to become more familiar with them. Here they are:

1. **Total Income**	Line 150 of the Tax Return
2. **Net Income**	Line 236 of the Tax Return
3. **Taxable Income**	Line 260 of the Tax Return
4. **Non-Refundable Tax Credits**	Line 350 of Schedule 1
5. **Taxes Payable**	Line 435 of the Tax Return

Total Income takes into account the taxable amounts of all your income sources, for example:

- *Ordinary income.* The full amount of employment and pension income and interest earnings received or accrued every year. These income groups are also referred to as "ordinary income" because 100% of them are included in total income.
- *Grossed-up dividends.* These are the actual dividends you received, but for tax purposes they are "grossed up" to a higher amount which roughly represents the before-tax earnings of a corporation. Later on the return, a dividend tax credit offsets this grossed-up dividend for

an advantageous tax result. However, the gross-up will reduce refundable and non-refundable tax credits.

- *Net rental income* and *net business income* from a proprietorship or partnership. This is what's left after reasonable expenses have been deducted from gross earnings.
- 50% of net capital gains, calculated as the amount after outlays and expenses and capital losses of the year are applied.

Net income, on the other hand is used to determine the level of refundable and non-refundable tax credits a taxpayer is entitled to. Those non-refundable tax credits are found on Schedule 1; whereas the refundable credits are often simply calculated automatically by the government and sent directly to you. In some cases the figure on Line 236 can also affect provincial user fees, like per diem rates at nursing homes, for example. It's a very important line, therefore, because it influences how much you'll receive in income redistribution. The deductions leading to net income are also very valuable—increasingly so the higher your income. Often missed are lucrative claims for child care or moving expenses, employment expenses or carrying charges and of course, the deduction for your RRSP contributions.

Following line 234 you'll find line 235: Social Benefit Repayment. This line is used to subtract any amounts of Employment Insurance, Old Age Security and Net Federal Supplements that must be repaid because the taxpayer's net income before these repayments (line 234) is too high. When planning for income levels, especially in retirement, it's important to stay clear of the applicable "clawback zones" for these benefits. See the next chapter for details.

Taxable income is the figure upon which provincial and federal taxes are calculated. Federal taxes are reduced by non-refundable tax credits like the Basic Personal Amount which is standard for everyone on the federal return, but this amount may vary on the provincial portions of the return.

Non-Refundable Tax Credits. From the BPA to the spousal amount, amounts for dependants under 18, medical expenses and charitable donations, public transit use, children's fitness and arts activities and amounts for disabled dependants as well as students, these amounts have the same value no matter what your income level is. However, to use them you must have taxable income. They are worth nothing to you otherwise and they cannot be carried forward to a future tax year if you don't need them.

With the exception of the donation credit, taxes are reduced on the federal tax return by 15% of the credit amount. To illustrate this, consider a taxpayer whose federal tax rate is 29%. A $1,000 deduction reduces taxes payable by

$290 ($1,000 x 29%) but a personal amount of $1,000 reduces taxes payable by $150 ($1,000 x 15%).

Each taxpayer is eligible to claim the *basic personal amount* ($10,822 for 2012). This means that each taxpayer in a family may earn up to $10,822 income without paying any income tax. This is an important figure for reducing income taxes within a family unit. In Ontario in 2012, for example, the income taxes payable on $43,244 earned by taxpayer in a family of four would have to pay $3,832 income taxes. If each of the family members earned $10,822 (same total income) then the family would pay no taxes at all.

The *age amount* is available only to taxpayers who are over age 64. The amount is reduced by 15% of the taxpayer's net income in excess of the base amount ($33,884 for 2012). This reduction in the age amount is equivalent to an additional 2.25% tax on seniors whose income is in the range $33,884 to $78,684 (for 2012).

The *amount for a spouse or common-law partner* (as well as the amount for an eligible dependant) is the same as the basic personal amount but is reduced by the dependant's net income (and eliminated when the dependant's net income reaches $10,822 (in 2012)). New for 2012, this amount is increased by $2,000 if the dependant is infirm.

The *pension income amount* of $2,000 is available to taxpayers who have eligible pension income. If the taxpayer's eligible pension income is less than $2,000 the amount is limited to the amount of the income.

The amount for *charitable donations* is the only non-refundable credit where the tax reduction is not 15% of the amount claimed. For charitable donations in excess of $200, the credit rate is 29%. For taxpayers with income below $128,800 (for 2012) this means that the credit for donating amounts over $200 is more than the taxes paid on the amount donated.

Taxes Payable, Line 435. This is, of course, the most interesting number of all… total taxes payable to federal and provincial governments. What's on your line 435? Are you aware of the total taxes you are required to pay? Most people are not. If you think that number should be lower, now is the time to plan how to do it, all year long.

Social Assistance. It's worth mentioning that at the bottom of page 2 of your tax return is a list of non-taxable sources of income including

- Workers' compensation benefits
- Social assistance payments
- Net federal supplements

While these amounts increase total and net income, they are not used in the calculation of taxes, deductions or credits; rather the amounts reduce benefits from some other government programs because they increase net income, the figure on which most refundable and non-refundable tax credits are calculated. This income is deducted at line 250 so that it is not included in taxable income.

Tax Strategy

Everyone should try to file their own tax return at least once. It's a life skill that's not bound to disappear—you will be paying income taxes for the rest of your life, so learn about the structure of the tax system so you can exercise your rights and make better decisions all year long.

CHAPTER 9

Clawback Zones

When a taxpayer's income falls into a clawback zone—for example where a portion of a social benefit like OAS or EI must be repaid or a refundable tax credit such as the Canada Child Tax Benefit is reduced, the taxpayer's marginal tax rate could be significantly higher than those who are not subject to a clawback. That's because not only do you pay more taxes as your income rises, but your eligibility for certain benefits decreases too. That "double whammy" hits low to middle income earners harder than other taxpayers.

For these reasons, an RRSP contribution for those who have the qualifying earned income and are age eligible, can be very valuable, as the RRSP deduction will decrease the net income upon which the clawbacks are determined. Two clawbacks are particularly vexing to taxpayers: the clawback of the EI benefits and the clawback of the Old Age Security Benefits.

EI Benefits Repayment. Taxpayers who receive *regular* EI benefits more than once in any 10-year period are required to repay the lesser of 30% of the benefits received and their income in excess of the base amount. This is generally the case for seasonal construction workers or others who work part of the year only.

For 2012, the base amount for EI repayment is $57,375. This means the taxpayer, who may be paying tax at a marginal tax rate of say 32% will pay taxes at a whopping 62% if they are required to repay EI and have income over this amount. Here's an example to illustrate this:

Example > Andre was laid off late in the year and received $3,000 in regular EI benefits. His T4E slip shows he is required to repay his benefits at a rate of 30% because he previously made a claim for regular benefits when his former employer became insolvent. On his T1 Andre's net income before adjustments is $60,000. He will need to repay the lesser of:

- 30% x $3,000 = $900 and
- 30% x ($60,000 – $57,375*) = $787.50

As Andre lives in Ontario, his marginal tax rate is 31.15% (i.e. he'd pay $31.15 more taxes if he earned $100 more in taxable income). A $100 RRSP deduction would reduce his tax bill by $61.15 when the EI clawback is taken into account. Taxpayers in this situation can obviously benefit handsomely from an RRSP contribution!

*Note this amount is indexed year over year.

Repayment of OAS Benefits. Taxpayers who receive Old Age Security benefits and have income in excess of the annually adjusted "base amount" must repay the lesser of the Old Age Security benefits received and 15% of their net income (before adjustments) in excess of the base amount.

For 2012, the base amount is $69,562. This means that a taxpayer with net income before adjustments of $70,000 whose marginal tax rate would be 35% would be paying an effective rate of 50% on any additional income. Here's an example to illustrate this.

Example > Tonia has a net income before adjustments of $75,000. She received $6,500 OAS during the year. Because of her income level, she will have to repay some of that: the lesser of

- $6,500 and
- 15% x ($75,000 – $69,562*) = $815.70

*Indexed year over year.

Tax Strategy

Clawbacks of social benefits increase your marginal tax rates significantly. You'll want to learn at what level of income this happens. Then plan not to cross over the clawback zone by planning your income sources and their realization for tax purposes to stay within income levels that are less punitive.

CHAPTER 10

Recovering Errors and Omissions

It may be too good to be true… if you learn something new in reading this book and find that you have missed lucrative tax provisions on prior tax returns, you may be able to recover tax gold by adjusting those prior filed returns. To do so, you'll need to keep track of dates, so put your Notice of Assessment or Reassessment, which you'll receive with your refund cheque or balance due notice after filing your return, in a safe place.

The *Income Tax Act* contains a definition of a "normal reassessment period," which is often referred to as the "statute of limitations" since it limits CRA's ability to reassess any tax year to the period that ends three years after the mailing of the original Notice of Assessment or Reassessment for the tax year.

If however, CRA suspects willful tax evasion, there is no time limit. You can avoid gross negligence or tax evasion penalties by voluntarily complying with the law to correct errors or omissions. In other words, get those unfiled returns filed or those returns that overstated deductions or understated income corrected by CRA comes knocking at your door.

Here's the tax secret > You can adjust prior filed returns to correct errors and omissions up to 10 years back.

Taxpayers can request adjustments to prior filed federal T1 returns within ten years after the end of the taxation year being adjusted. This is a great way to recover "gold" from prior years. Many taxpayers miss claiming all the deductions and credits they are entitled to; be sure you're not one of them.

Adjust your tax return by completing Form T1-ADJ, and follow these instructions:

- If you think you missed claiming something on a prior filed return, call your tax practitioner to make an adjustment or do it yourself using form T1-ADJ, available on the CRA's website.
- You can also adjust electronically on the CRA website. Log on to "My Account" and choose the "Change my return" option.
- Have supporting documentation available in case of audit.
- Never file a second tax return.

Some Exceptions Apply. Note that the statute of limitations for filing adjustments to provincial tax provisions is usually only 3 years. To claim refundable tax credits you have missed, you can go back only 11 months, except in hardship cases.

Checklist of Common Errors. Most common filing errors appear in the checklist below; review your prior filed returns each year to be sure you haven't missed something:

Errors in Reporting Income

- **Taxable benefits double reported**
  Example > If your employer pays your premiums to a private healthcare plan, the amount is shown in Box 40 of your T4 slip. It's also included in Box 14. If you add the amount in Box 40 to the amount in Box 14, you'll report that taxable benefit twice.

- **Missed premium deduction on wage loss replacement benefits received**
  Example > While you can't deduct your wage loss replacement premiums in the year that you pay them, if you pay part of the premiums and your employer pays part, then you can deduct the premiums you paid from the taxable benefits received under the plan.

- **Failure to report taxable foreign pension from Germany, U.S.**
  Example > You receive a U.S. Social Security pension. You must report that income on your Canadian tax return. If you began receiving the pension after 1995, then you can claim a deduction for 15% of the amount received.

  Example > You receive a Social Security pension from Germany. You must report the amount received (in Canadian dollars) on your Canadian return. A portion of that pension will be non-taxable and you can claim a deduction for the non-taxable amount. The non-taxable portion will depend on what year you began receiving the pension.

- **Missed self-reporting interest on mortgage held privately**
  Example > You sold a rental property and took back a mortgage. You must report the interest you collect on the mortgage each year.

- **Missed reporting tips and gratuities**
  Example > You work in the service industry and receive tips. These tips are taxable and must be reported as "other employment income" on your tax return. You can also elect to make contributions to the CPP on this income.

Errors in Claiming Deductions

- **Missed claiming brokerage fees**
  Example > You purchased and sold stock. When calculating your capital gain, you must add the brokerage fee for the purchase to the adjusted cost base of the shares and you must deduct the brokerage fee for the sale from the calculated gain.

- **Incorrect adjusted cost base due to missed capital gains election**
  Example > You claimed a capital gains election in 1994 on a property you still own. When you sell the property the adjusted cost base of the asset is based on the elected amount rather than on the amount you paid for the property. This is a common error made by executors who were not aware of the election. The result can be an overstated capital gain.

- **Child care expenses claims not made by high income earner**
  Example > You incurred child care expenses for a period while the lower income spouse was unable to care for the children because they were a full-time student. The higher income earner can claim the child care expenses for that period.

- **Moving expenses—missed real estate commissions**
  Example > When you sell your home and move at least 40 km to a new work location, you can claim moving expenses. Usually the largest of these expenses is the real estate commission on sale of the old residence. Be sure to claim that amount as part of your moving expense claim.

- **Missed safety deposit box fees**
  Example > You have a safety deposit box for storing investment documents. The fees for that box may be claimed as a carrying charge.

- **Prior year capital losses not recorded**
  Example > You sold stock for less than you paid for it. There are no other capital gains in the year. Even though the capital loss cannot

be claimed against other income you should still report the loss as it can be carried forward to future years to reduce any capital gains in a future year.

Errors in Non-Refundable Tax Credits

- **Spousal amount—gross rather than net income used**
  Example > Your spouse has a small business. The business took in $10,000 last year but expenses totalled $6,000. Your claim for the spousal amount must only be reduced by the $4,000 net income, not the $10,000 income the business grossed.

- **Amount for eligible dependants—file when marital status changes**
  Example > Last year you and your spouse separated and each of you was granted custody of one of your children. Although your marital status was married at the beginning of the year, you can claim the amount for 'eligible dependant' for the child that lived with you after the separation.

- **Caregiver amount—missed claiming for parent or other infirm dependant**
  Example > Your mother moved in with you last year and you supported her. If her income is low enough, you may claim the caregiver amount for her.

- **Disability amount—missed claim for sick child**
  Example > Your child was born with a severe disability. You are eligible to claim the disability amount for the child once you get a doctor to sign a disability certificate for the child.

- **Tuition, education and textbook credits—missed transfer to parents**
  Example > Your son is a student at university. His income is not high enough to use up his claim for the tuition, education and textbook amount. By having him complete the back of the T2202A form, a portion of the unused tuition, education and textbook amount can be transferred to your return, to a maximum of $5000.

- **Amounts transferred from spouse—missed transfer of age credit**
  Example > Your spouse is over age 65 but does not have enough income to use the age amount. By completing Schedule 2, you can transfer the amount that is not needed to your return.

- **Medical expenses—missed multiple expenses**
  Example > In addition to the normal doctor's fees and prescriptions, there are a number of other medical expenses that are often missed,

such as private health care insurance premiums, including medical travel insurance and the costs of transportation to receive medical care not available locally.

- **Donations—claim on return of one spouse**
  Example > Both you and your spouse make charitable donations. Each of you claims your own donations. By combining the claim on one return, the amount of the claim is bigger because the rate applicable to the first $200 of each claim is less than the rate applicable to claims over $200.

- **Instalment payment reduction request missed**
  Example > You received an instalment payment notice from CRA based on your income last year. This year your income will be substantially less. You should not continue to make the instalments based on the prior year income but should recalculate the amount based on this year's estimated income.

Errors in Tax Calculations
- **Dividend tax credits not claimed**
  Example > You received eligible dividends. These dividends are eligible for the dividend tax credit claimed on Schedule 1. If your spouse's income was very low you may be able to transfer the dividends and the dividend tax credit to your return for a better after-tax result for the whole family.

- **Foreign tax credits not claimed**
  Example > You received dividends from a U.S. corporation from which U.S. taxes was withheld. You must report this income (in Canadian dollars) on your Canadian return and pay taxes to Canada. You are eligible to reduce those Canadian taxes because taxes were already paid to the U.S. Complete form T2209 to claim the federal credit and Form T2036 to claim the provincial credit.

Tax Strategy

There is gold in tax recovery: go back up to 10 years from December 31 to recover missed provisions and do file tax returns to build unused RRSP contribution room and report capital losses. These are tax planning tools that can save your thousands of dollars in the future. But remember, never file a second tax return.

Essential Tax Facts

Follow these simple rules to take charge:

File by April 30. Even though proprietors and their spouses have until June 15 to file their returns before late filing penalties kick in, it makes sense to file by midnight April 30 to avoid interest charges if you have a balance due. If you can't file by April 30 and you will owe, at least pay the estimated tax by that date. File earlier to recover your tax refunds as quickly as possible.

Mind Your Fs and Ps. Federal tax returns are required to be filed by all Canadians who have a balance due or file to recover overpaid taxes or refundable tax credits. Provincial taxes for the whole year are based on your province of residence on December 31. Moves to more highly taxed provinces should therefore be planned for the start of a tax year. Moves to provinces with a lower tax rate are best planned for later in the year so that the lower rate applies to the whole year.

Repurpose Your Income. There are many different definitions of "income" on the tax return. Active income sources which qualify as "earned income" for RRSP purposes, or "earned income" for the purposes of claiming child care expenses. A variety of income sources with different tax attributes can help you to "average down" the taxes you pay.

Use Tax Free Zones. Everyone in Canada qualifies for the Basic Personal Amount (BPA). These days that means you can earn just over $900 every month tax-free. Make sure everyone in the family does… it's your starting point for personal productivity and tax planning.

Reduced Net Income Pays Off in Spades. Keep an eye on net income, Line 236 of your T1 return. It's one of the most important lines because of its impact on the size of your refundable and non-refundable tax credits. You can reduce your net income by making an RRSP contribution. That will increase your credits and your after-tax cash flow, too.

Combined Family Net Income is Required. You can have zero income and pay zero taxes but still receive refundable tax credits in Canada—simply by filing a tax return. But because many of these credits are based on "family" rather than "individual" net income, you and your spouse need to file tax returns together. Planning to reduce your net incomes together, instead of individually, is therefore smart, and a focus for family tax planning.

Preserve Your Appeal Rights. You are in a relationship with the CRA, so you need to know some key parameters. April 30 is the tax filing due date for most, and the date on your Notice of Assessment or Reassessment—CRA's response—is used to determine your further appeal rights, in case your taxes are in dispute. The Statute of Limitations for the correction or errors or omissions will apply to this date too. Keep the form with your permanent tax records.

PART III

The Tax Savvy Family

CHAPTER 11

Your Family—An Economic Unit

Back in 1972, tax reform discussions centred around whether the family, including dependants living in the home, should be taxed as one unit on one tax return.

Despite the fact that economic decisions—including spending and investing—are generally made as a family unit, the thinkers of the day struggled with this question. They wanted to ensure there was no "tax on marriage." Specifically, people with two incomes should not be taxed as if there was only one, thereby bumping the whole family into one larger tax bracket.

And so, today, not only do we have a much broader definition of what a "conjugal relationship" is for tax purposes, but each member of the family is taxed as an individual. Everyone is entitled to a Basic Personal Amount (about $11,000 at the time of writing) and individual incomes are subject to progressive tax rates. That is, you pay more as you earn more, but the family unit is not bumped into one large tax bracket.

That is, except when it comes to certain refundable tax credits. Net family income—the income of both spouses—does have to be taken into account for the purposes of measuring how much of these credits your family unit will receive.

There is another problem. As a result of the tax reforms of the early 70s, capital gains because taxable for the first time in 1972. Bear in mind that, as a result, that on the final tax return of the last remaining spouse, there is a deemed disposition of all taxable assets, and unspent pension accumulations too. That makes the government a substantial beneficiary of your family's lifetime economic results, the one who stands in line first to receive its share of the residue.

Here's the tax secret > Modern families that are successful in accumulating wealth over time use the power of their economic unit to get the best after-tax results during their lifetimes and with a tax-efficient, intergenerational wealth transfer in mind.

It's not unusual for everyone in the family to participate in the economy in a significant way: the money the kids earn at babysitting, doing lawn care, or working at the local hamburger joint, mom and dad at employment or self-employment activities, in the case of stay-at-home parents, the raising of children, caring for the vulnerable, studying for self-improvement or the home-based entrepreneurial activities which all grow into enormous economic contributions.

Have you ever tracked the value of those activities? It's a worthwhile exercise that helps you optimize family filing provisions on all the tax returns and in making investment decisions.

Your Tax Time Focus. Your focus at tax filing time needs to be on two things: reducing taxes on income earned by each family member as a starting point; then in making sure you gather all the refundable tax credits your family is entitled to.

Your Family Management Focus. While discussions about money are often difficult for families, the reality is that at some point, family life events demand a joint financial accounting: at tax filing time, at marriage, divorce, incapacity, retirement and at death.

In anticipation of those events, it's important to think more strategically: how can you build and protect from tax the asset pools each member in the family unit is building? Is money being saved at all? Is it in the right accounts? Which accounts should be funded first?

Annual Family Financial Checkup

Financial Facts	Dad	Mom	Child 1	Child 2
Gross Income				
Net Income				
Taxes Paid				
Tax Credits				
TFSA				
RRSP				
RESP				
Other Savings				
Debt—Home	( )	( )	( )	( )
Debt—Other	( )	( )	( )	( )

This is a very simple accounting of income and net worth for the family as a whole that may help you think about the kinds of financial decisions you should be making at year end, at tax time and throughout the rest of the year. It will instill the knowledge and skills your family needs about money management as a whole and then help your family unit make confident decisions about tax strategies and investment outcomes together with your professional financial and tax advisors.

Tax Strategy

When it comes to smart family tax filing, know that it's possible to transfer various tax credits on the tax return, as well as to split and shift certain income sources from higher to lower-taxed individuals to get better overall results. Your goal is to structure a "tax-efficient family income" and this may involve the transfer of assets into the right hands throughout various life stages and at the end of life, too.

CHAPTER 12

Tax Benefits for Your Dependants

To begin to understand the tax consequences of living together as a family unit, it's important to define who your family members are for tax purposes. It would seem to be a simple question, but that's not always so in today's complex, blended family units.

Here's what you need to know about your primary "conjugal" relationship with your "significant other":

- A *spouse*, for tax purposes, is someone to whom you are legally married.

- A *common-law partner*, for tax purposes, is someone who is not your spouse but is:
  - a person of the same or opposite sex with whom you lived in a relationship throughout a continuous* 12-month period, or
  - someone who, at the end of the tax year, was the actual or adoptive parent of your child.

*Note that separations of less than 90 days do not affect the 12-month period.

For income tax purposes, all rules that apply to a spouse apply equally to a common-law partner, and for the purposes of this book, when we refer to a spouse we include the common-law partner in the term. You will claim a spouse on your tax return under the Spousal Amount if net income levels are low enough; you will also qualify to transfer certain other provisions, described below.

In addition—and this is where expensive mistakes can occur—you will have to combine net income levels for the purposes of claiming refundable tax credits. If you receive credits by claiming them based on one income only, repayment, with interest can create hardship; best to file correctly at the outset.

The family unit will also be allowed one tax exempt family residence, not two and so valuations are required when spouses who each have a residence, cohabitate. One of those properties will become a taxable residence.

Dependants. Taxpayers who support minors or adult dependants, or both, may qualify for additional tax benefits. A dependant is generally defined as:

- a child of the taxpayer,
- the taxpayer's parent or grandparent or
- a person related to the taxpayer who is under 18 years of age or if over 18, wholly dependent on the taxpayer because of mental or physical infirmity.

These qualifications need not be met throughout the whole year but must be met at some time during the year. The supporting individual may claim medical expenses for these dependants as well as provisions for providing care in the case of incapacity.

The rules for the definition of infirmity can be confusing, however, and because this is an emerging issue for families and a new focus on the tax return, it makes sense to take some time to define it now. In CRA's Interpretation Bulletin IT-513, it means "lacking muscle or mental strength or vitality."

Caring for Infirm Dependants. In 2012 the federal government introduced a new *Family Caregiver Tax Credit* (FCTC) which provides a $2,000 increase to five non-refundable tax credits when a dependant is mentally or physically infirm. The credits are:

- The Spousal Amount
- The Amount for Eligible Dependant (Equivalent-to-Spouse Amount)
- The Amount for Children under 18
- The Amount for Infirm Adult
- The Caregiver Amount

A child under 18 will be consider to be infirm only if they are likely to be, for a long and continuous period of indefinite duration, dependant on others for significantly more assistance in attending to personal needs compared to children of the same age. It's important to draw the distinction between "infirm" and "disabled." As defined above, an infirm dependant is one who is "lacking muscle or mental strength or vitality." A disabled dependant is one who has a "severe and prolonged impairment in mental or physical functions." To qualify as disabled, a Disability Tax Credit Certificate (T2201) must be completed and signed by medical practitioner to certify that the individual is disabled. Credits for infirm and disabled taxpayers include:

- *Child Care Deduction*—An enhanced child care deduction of up to $10,000 can be claimed for disabled dependants but only if they qualify for the Disability Amount and have a Disability Tax Credit certificate, signed by a medical practitioner.
- *Disability Supports Deduction*—A medical doctor must certify that the supports, including attendant care are required; a Disability Tax Credit certificate is not required.
- *Disability Amount*—claimed for severe and prolonged disabilities expected to last more than 12 months. A Disability Tax Credit certificate signed by a medical practitioner is required to make this claim.
- *Caregiver Amount*—You can claim this amount if you live with and care for parents over the age of 65 or other infirm relative. To qualify for the additional $2,000 FCTC however, the dependant must be dependant due to a mental or physical infirmity.
- *Infirm Adult over 18*—You can claim this amount if you are supporting the infirm relative in their home, hospital or nursing home. It's possible for you and a sibling to share this amount as long as no more than one full credit is claimed. This amount does not require a Disability Tax Credit certificate but the individual must be dependent upon you for support due to mental or physical infirmity.
- *Medical Expenses*—The amounts claimable here are for your own nuclear family and the infirm adults you may be supporting. More detail follows.

Transferring Deductions and Credits. When you file family tax returns at the same time, starting with the lowest income earner and working your way up to the highest, you'll ensure that income is taxed at the lowest possible rates and the family net income is as low as possible to maximize eligibility for available tax credits. The chart below can help.

Tax Provision		Claimed By
Income	Canada Pension Plan Benefits	After age 60, split CPP income by making an equal assignment of benefits to each spouse.

Tax Provision		Claimed By
Income (continued)	Taxable Dividends	Dividends can be transferred to high-earning spouse if by doing so a Spousal Amount is created or increased.
	Eligible Pension Income	Up to 50% can be transferred to the other spouse by election each year.
Deductions	Safety Deposit Box	Either spouse may claim if it holds household investment documents.
Non-Refundable Tax Credits on Schedule 1	Basic Personal Amount	Not transferable.
	Age Amount, Pension Income Amount, Disability Amount, Tuition, Education and Textbook Amounts, Amount for Dependent Minors	These five amounts are transferable to the higher earner if the lower earner is not taxable. For the Disability Amount; Tuition, Education and Textbook Amounts transfers from other dependants may also be made.
	Claims for Spouse or Eligible Dependant	They are claimed by the supporting individual with higher taxable income.
	Claims for Infirm Adults, Caregiver, Donations, Adoption Expenses	Can be claimed by either spouse or shared between them.
	Medical Expenses	Usually claimed by spouse with lower net income for best benefit (if that spouse is taxable). Medical expenses for other dependent adults can be claimed by either spouse.
	Canada Employment Amount	Not transferable.

Tax Provision		Claimed By
Tax Credits on Schedule 1 (continued)	Public Transit Amount	Can be claimed by either spouse or shared between them.
	Children's Fitness and Arts	Can be claimed by either spouse or shared between them.
	New Home Buyers' Amount	Can be claimed by either spouse.

Keep these transfer provisions in mind when you plan investment activities throughout the year and account for them at tax time. You will be in a position to ask better questions about the tax and investment planning decisions you would like to make; for example:

- How are tuition, education and textbook credits transferred from our children?
- How can we increase the Canada Child Tax Benefits we receive?
- Will an RRSP help? Who should contribute?
- Should we pay down the mortgage first, then invest in the RRSP?
- How should we invest the Child Tax Benefits received? In whose account?
- How can we split income between family members to reduce taxes?
- What should we do with our family's tax refunds?
- Who should own a TFSA?
- Is an RESP a good idea for our family?
- Should we borrow money to invest? If so who should do this?
- Should we consider buying life insurance and how should we fund this?

Tax Strategy

There are a number of tax benefits available when you have dependants. Many of these provisions can be transferred between family members, the result of which is more new money with which to invest. Getting the returns right will allow you to shift your focus to decisions about tax savvy investments, starting with the use of an RRSP and a TFSA for eligible family members.

CHAPTER 13

Maximizing the Tax Credits

Families with children are eligible for two significant sources of income redistribution: the *Universal Child Care Benefit (UCCB) and the Canada Child Tax Benefit (CCTB)*. They can also take advantage of the non-refundable tax credits specific to their support of dependants. Learning more about how to get more of each of these, will help you save and create wealth for your family. That's the subject of this chapter.

Universal Child Care Benefit (UCCB). The UCCB is a $100 per month amount paid for each child under the age of 7 no matter what the family income level. In a two-parent family situation, the UCCB must be reported by the spouse with the lower net income thereby minimizing the income taxes payable on the UCCB. In a single-parent family this amount may be reported by the parent or be included in the income of the child for which the amount for an eligible dependant is claimed.

Be sure to save this money in a separate account in the name of each child. Earnings will be reported by that child, as you'll learn more about in the next chapter. But in addition, this is a great start to an education fund, and a great way to instill financial literacy lessons in children.

I remember taking my small sons to the bank every month with this "bonus" showing them not only where and how to save money for their futures regularly, but also instilling in them the non-negotiable goal of a post-secondary education. They are very fine young men now, well educated, giving much back to their communities and, best of all, they graduated without debt.

Canada Child Tax Benefit (CCTB). The CCTB is a refundable tax credit that is based on family net income (Line 236 of your tax returns) and the number of eligible children you have. In most cases the CCTB is paid to the mother of the children although it may be split between parents when parents are separated and share joint custody. The amount of the CCTB is not shown on the tax return at all; rather CRA calculates this automatically for you.

The CCTB must be applied for, generally when child is born (or when a family immigrates). In order to continue receiving the CTB, *both spouses must file a tax return each year* so that family net income can be determined. The benefit year is July to June based on family net income for the previous year. Most provinces provide an additional child benefit which is paid along with the CCTB.

How much you will receive changes from year to year due to indexing. See Appendix 1 for this year's details. What's important is that the size of your family net income will determine how much you get. The more you earn, the less you get. However, that clawback can be very expensive, as outlined below:

1. Your basic benefit is reduced by 2% of net income in excess of approximately $43,000 if there is only one eligible child and 4% of income in excess of this if there are two or more eligible children.

2. The national child tax benefit supplement is reduced by a percentage of family net income in excess of approximately $25,000. The clawback rate is:

    (a)   12.2% for one child
    (b)   23% for two children and
    (c)   33.3% for three or more children

3. Note that for disabled children the child disability benefit is also available.

Here's the tax secret > With clawback rates of 12.2% to 33.3%, taxpayers with relatively low family income levels are subject to marginal tax rates of 50% or more, when regular tax rates on income are factored in. It is good planning for families to make RRSP contributions to reduce net incomes, and cut the impact of the clawback zones.

Focus on Family Net Income. Family net income can be reduced in a number of ways, but one of the most popular ways, is to make a contribution to an RRSP. This can still be done within 60 days after the end of the tax year, thereby making it possible to create higher refundable tax credits in the next "benefit year" which runs from July 1 to June 30. If it's too late for this year, be sure to get a handle on those clawback zones for next year and plan now to contribute to an RRSP.

Some of the other deductions that reduce net income on the tax return appear below. Another strategy is to make sure you have indeed claimed every one that you are entitled to:

- Contributions to employer-sponsored Registered Pension Plans (RPPs). Check your T4 Slips for these numbers.
- Contributions to RRSPs
- Elected split pension amounts (from eligible pensions)
- Union and professional dues
- Universal child care benefit repayments
- Child care expenses
- Disability supports deduction
- Business Investment Losses
- Moving expenses
- Spousal support payments
- Carrying charges and interest expenses
- Deductions for the CPP contributions on self-employment income
- Exploration and development expenses
- Clergy residence deductions
- Other deductions like certain legal fees or social benefit repayments like clawbacks of Employment Insurance and Old Age Security benefits

Non-Refundable Tax Credits. While refundable tax credits are automatically calculated by government and sent directly to Canadian homes, or electronically into your bank accounts when you file family tax returns, non-refundable tax credits must be proactively chosen on your tax return. These credits will reduce your taxes payable, so are really not of benefit to you unless you have taxable income.

You should be familiar with many of them because, if you are an employee, your employer will require you to indicate which ones you qualify for so that he or she can reduce your tax withholdings to reflect the costs of supporting family members. These credits also include amounts to account for special expenditures like public transit costs, amounts paid for children's arts or fitness activities, medical expenses and charitable donations.

Non-refundable credits are totaled on Schedule 1 and then multiplied by the lowest tax rate, to get the real dollar value in reducing taxes payable. Check out the federal Schedule 1 but also the equivalent provincial form. The numbers are not necessarily the same. The provinces extend tax reductions through personal amounts as well, but here the two tax system part ways, with several provinces embellishing on the tax credits, or deciding on their own whether or not to index them for inflation.

Let's review now, some of the more common non-refundable tax credits for their family members, all of which increase tax-free zones, thereby saving you money:

Amount for Eligible Children Under 18. The full amount of this credit can be claimed for the entire year including the year of birth, death or adoption, even if these life events happened right at the end of the year. Also know that:

- Either parent may claim the credit.
- Unused credits can be transferred between spouses and common-law partners.
- Where parents are estranged, the credit can be claimed only by the parent who would be eligible to claim the "eligible dependant credit" if that child were the parent's only child.
- Unused credits cannot be carried forward.

If the child is infirm, an addition $2,000 Family Caregiver Tax Credit can be claimed.

Amount for an Eligible Dependant. An equivalent-to-spouse or amount for "eligible" dependant is possible if you were single, separated, divorced, or widowed and supporting a dependant if these rules are followed:

- only one person can claim the amount for an eligible dependant in respect of the same dependant,
- no one may claim the amount for an eligible dependant if someone else is claiming the amount for spouse or common-law partner for that dependant,
- only one claim may be made for the amount for an eligible dependant for the same home,
- where more than one taxpayer qualifies to make the claim, the taxpayers must agree who will make the claim or no one will be allowed to,
- if a claim for the amount for an eligible dependant is made in respect of a dependant, no one may claim the "Amount for Infirm Dependants" or the "Caregiver Amount" in respect of the same dependant.

Amount for Infirm Dependant Adults. If you support a dependant who is:

- at least 18 years of age, and
- dependant on you because of mental or physical infirmity,

you may claim certain tax credits in respect of that dependant. To qualify, the dependant must be:

- the child or grandchild of you or your spouse or common-law partner, or
- the parent, grandparent, brother, sister, uncle, aunt, niece or nephew of you or your spouse or common-law partner and resident in Canada at any time in the year.

If the adult is disabled, an addition $2,000 Family Caregiver Tax Credit can be claimed.

Caregiver Amount. If you support a dependant in your own home who:

- meets the qualifications for the amount for infirm dependant adults or
- is your parent or grandparent and is age 65 or older

you may claim the caregiver amount in respect of that dependant.

If the adult is disabled, an addition $2,000 Family Caregiver Tax Credit can be claimed.

Transfers of unused credits from spouse or common-law partner. If your spouse's income is too low to claim any of the following credits to which they are entitled:

- Age Amount
- Pension Income Amount
- Disability Amount
- Tuition, Education and Textbook Amount
- Amount for Dependent Minors

then you may transfer the portion that they do not need to your return.

Transfer of Disability Amount or Tuition, Education and Textbook Amounts from Children. If your child is eligible to claim the Disability Amount or the Tuition, Education and Textbook Amounts but does not need those credits, you may claim them on your return. For the Disability Amount, you may claim whatever portion your dependant does not need with no additional documentation (other than the Disability Tax Credit Certificate). For the Tuition, Education and Textbook amount, your child must complete the back of the T2202A slip they receive from their educational institution. This transfer is limited to $5,000 less the amount used by the child.

Amount for Adoption Expenses. If you adopt a child, you may claim a credit for the adoption expenses in the year that the adoption becomes final. This amount may be claimed by either spouse.

Amount for Children's Fitness and Amount for Children's Arts. If you enrol your child (under age 18 if disabled or under age 16 otherwise) in a program that qualifies for either of these credits, you may claim the lesser or the qualifying expense or $500 for each credit. An additional $500 claim is allowed if you spend at least $100 and the child is disabled.

Tax Strategy

Claiming all the non-refundable tax credits on your TD1 *Tax Credit Return*, which determines the amount of your withholding taxes, as well as on your T1 *Income Tax and Benefits Return* will put more money into your pocket as you earn it, and when you file your tax return, too. For the credits such as charitable donations not listed on the TD1 form, use form T1213 *Request to Reduce Tax Deductions at Source* to authorize your employer to reduce withholding. Reducing family net income with an RRSP contribution can increase your Canada Child Tax Benefits and other refundable tax credits.

CHAPTER 14

Family Income Splitting

Family income splitting is the process of shifting investment income from one family member who has a fairly high marginal tax rate to be reported and taxed in the hands of family members who have lower marginal tax rates.

There are several methods of income splitting such as inter-spousal loans, loans to non-arm's length minor children, and transferring assets. But, because of advantages the tax-efficient investor may realize from these strategies, the *Income Tax Act* has many rules that restrict certain transactions. The test for the vast majority of these restrictions is whether the transaction was between non-arm's length or related individuals.

The Attribution Rules, for example, clearly set out what's allowed and what isn't when it comes to the transfer of income and assets amongst family members.

Attribution Rules. The Attribution Rules are triggered by non-arm's length transactions. The *Income Tax Act*, essentially removes the opportunity for families to take advantage of provisions aimed at individuals—the use of tax free zones and tax brackets and rates, which increase as income rises. Here's what's not allowed:

- *Transfers and loans to spouse or common-law partner.* If you transfer or loan property either directly or indirectly, by means of a trust or any other means to a spouse or common-law partner for that person's benefit, any resulting income or loss or capital gain or loss from that property is taxable to you.
- In addition, where one spouse guarantees the repayment of a loan to the other spouse, made for investment purposes, attribution will apply to any income earned from the loaned funds.

- *Transfers and loans to minors.* Where property is transferred or loaned either directly or indirectly to a person who is under 18 and who does not deal with you at arm's length or who is your niece or nephew, the income or loss resulting from such property is reported by you until the transferee attains 18 years of age. Capital gains or losses do not, however, attribute back to you.

  In other words, income resulting from assets transferred to a minor child will trigger attribution of rental, dividend or interest income, but not capital gains.

As you can seem these rules thwart an otherwise perfect investment opportunity: the transfer of assets from the higher earner to the lower earners in the family so that tax on income is paid at lower tax brackets, leading to lower overall family taxes payable.

Here's the tax secret > There are ways to get around the Attribution Rules.

The following are examples of transactions you can undertake in the family to stay onside with the Attribution Rules and still accomplish income splitting and asset transfers, within the framework of the law.

- *Tax-Free Savings Accounts.* If you make contributions to a Tax-Free Savings Account for your spouse or adult children they will earn income on those deposits with no income tax payable, either by them or by you, so long as the contribution is a true gift and not a scheme to allow you to earn that income on a tax-free basis. These earnings will have no effect on your ability to claim the Spousal Amount.
- *Spousal RRSPs.* Attribution does not apply to contributions made to a spousal RRSP, unless there is a withdrawal within three years.
- *Wages paid to spouse and children.* Where a spouse or children receive a wage from the family business, the attribution rules won't apply if the wage is reasonable, and is included in the recipient's income.
- *Interest income from Child Tax Benefit (CTB)* or *Universal Child Care Benefit (UCCB)* payments. If CTB or UCCB payments are invested in the name of a child, the income will not be subject to attribution. In other words, interest, dividends and other investment income may be reported in the hands of the child. Be sure this account remains untainted by birthday money and other gifts.

- *Joint accounts.* T5 Slips are issued by banks in the names of the account holders to report earnings on investments including interest and dividends. This does not mean that the income on those slips is taxable to those whose names are on the slips. Instead, report income on the return of the individuals who contributed the funds to the account in the proportion that the funds were supplied. For example, if only one spouse in a family works and is the source of all of the deposits, then all of the interest earned on the account is taxable to that person, no matter whose name is on the account.
- *Property transfers to a spouse.* A special rule applies when property is transferred to a spouse. Normally, such property transfers at tax cost, so that no gain or loss arises. This is true even if the spouse pays fair value for the property. The property will not transfer at tax cost, but at fair market value, provided the transferor files an election to have this happen with the tax return for the year of transfer and the spouse has paid fair value consideration.
- *Transfers for fair market consideration.* The Attribution Rules will not apply to any income, gain or loss from transferred property if, at the time of transfer, consideration was paid for the equivalent of fair market value for the transferred property by the transferee. The person acquiring the property must use his or her own capital to pay for it.
- *Transfers for indebtedness.* The Attribution Rules on investment income will not apply if the lower income spouse borrowed capital from the higher earner, and the parties signed a bona fide loan that bore an interest rate which is at least the lesser of:
  - the "prescribed" interest rates in effect at the time the indebtedness was incurred and
  - the rate that would have been charged by a commercial lender.

Note that the prescribed interest rate used in establishing bona fide inter-spousal loans is set quarterly by the CRA. It is based on average yields of 90-day Treasury Bills for the first month of the preceding quarter.

Payment of interest on inter-spousal loans. Interest must actually be paid on the indebtedness incurred by the spouse, under a formal loan agreement described above, by January 30 of each year, following the tax year, or attribution will apply to income earned with the loaned funds.

- *When spouses live apart.* If spouses are living separate and apart due to relationship breakdown, they can jointly elect to have Attribution

Rules not apply to the period in which they were living apart. The Attribution Rules do not apply after a divorce is finalized.

- *Assignment of Canada Pension Plan Benefits.* It is possible to apply to split CPP benefits between spouses, thereby minimizing tax on that income source in some cases.
- *Pension income splitting.* The election to split pension income between spouses does not involve the actual transfer of funds from one spouse to another but is an election to have the split pension taxed as if it were the other spouse's income. As such, the attribution rules do not apply. (However, if funds are actually transferred from one spouse to the other, the attribution rules will apply to any income earned on the transferred funds).
- *Investments in spouse's business.* Investments in the spouse's or common-law partner's business venture are not subject to Attribution Rules as the resulting income is business income rather than income from property.
- *Second generation earnings.* While the income earned on property transferred to the spouse must be reported by the transferor, any secondary income earned on investing the earnings is taxed in the hands of the transferee.
- *Spousal dividend transfers.* One spouse may report dividends received from taxable Canadian corporations received by the other spouse if by doing so a Spousal Amount is created or increased.
- *Inheritances.* Attribution does not apply to inheritances.
- *Assets transferred to an adult child (over 18).* This will, in general, not be subject to attribution. However, when income splitting is the main reason for the loan to an adult child, the income will be attributed back to the transferor. An exception again occurs when fair market value consideration is paid or a bona fide loan is drawn up with interest payable as described above, by January 30 of the year following the end of the calendar year.
- *The Kiddie Tax.* The Attribution Rules will not apply when an amount is included in the calculation of Tax on Split Income on Schedule 1 of the tax return. This special tax is assessed on income earned by minor children from their parents' or other relatives' ventures. Specifically, dividends or shareholder benefits earned either directly or through a trust or partnership, from a corporation controlled by someone related to the child, are extracted from the normal tax calculations and reported on Form T1206 so that tax on this income can be calculated

at the highest marginal rates, thereby eliminating any tax benefits of such an arrangement. Beginning in 2011, capital gains on the sale of shares in the business are also subject to the Kiddie Tax.

Tax Strategy

Consider having the higher income spouse pay household and personal expenses, and the lower income spouse acquire investment assets with income earned in his or her own right. You can also reinvest spouse's income tax refunds and refundable tax credits to create income in his or her "own right," so that resulting earnings are taxed to them.

CHAPTER 15

The Importance
of the Family RRSP

For the vast majority of working taxpayers and their families, the most powerful, tax-efficient investment is the *Registered Retirement Savings Plan (RRSP)*. To work well, it requires planning, however, not just when you fund it, but when you later withdraw from it, too.

Because the RRSP accumulations can grow significantly and make you rich, your goal is to plan how the money can later be taxed at the lowest possible marginal tax rates when it is withdrawn to create a pension for you. The plan includes avoiding the "super taxes" that might arise when the last surviving spouse in the family dies with untaxed deposits. You can do that by generating the tax at lower tax brackets along the way and then saving the money in a TFSA or other non-registered account.

That's the end game. Along the way, the RRSP plays many very important roles in building family wealth, and those who are less tax astute may forget about them:

- The RRSP investment results in a tax deduction which provides and immediate return in tax savings
- It can help reduce withholding taxes throughout the year so you have more to invest with
- It will also reduce net income, the figure on which your refundable tax credits like the Canada Child Tax Benefit and the clawbacks of social benefits like the Old Age Security and Employment Insurance are based. That creates and preserves income for you throughout the year.
- The money inside the plan grows on a tax deferred basis—you don't pay tax on the earnings until you withdraw them

- The RRSP is not just for retirement—you can tap into the money on a tax-free basis if you buy your first home or go back to school, although, this may interrupt your retirement savings.
- Upon withdrawal to create a regular retirement pension benefit, both principal and earnings are taxed as "ordinary income"—100% is added to income, but income splitting is possible with your spouse once you turn 65.
- You'll miss tax savings opportunities if you wait until the end of the year in which you turn 71—the age at which you must convert your savings in an RRSP to a RRIF or annuity. Better planning involves "averaging down" the tax owing on these deposits over a longer period of time.

Why the RRSP First? So what should you invest in first, a Tax-Free Savings Account (TFSA) or an RRSP? That's a hotly debated question these days. Should you consider an RESP or an RDSP if you have students or disabled dependants to support?

From an income perspective, it's tough to beat the advantages of the *Tax-Free Savings Account* (TFSA), because all your earnings will remain tax-free, while the money is in the account and after when you withdraw your earnings, too. However, the savings you invest in that plan is money upon which someone in the family has likely already paid taxes; and no tax deduction is created when you invest. Also, your annual investment is limited to a maximum of $5,000 (indexed, depending on future inflation rates.) This topic will be raised again as we discuss investments later in the book.

The *Registered Education Savings Plan (RESP)* and the *Registered Disability Savings Plan (RDSP)* are also important tax shelters. In both cases, the government adds grants and bonds to sweeten the investment. Free money is always a good thing and so that's an important advantage to be considered, too. Again, funding for these plans comes from tax-paid savings, and there are contribution maximums to consider.

> *Here's the tax secret* > Neither the TFSA, RESP or RDSP will help you decrease your family's tax burden today, nor will they help you maximize social benefits. That's where the RRSP can really pull rank. If you want to accumulate savings, grow your money exponentially, and maximize all the family tax filing benefits available to you, it pays to invest in an RRSP, because it reduces both net and taxable income, as further explained below.

RRSP Eligibility. To participate, you do need to be age-eligible (under age 72—or have a spouse under 72) and have the required "unused contribution room." This room can only be created by filing a tax return, and the taxpayer must earn the requisite "earned income" sources; most commonly, income from employment, and self-employment. The actual contribution is limited to 18% of earned income in the previous tax year to an annual dollar maximum.

There are seven main benefits to the family in making an RRSP contribution:

- *Decreased taxes for each individual.* A tax deduction is created for the contribution made to the plan, up to your available contribution room. That deduction will reduce the taxpayer's net income. It can be carried forward to a future year, too, if income is too low for tax benefits this year. That's a powerful coup in cases where incomes fluctuate (seasonal employment/self-employment, commission sales, bonus, severance receipts). However because this contribution room is not indexed to inflation, it pays to use it sooner rather than later.
- *Increased social benefits and preserved monthly income.* The reduction in net income will ultimately trickle down to reduce taxes payable. Where applicable, it will also increase social benefits received from federal and provincial refundable tax credits or the Old Age Security, by decreasing clawbacks. Those on Employment Insurance may be subject to clawbacks of that income source too in some cases. Again an RRSP contribution can help preserve that income.
- *Tax deferred income growth.* The income earned on the principal invested loses its identity within the plan. That means the whole amount—principal and earnings—will be taxed as income on withdrawal. Plan your future affairs to withdraw the money out of your "RRSP Bucket" over a longer period of time to "average down" tax rate exposure. Remember, while in the plan, the earnings are not taxable, providing for a tax deferral and an opportunity for more rapid growth than if the funds were held outside this registered account.
- *Tax leveraging.* The tax savings generated by the RRSP contribution will be in the double-digit zones, depending on the taxpayer's marginal tax rates and these large and immediate tax savings can be leveraged into other tax-efficient investments. Depositing your refund to a TFSA may make the most sense, as the money can now accumulate tax-free forever—and there is no upper age barrier. Seniors who become age-ineligible for RRSP purpose, can shelter at least some savings in the TFSA. However, you may have some debt and risk management issues to consider first.

- *Debt management.* Given higher costs of servicing debt vs. the lower returns on investments in recent times, advisors and clients will want to review using the tax savings generated by the RRSP to paying off debt that results in high, non-deductible interest cost savings immediately.
- *Risk management.* Life or critical illness insurance can be secured with the tax savings from the RRSP.
- *More than retirement savings*—home buyers and students benefit too. By making another RRSP contribution, which leads to a bigger tax refund and more new capital for investment purposes, taxpayers can continue to build wealth for the future in retirement. The RRSP can also be used to supplement home ownership and education on a tax-free basis, by allowing tax-free withdrawals under the Home Buyers' Plan and the Lifelong Learning Plan. That makes it a versatile and important investment for taxpayers of all ages.

Calculating Your RRSP Room. You'll find your RRSP Contribution room on your Notice of Assessment or Reassessment from CRA. It's not always right, though, especially if you missed filing a tax return on which you had qualifying "earned income" in the past 10 years. Be sure not to miss out on creating this valuable pension savings room. File a tax return within the 10-year Statute of Limitations for the correction of errors or omissions.

There is so much flexibility in planning your financial freedom if you do. Your contribution room is decreased by any RRSP contributions deducted on your tax return. But, if you don't contribute, the unused RRSP contribution room may be accumulated and carried forward for use in the future… indefinitely. Check it out, you may have a large number there now—it's ready for you to fund anytime in your future. When you do, you'll get a tax deduction.

Consider the Spousal RRSP. You now know there is no lower age limit for contributing to an RRSP; however, the RRSP accumulations you have must be collapsed by the *end of the year in which you turn 71.* However, it's still possible to fund a spousal RRSP, if your spouse is younger and you have RRSP room. The benefit of doing this is that you get to take the tax deduction, but you also get to split retirement income accumulations with your younger spouse. So, unused RRSP contribution room can be an important bonus in reducing net income for retirees who are no longer age-eligible for RRSP contributions if they have a spouse who is under age 72. This can preserve your indexed Old Age Security pension as an added benefit.

Example > Jasper is 72 with a net income of $75,000 after pension income splitting. He is subject to a clawback of part of his Old Age Security income because his income level exceeds the OAS threshold. Jasper's wife Elaine is 69. Because Jasper has unused RRSP contribution room of $10,000, he can make a $5,000 spousal RRSP contribution and reduce his net income to $70,000 eliminating most of the OAS clawback. This technique could be used again in the following year using up his available contribution room and eliminating the clawback next year.

Assets transferred to the spouse using a spousal RRSP become the spouse's income when they are removed from the RRSP, but any contributions made in the same or prior two calendar years are income to the contributor. Therefore to accomplish pension income splitting at age 60 using a spousal RRSP, contributions must be made before the spouse is 57 years old.

Example > Kenneth has contributed $3,000 annually to a spousal RRSP for his wife Fiona for the past ten years. This year he made no contribution and Fiona withdrew $10,000 from her RRSP. Because Kenneth had contributed a total of $6,000 in the current and prior two calendar years, Kenneth would have to report $6,000 of the withdrawal and Fiona would report the remaining $4,000. All subsequent withdrawals from the RRSP would be Fiona's income.

Tax Strategy

Careful planning is required when you withdraw funds from the RRSP account so that you avoid unusual spikes to marginal tax rates (and an incrementally higher erosion of the capital invested) or a clawback of Old Age Security, EI or tax credits. Whether the money should go into a spousal RRSP and what the optimal age to start making taxable withdrawals is should be planned in advance. But in the meantime, don't miss out on claiming increased tax refunds and credits as a result of your RRSP contribution.

CHAPTER 16

Your Tax-Free Future—The TFSA

You have already learned a lot about planning to file a more timely and accurate tax return and how to structure your net and taxable income sources to be more tax efficient. From a planning point of view, there is one more thing you need to know about your tax filing "basics": a cornerstone of every tax plan is the inclusion of a *Tax-Free Savings Account* in the taxpayer's investment portfolio.

Here's the tax secret > If you contribute to your TFSA regularly and to the annual maximum throughout your lifetime, you will have a completely tax free pension when you retire—putting you light years ahead of generations before you in the opportunity to secure peace of mind.

There is nothing but good news. Taxpayers over the age of 17 may contribute up to $5,000 each year (indexed each year to the nearest $500) to such an account, or their relatives and supporting individuals may make contributions for them. The TFSA is exempt from the normal "Attribution Rules" which require higher earners who transfer or loan money to their spouses to report earnings on the transferor's return so long as the funds stay in the TFSA.

And despite the fact that you might think it's almost too good to be true, indeed, investors may take the money out of their TFSA for whatever purpose they wish and *then put the money back into the TFSA to grow some more.* You do not lose your TFSA contribution room when the money comes out.

However, there are penalties for "re-contributing" at the wrong time. You have to wait until the required contribution room is created: January 1 of the next year. There are three parts to this "Contribution Room," which must be considered however:

1. New Contribution Room created at January 1 of each new year. ($5,000 per year plus indexing, when applicable)

2. "Re-Contribution" Room based on prior year withdrawals. This "re-contribution room" is created at *January 1* each year.

3. Carry forwards of the contribution and "re-contribution" room created above if left unfunded.

Neither withdrawals nor earnings can be included in income for any income-tested benefits, such as the Canada Child Tax Benefit or Goods and Services Tax (GST) Credit. Investors at lower income levels can therefore save and earn on a tax exempt basis while continuing to benefit from income redistribution provisions.

Following are some additional facts about TFSAs you may find helpful as you consider adding this investment to the portfolio of each adult in the family:

- **TFSA Eligible Investments.** The same eligible investments as allowed within an RRSP are allowed in the TFSA. A special rule prohibits a TFSA from making an investment in any entity with which the account holder does not deal at arm's length. For example, the TFSA cannot hold shares in the owner's small business corporation. For occurrences after October 16th, 2009, a 100% penalty tax on the income earned on such investments will apply.

- **TFSA Excluded Investments.** Prescribed excluded property for these purposes includes any obligation secured by mortgage so that individuals cannot hold their own mortgage loan as an investment in their TFSA.

- **Interest Deductibility.** Interest paid on money borrowed to invest in the TFSA is not deductible. It should be noted that rules are in place so that if the loan is not an arm's length arrangement or was made to allow another person (or partnership) to benefit from the tax-free status of the TFSA, the TFSA will be deemed to no longer be a TFSA.

- **Stop Loss Rules.** A capital loss is denied when assets are disposed into a TFSA. This means you can't claim a loss if you transfer your losing shares into your TFSA.

- **Using TFSA as Security.** A TFSA may be used as security for a loan or other indebtedness.

- **Excess Contributions.** When taxpayers make contributions over the allowed maximum, they are subject to a 1% per month penalty until the amounts are removed. However, if taxpayers are willing to pay the penalty tax in order to keep the money in the plan, hoping to reap an even higher tax-free return on the excess contribution, 100% of the gains will be subject to tax when deliberate overcontributions occur after October 16th, 2009.

- **Swapping for Tax-Free Gains.** When taxpayers swap investments from non-registered accounts for cash in the TFSA, and then swap them back out for a revised, higher price point, thereby leaving gains in the TFSA to be tax-free, 100% of the gains are subject to tax, after October 16th, 2009.
- **Departure Tax.** The TFSA is not caught by the departure tax rules. In fact, a beneficiary under a TFSA who immigrates to or emigrates from Canada will not be treated as having disposed of their rights under a TFSA. No TSFA contribution room is earned for those years where a person is non-resident and any withdrawals while non-resident cannot be replaced. However, it will make sense to remove capital properties from the TFSA on a tax-free basis immediately prior to emigrating and then trigger the deemed disposition on departure to avoid taxation in the destination country.
- **Marriage Breakdown.** Upon breakdown of a marriage or common-law partnership, the funds from one party's TFSA may be transferred tax-free to the other party's TFSA. This will have no effect on the contribution room of either of the parties.
- **Death of a TFSA Holder.** Upon the death of the TFSA holder, the funds within the account may be rolled over into their spouse's TFSA or they may be withdrawn tax-free. Any amounts earned within a TSFA after the death of the taxpayer are taxable to the estate.

Tax Strategy

It's worth mentioning again—especially to young adults—that the TFSA is an absolute gift to your future financial freedom. *It will help you create a tax-free pension.* Given its full accumulation period (age 18 to date of death), every resident of Canada has the opportunity to become a millionaire, by simply investing $5,000 each year. Being very conservative, if you deposit $5,000 each year, indexed by 2%, for 50 years in a TFSA that earns only 4.5% interest on those deposits, the balance after the last deposit will be over $1,103,000.

CHAPTER 17

Education Planning With RESPs

A *Registered Education Savings Plan (RESP)* is a tax-assisted savings plan set up for the purposes of funding a beneficiary's future education costs. It also serves as a way to split income earned in the plan with the beneficiary, who will be taxed at a lower rate than the contributor, as a general rule, when earnings are withdrawn.

Most important, and what gives it weight as an important family investment, is that the federal government encourages family educational savings by contributing to your efforts with the Canada Education Savings Grants and Bonds.

A contributor can invest up to $50,000 per beneficiary as a lifetime maximum. Annual contribution limits in place prior to 2007 are no longer in effect however, government contributions are maximized if contributions are spread over time rather than in one lump sum. However, the following rules apply to RESPs:

- The plan must terminate after 35 years (unless the beneficiary is disabled).
- Minor siblings can substitute as plan beneficiaries if the intended beneficiary does not become a qualifying recipient.

Transfers may be made between RESPs with no income tax consequences. In fact, tax-free transfers between individual Registered Retirement Savings Plans (RESPs) for the benefit of siblings will now be allowed without triggering the repayment of Canada Education Savings Grants (CESGs) so long as the beneficiary of the recipient plan is less than 21 years old at the time of the transfer. This change applies to asset transfers after 2010.

There are several tax advantages to an RESP investment. The subscriber, who contributes money into the plan, does not receive a tax deduction at the time of investment. However, income earned within the plan on the contributions is tax-deferred until the beneficiary student qualifies to receive education assistance from the plan by starting to attend post-secondary school, either on a part-time or on a full-time basis.

Here's the tax secret > The sweetener to these savings is the **Canada Education Savings Grant (CESG)** which provides additional funds for education. This grant is added to the RESP each year by Human Resources and Skills Development Canada. The grant is received on a tax-free basis by the plan. Started in 1998, it provides for a federal grant of 20% of the first $2,500 contributed to an RESP for children under the age of 18. The lifetime maximum CESG is $7,200.

To receive the money, the beneficiary of the RESP must have a Social Insurance Number. The CESG room of up to $500 a year (20% of $2,500) can be maximized each year including the year the child turns 17. Unused CESG contribution room can be carried forward until the child turns 18, however, the grant may not exceed $1,000 a year. This means that the catch-up of the grants is limited to two years at a time so it's better to make contributions each year rather than in a lump sum.

An additional CESG is available if the family net income is low enough. For families with net income in the lowest tax bracket (below $42,707 in 2012), an additional grant is 20% of the first $500 deposited (maximum $100 additional grant). For families with net incomes in the second tax bracket (between $42,707 and $85,414 for 2012), the additional grant is 10% of the first $500 deposited (maximum $50 additional grant).

The Canada Learning Bond (CLB). There's more good news. The first time a child becomes eligible to receive benefits under the National Child Benefit, which is part of the Child Tax Benefit calculations, an initial Canada Learning Bond entitlement of $500 is available. This will generally happen under one of two circumstances:

- the year of birth or
- a subsequent year if the family net income is too high in the year of birth.

The entitlement is $100 in each subsequent year that the family qualifies for the NCB until the year the child turns 15. Once 16, the CLB is no longer allocated to the child.

In order to turn the entitlement into real money, the Canada Learning Bond must be transferred into a Registered Education Saving Plan (RESP) for the benefit of the child. This can be done at any time before the child turns 21. If the CLB is not transferred to an RESP by the time the child turns 21, the entitlement will be lost.

The Canada Learning Bond transfers to an RESP do not otherwise affect the limits of contributions to the RESP and CLB amounts are not eligible for the Canada Education Savings Grant. No interest is paid on unclaimed Canada Learning Bonds so it is important that the CLB be transferred to an RESP as quickly as possible so that the amount can begin to earn income within the plan.

In the year the child is born, if the parents are eligible for the National Child Benefit Supplement, the parents should:

- obtain a social insurance number for the child (required for an RESP)
- open an RESP account with the new child as beneficiary*
- apply to have the Canada Learning Bond amount transferred to the new RESP.

*An extra $25 will be paid with the first $500 bond to help cover the cost of opening an RESP.

Education Assistance Payments (EAPs). When a student is ready to go to post-secondary school full time, payments can be made out of an RESP. These are called Education Assistance Payments (EAPs). The amounts represent earnings in the plan as well as government contributions and are taxable to the student on Line 130 of the return. The actual contributions may be either returned to the subscriber or paid to the student with no income tax consequences. The CESG will form part of the EAPs.

For full-time studies, the maximum EAP is $5,000 until the student has completed 13 consecutive weeks in a qualifying education program at a post-secondary educational institution. Once the 13 weeks have been completed, there is no limit to the amount that may be withdrawn from the plan.

For part-time students, who spend a minimum of 12 hours a month on coursework, the maximum EAP is $2,500 per 13-week semester. Beneficiaries under an RESP are allowed to receive EAPs for up to six months after ceasing enrolment in a qualifying educational program. However, if, for a period of 12 months, the student does not enroll in a qualifying education program, the 13-week period and the $5,000 limitation will be imposed again.

Beginning in 2011, the 13-week period for full-time students is reduced to 3 weeks for students studying outside Canada.

If amounts are withdrawn from the RESP for purposes other than EAP payments, the lesser of the undistributed CESG amounts and 20% of the amount withdrawn will be returned to the HRSDC by the RESP. Should the beneficiary be required to repay any CESG amounts received as Educational Assistance Payments, a deduction for the amount repaid may be taken.

Accumulated Income Payments (AIPs). If the student does not attend post-secondary school by the time s/he reaches the age of 31, and there are no qualifying substitute beneficiaries, the contributions can go back to the original subscriber. If this happens, the income earned in the plan over the years will become taxable to the subscriber, and the income is subject to a special penalty tax of 20% in addition to the regular taxes payable. Such income inclusions are called "Accumulated Income Payments" or AIPs. Form T1172 must be completed to compute this tax.

As an alternative, if the subscriber has unused RRSP contribution room, AIPs can be transferred into the subscriber's RRSP, up to a lifetime maximum of $50,000. If amounts are transferred to an RRSP, Form T1171 may be used to reduce or eliminate tax withheld on the AIP.

Tax Strategy

You may want to consider using a Tax-Free Savings Account as an adjunct to an RESP for accumulating funds for your adult child's education. Although the TFSA does not have the added incentives of the CESG or CLB, it does offer flexibility that is not available in the RESP. There are no time limits on the contributions, no age limits on the beneficiaries, and no limits to the amount that can be withdrawn in any given year, and the withdrawals will not have to be reported in income—whether the beneficiary becomes a student or not.

CHAPTER 18

RDSPs: Dignity in Disability

Many families take care of disabled people who are vulnerable in every way, including the staffing shortages that the public health care system is often challenged with. Fortunately, it is possible to save in a tax-assisted way to create the funds to privately supplement gaps when they occur in your family.

In 2008 a new type of registered saving plan was introduced in Canada, designed to accumulate funds for the benefit of a disabled person in the family. The *Registered Disability Savings Plans (RDSPs)* are structured very much the same way as RESPs are, which allows for tax-assisted grants and bonds that can significantly enhance your savings.

Any person eligible to claim the Disability Amount can be the beneficiary of an RDSP and the plan can be established by the disabled person or by an authorized representative. Anyone can contribute to an RDSP—they need not be a family member—but contributors can never receive a refund of their contributions.

Where it is not clear whether the disabled individual is contractually competent and they do not have a legal representative, certain family members (spouse or common-law partner or parent) will be allowed to become the plan holder for the disabled adult. If subsequently it is determined that the disabled individual is able to enter into a contract, they will replace the family member as the plan holder. Where the disabled individual is found not to be contractually competent, a legal representative of the disabled individual may replace the family member as the plan holder. This new measure will be in effect until December 31, 2016.

Tax Treatment. While contributions are not deductible, income accumulates in an RDSP tax free. Contributions withdrawn from an RDSP are not taxable either, but all other amounts—accumulated investment income, and the lucrative government grants and bonds (discussed below)—are taxable in the hands of the beneficiary as withdrawn. When RDSP income is withdrawn, it is reported to the taxpayer in Box 131 of a T4A slip. These amounts must be included in income on line 125.

Here's the tax secret > There is no annual limit on contributions to an RDSP but lifetime contributions cannot exceed $200,000. Contributions are permitted until the end of the year in which the disabled beneficiary turns 59. That means that windfalls, like inheritances can be contributed to the RDSP, but it may not be a good idea to do that in a lump sum, because you'll want to time the contributions to maximize the Canada Disability Grants and Bonds.

Government Support. The Federal government will provide direct financial assistance to RDSPs in two ways: with a *Canada Disability Savings Grant (CDSG)* and *Canada Disability Savings Bond (CDSB)*

1. **Canada Disability Saving Grant** will match RDSP contributions as follows:

Family Net Income (2012)

Up to $85,414	Over $85,414
First $500—300% (maximum $1,500)	First $1,000—100% (maximum $1,000)
Next $1,000—200% (maximum $2,000)	
Therefore: $1,500 contributed to RDSP generates $3,500 CDSG	Therefore, $1,000 contributed to RDSP generates $1,000 CDSG

Family income is calculated in the same manner as it is for Canada Education Savings Grant purposes except that in years *after the beneficiary turns 18 family income is the income of the beneficiary and their spouse or common-law partner.* There is a lifetime maximum of $70,000 that will be funded under the CDSG and an RDSP will not qualify to receive a CDSG from the year in which the beneficiary turns **49**.

2. **Canada Disability Savings Bond.** Unlike the CDSG, there is no requirement that a contribution be made to a RDSP before a savings bond contribution is available. The maximum annual CDSB contribution is $1,000 and is earned where family income does not exceed $24,863

(2012). The CDSB amount is phased out completely when family income is $42,707 (2012).

There is a lifetime maximum of $20,000 for CDSBs. Like the CDSG, CDSBs will not be paid after the beneficiary of the RDSP turns **49**.

Catch-Up of RDSP Grants and Bonds. When an RDSP is opened, CDSG and CDSB entitlements will be calculated for the 10 years prior to the opening date (but after 2008) based on the beneficiary's family income in those years. CDSB entitlements from the catch-up period will be paid into the plan in the year the plan is opened. When contributions are made to the plan, the CDSG rate earned by those contributions will be paid as if the contributions were made in the year that the entitlements were earned.

Example > Ivan opened an RDSP for his disabled son Brad in 2012 and contributed $10,000. Brad is 24, single and his net income has never exceeded $40,000. Because the catch-up of grants and bonds is allowed, the $10,000 contribution is treated as if it were $1,500 deposits in 2009 to 2011 and the remaining $5,500 in 2012. In each year, those deposits would be eligible for grants of $3,500 so the total CDSG generated by the one $10,000 deposit is $14,000. In addition, CDSBs will be generated based on Brad's actual net income in years 2009 to 2012.

Withdrawing an RDSP Pension. Only the beneficiary and/or the beneficiary's legal representatives can withdraw amounts from an RDSP. That beneficiary must start to withdraw funds from the RDSP in the year he or she turns 60. Maximum annual withdrawal amounts are to be established based on life expectancies but the beneficiary may encroach on the capital sooner, although a portion of the grants and bonds may have to be repaid if that is within 10 years of the plan start date.

For withdrawals made after 2013, the maximum *Lifetime Disability Assistance Payment* (LDAP) will be increased to no less than 10% of the fair market value of the assets in the plan at the beginning of the year. Where the maximum amount under the existing LDAP formula exceeds 10% of the asset value, a different formula is used.

Also, beginning in 2014, the current RESP rollover provisions to RRSPs will be extended to RDSPs. That is, RESP investments, after CESG and CLBs have been repaid, may be rolled over to an RDSP so long as the plan holder has sufficient RDSP contribution room. These contributions will not generate CDSB or CDSGs. Withdrawals of rolled-over RESPs will be taxable.

Specified Disability Savings Plans. Where a beneficiary has a shortened life expectancy, a repayment of grants and bonds will not be required if a DAP, up to a specified limit, is made to the beneficiary. In this case, the plan holder must file the prescribed form along with a letter from a medical doctor certifying that the beneficiary is not likely to survive more than five years, with the RDSP issuer. The RDSP issuer must then notify the Minister of Human Resources and Skills Development. Once the election has been made, the RDSP will be considered a Specified Disability Savings Plan (SDSP).

The following rules apply to Specified Disability Savings Plans:

- lifetime disability assistance payments must begin in the year following the year the plan became an SDSP,
- the maximum amount of taxable DAPs that can be withdrawn from the plan each year is $10,000 (or more if required to satisfy the minimum withdrawal requirements if the beneficiary is 60 years of age or older),
- no further contributions can be made into the plan, except for the rollover of a deceased individual's RRSP or a RRIF proceeds to the SDSP of a financially dependent disabled child or grandchild,
- no new grants and bonds will be paid into the plan, and
- no carry forward of unused entitlements to grants and bonds will be permitted, except for the year in which the plan became an SDSP.

Repayment of Grants and Bonds. For withdrawals from RDSPs after 2013, the "10-Year Replacement Rule" will be replaced with a "Proportional Repayment Rule." Under the old rule, if any amount is withdrawn from the RDSP any CDSG and CDSB amounts received in the past ten years must be repaid (except for SDSPs). Under the new rule, the repayment amount will be the lesser of

- the amount removed x 3 and
- the amount of the CDSG and CDSB amounts received in the past ten years.

Death or Cessation of Qualification. When an RDSP beneficiary ceases to qualify for the Disability Amount, currently, the RDSP must be terminated immediately. Beginning in 2014, when this happens, the beneficiary may make an election to continue the plan for up to four calendar years after the end of the calendar year in which the beneficiary ceases to be eligible for the Disability Amount. During the election period:

- No contributions will be permitted.
- No new CDSB or CDSGs will be paid into the plan.

- Withdrawals will be permitted subject to the new Proportional Repayment Rule.

Current RDSPs which would be required to be terminated before 2014 will not be required to be terminated until the end of 2014.

Impact on Other Means-Tested Support. RDSP withdrawals will not affect any other means-tested support delivered through the income tax system including, in particular, the clawback of OAS or Employment Insurance benefits.

Tax Strategy

It takes a village to raise a family. When that village can collaborate to build a private pension for the disabled, it's a wonderful thing. If you support a disabled adult, look into funding their future, with the help of the generous matching provided by the federal government.

Essential Tax Facts

Follow these simple rules to take charge:

Make Your Family a Tax-Efficient Economic Unit. Getting the best tax results for each individual in the family is smart. But families that plan for the creation of both income and capital as a unit, get great after-tax results. File family tax returns together as a starting point.

Work With Tax Free Zones. Every Canadian can earn about $11,000 of tax free income, thanks to the Basic Personal Amount. In principle, one person making $44,000 will pay more tax than four making $11,000 each, as they pay none. Income splitting can make a big difference to the accumulation of family wealth.

Claim Refundable Credits. There are three important refundable tax credits to claim by filing a tax return: The Canada Child Tax Benefit (CCTB), the GST/HST Credit and the Working Income Tax Benefit. Provincial governments can offer more. Keep your family net income below income testing thresholds to take full advantage.

The RRSP: Both for Now and Later. Every family member with "earned income" can create RRSP contribution room, with a tax deduction resulting for any contributions. Used at your option this year or in the future, the deduction reduces income taxes payable; also earnings are not taxed while the funds remain in the plan. Quite simply, it can double your savings due to the tax free compounding of all the principal in the plan. These plans offer income splitting opportunities later in life, too.

Reduce Withholding Taxes With an RRSP. Put more money in your family's saving funds all year long by reducing your withholding taxes as a result of your RRSP contributions. Ask your tax advisor about filing Form T1213 to do so.

Plan for Tax-Free RRSP Withdrawals. All amounts removed from an RRSP are taxable as ordinary income unless they are withdrawn under the Home Buyers' Plan or the Lifelong Learning Plan. For those purposes they are tax-free, as long as a specified payment schedule is met. In addition, any amounts withdrawn when income is below the personal amounts available to an individual taxpayer, will be tax-free.

Set Up Spousal Retirement Income. Spousal RRSPs provide a means of transferring assets from one spouse to another so long at the funds are not removed from the plan until at least three calendar years after the last spousal contribution. In the meantime, the contributor gets the tax deduction.

Work Around the Attribution Rules. They make income splitting and joint asset accumulation more difficult with spouses and minor children, but opportunities exist if you follow proper procedures. You've seen the opportunities with RRSPs. Transferring other sources of income and capital will save you money, too.

The TFSA is Your Ticket to Tax Freedom. Make sure you contribute $5,000 for each resident adult in the family every year. Earnings are not taxed either in the plan or when they are removed. It provides an excellent parking place for transferred assets from the higher-income taxpayer to lower-income taxpayers in the family.

Build Education Funding with Sweeteners. The RESP is a registered plan designed to fund post-secondary education costs. Contributions are not tax deductible, but government assistance is made through Canada Education Savings Grants and Bonds, and that sweetens the opportunity to save more money in an investment which will result, statistically, in higher individual earnings and wealth accumulation.

Plan Student Income Wisely. Amounts contributed to RESPs may be returned tax-free to the contributor but grants, bonds and earnings are taxable to the beneficiary if they become a student or, if not, grants and bonds must be returned and the remaining earnings in the plan are taxable to the contributor and subject to a 20% penalty tax. Seek professional advice if study plans get put on hold or stop completely.

Build Private Pensions for the Disabled. Health care and home care is expensive to governments and can leave gaps in services that you may find unacceptable for your loved one. An alternative is private funding for additional care. The RDSP can help. It is a registered plan set up for a disabled individual. Contributions are not deductible but generous government assistance is available in the form of Canada Disability Savings Grants and Bonds. It's a good way to ensure dignity in disability.

Withdraw RDSPs With Caution. Amounts withdrawn from RDSPs are taxable to the beneficiary as Disability Assistance Payments. If grants and bonds are withdrawn within ten years, some portion may need to be repaid, except in the case of a specified disability savings plan (where the beneficiary has a life expectancy of not more than five years).

PART IV

Creating Tax Effective Wealth

CHAPTER 19

The Rules of the Rich

The recent global financial meltdown has reduced the net worth of millions of people, yet there are even greater threats to family wealth on the horizon—too much debt, increasing interest rates, more tax and inflation erosion.

Throughout these tough financial times, one of the biggest threats to your family's wealth could be the inappropriate financial actions you may be tempted to take—or not take. The solution to creating wealth despite difficult times, can often be found in using a simple set of rules, used consistently to guide your financial decisions. Thinking "tax" in making those decisions will make you richer.

What are those "rules of the rich"? Over the years, in working with taxpayers and writing about and teaching taxes, I have met average people who became very wealthy by focusing consistently on four elements of wealth management throughout their lifetimes: the accumulation, growth, preservation and transitioning of their wealth. That money became "real" when it held its purchasing power—what was left after taxes, inflation and fees. Those four elements and three wealth eroders are what we focus on in working with advisors and their clients at the Knowledge Bureau. We call this strategic process to managing wealth, Real Wealth Management™.

We have found that people who become richer follow a consistent, purposeful process for thinking about their earning and savings activities. They use a series of principles, processes and habits that work not only in one generation, but in many. And the wealthier they are, the more focused they become on their biggest wealth eroder, taxation.

Tax erosion is inter-generational. You are taxed on your income along the way; you will also be taxed on the capital you have accumulated before it passes along to your children. That's way a strategic focus, process and plan is required as you accumulate more wealth.

Your financial experiences will provide the backdrop for both the money and the financial wisdom you pass along to your heirs, and this is very important. You will likely accumulate more as you age, and this means your money will require management—rules to grow by, and rules to protect and transition it. In addition, you'll need help when you no longer can make financial decisions for yourself and your family.

How do you know where to start in making those important financial decisions, adding a tax focus and then laying the groundwork for a plan that will sustain your wealth over time? You may find it easier to move forward if you understand how to measure your financial stability, today.

How to Measure Financial Stability. Just how well are you doing compared to where you were a year ago, three years ago, etc.? We measure all kinds of things regarding our physical health—our weight, our fitness level, our body mass. Most people don't measure their financial stability. How "financially stable" you are, however, really matters in these times.

Your financial stability is measured by net worth. The Department of Human Resources and Skills Development Canada has a great definition that speaks to the financial actions you may wish to take once you better understand how to measure your financial progress.

> Net worth, also referred to as wealth, is one measure of an individual's material well-being. It is the amount by which assets differ from liabilities or debt.

> Net worth represents the degree of flexibility Canadians have to respond to unexpected events (such as a job loss), or to opportunities (such as starting a business), or to needs that arise (such as paying for a child's education). Building up net worth is also a key part of retirement planning, enabling a more comfortable retirement.

The *Net Worth (Wealth) Indicator* shows the net worth of Canadian families, including their median net worth, assets and debt. In 2005, the median assets of Canadian families were $229,930 and the median debt was $44,500. Their median net worth was $148,350, 23.2% higher than in 1999. Stats Canada Quarterly Report second quarter 2012 reported that household net worth rose 1.2% to $6.8 trillion in the second quarter, following a 2.0% increase in the first quarter. Household per capita net worth increased from $192,500 in the first quarter to $194,100 in the second quarter.

Here's the tax secret > Your family net worth is the indicator of both your wealth and your financial stability. How well you manage your after-tax position both now and in the future can significantly increase both.

Getting Started. To get started on managing your tax-efficient wealth, you need three things: financial goals, common analysis tools and a consistent way to analyze your results.

- *Financial goals that lead to a long term vision.* This simply begins with a series of probing questions you may have about an important financial event—like buying a new home, or making retirement plans. Many individuals and families use the services of a variety of financial specialists—tax, legal, insurance, investment, retirement, business valuators, and so on, to help them and that's important. New financial decisions are required over your lifetime, and you can't be an expert at all of them. The object is to *plan* your financial priorities and then to help yourself to the services you need, like tax preparation or investment product selection, for example.
- *Common analysis tools*, that everyone can understand and work with. Your long term financial success will benefit from the consistent use of three documents that have tax implications: the tax returns for all the family members, the personal net worth statement, and your financial plans. The tax return reports on history—what happened last year. The personal net worth statement reports on your financial position at the present time; providing an accurate valuation of your assets and debt. These documents can provide a good picture of the after-tax income you have and the capital you need to meet family goals in the future. That's where your financial plans come in: to project how you will meet those future needs—with budgets, cash flow statements, investment plans, education and retirement plans, and so on.
- *A consistent process for the evaluation of results,* which will ensure that regular meetings with advisor are purposeful, that changes in net worth and personal taxes are understood and anticipated, and most important, to determine whether your net worth is growing or declining—after taxes, inflation and fees. Do you have sustainable wealth? Or will your wealth disappear as we manage through a variety of economic events? Adjustments to previous decisions can be made

if necessary. But more importantly decisions you have been putting off will become more obvious to you.

Armed with your vision and goals, and the documents you'll get to know better in analyzing your results, you are ready to accumulate, grow, preserve and transition your wealth.

Accumulation, the first element of Real Wealth Management, begins with the commitment of money (whether earned or received as a gift or social benefit) to a consistent savings plan. To accumulate with consistency, you may wish to consider the following checklist of questions in collaboration with your advisors:

- What are my savings goals, and the goals of each family member?
- How much should we start to save to reach those goals?
- When should we start saving, and in what accounts?
- What income can we generate in the short and the long term?
- What is the after-tax yield on our investments and why is this important?
- How do taxes and inflation affect these investments?
- What are the right investment products that will help us reach our goals?
- When should we buy and when should we sell?

There are several reasons for considering these questions:

Continual Accumulation. Do you know rich people who don't think they are wealthy? That's not unusual. The reason is simple: your capital will deplete and depreciate and must be replenished and/or replaced over time. That means you may find the need to continue to accumulate, no matter how old you are or how rich you are.

The Role of Human Capital. While there are many sources of wealth, and many ways to accumulate it, the role of "human capital" cannot be understated. This is your personal productivity which will add new income and ability to the management of your capital. Once your human capital stops contributing—perhaps due to disability—you must rely on the performance of capital to fund your wants and needs. Recently, the returns have been slim, and many people have decided to work longer to add to their capital.

The Role of Behavior. There are likely present-oriented people in your family who have difficulty saving money for the future. Sometimes this is simply behavioral; the person has no discipline in spending or saving money. Another person may not have a strong sense of future and this can change over a lifetime. However, future oriented people can delay immediate satisfaction to the future, by investing for the future through a strategy, a plan, a process and the right people to get disciplined results. There are challenges here too, because these folks might be afraid to spend, which can have expensive tax consequences, too.

You have learned that "sustainable wealth" keeps its purchasing power over time—after tax, after costs and after inflation. That takes both a short and long-term focus to expertly manage your family's wealth over several generations.

Planning your investments—short and long term. In the previous part of the book, we discussed the key investments to give you immediate tax-efficient results as you begin your savings process: the RRSP, the TFSA, the RESP and the RDSP. When you add a strategic process like Real Wealth Management to your decision-making, you will be able see a clearer path to the investments you need to make to get the results you want, and when to make them.

For example, once you have full funded registered investment opportunities, it's time to look beyond to other financial assets in non-registered accounts and other non-financial asset categories, like real estate for example. The chart below, can help you visualize how to categorize your investment decision-making into those four important elements, and make your plans tax efficient, too.

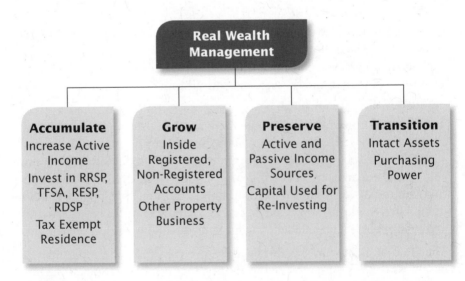

Real Wealth Management			
Accumulate	**Grow**	**Preserve**	**Transition**
Increase Active Income	Inside Registered, Non-Registered Accounts	Active and Passive Income Sources	Intact Assets Purchasing Power
Invest in RRSP, TFSA, RESP, RDSP	Other Property Business	Capital Used for Re-Investing	
Tax Exempt Residence			

Working with Your Advisors. Any strategic wealth management plan will be better served by a consistent, collaborative approach. Consider these five steps in making better tax-efficient decisions both with your advisors and your family members:

1. Develop financial questions that require decision-making.
2. Accumulate money by analyzing how you use it: in the present vs. in the future.
3. Grow personal and family net worth according to your vision and your goals.
4. Preserve the results of your human capital—your personal productivity that results in the actively earned income sources you are responsible for—by protecting what's left after tax, with astutely planned investments. Those investments should earn tax-efficient "passive income sources." Always re-invest capital for a long term result that retains your purchasing power.
5. Transition assets intact—after taxes, fees and inflation.

Tax Strategy

How you make your income—employment or self-employment—and how much you take home for needs and savings has a direct bearing on your ability to create wealth. When you add a tax-efficient lens to accumulating, growing, preserving and transitioning your wealth to other family members or the community, everyone will be wealthier.

CHAPTER 20

Maximizing Personal Productivity

The first stop in building wealth for most people is making money through employment. By investing in yourself, your ongoing education, your company, and the tax benefits available to employees, you'll soon kick start your own wealth creation.

When you work for someone else as an employee, you are in an "employer-employee relationship" which CRA defines as verbal or written agreement in which an employee agrees to work on a full-time or part-time basis for a specified or indeterminate period of time, in return for salary or wages. Under this type of arrangement, the employer has the right to decide where, when and how the work will be done.

Here's the tax secret > Most people understand they can negotiate for salary or wages, but it's the job perks—especially the tax free ones—that can be exponentially more valuable in accumulating personal wealth.

There are several sources of employment income within a master-servant relationship:

- Income from salary or wages, which is taxable in the year received
- Director's fees (these are subject to CPP but not EI premiums)
- Employee Benefit Plans like a self-funded leave of absence
- The value of benefits or perks, including your employer-provided car, vacations, education, uniforms, meals, memberships to fitness clubs, and so on. Some of these benefits are taxable, some are not. We'll discuss the tax-free ones in more detail in the next chapter.

Making Tax Remittances for You. The employer has several obligations to meet in this relationship, too. He or she is required by law to make statutory deductions from your gross pay for contributions to the Canada Pension Plan (CPP), Employment Insurance (EI) and Income Taxes (IT).

These are usually remitted once a month, although very small businesses have the option to remit each quarter. Minors do not contribute to the Canada Pension Plan; nor do those over 70.

Everyone who is employed must contribute to EI; that is, there is no age limit. Employees who earn $2,000 or less from employment will have their premiums refunded when they file their tax returns. This eliminates students or occasional workers from eligibility for EI as well.

Employment income is always reported on the cash basis—when received. You will also report your employment income on a calendar year basis— January to December—in every case. Sometimes, an opportunity for salary or income deferral to a following year may be available.

Salary Deferral Arrangements. Under a salary deferral arrangement, receipt of salary or wages is postponed into the future; generally the next tax year. However, here's a trap: the deferred amount is generally included in income in the current year or year of contribution—which means that no tax deferral is actually allowed.

Sabbaticals. In addition, however, it is possible to defer salary or wages for a self-funded leave or sabbatical. The employee who saves in this way will not be subject to tax in the year the leave is earned as long as salary is deferred for no more than six years and no more than ⅓ of the salary is deferred. The leave of absence must start no later than the seventh year and must be for a period of at least six months. The employee must then return to work for at least the same amount of time as the leave. The amounts are taxable in the year withdrawn.

Employee Benefit Plans. You should also be aware that there are numerous types of employee benefit plans available. Often the employee will not be taxed when contributions are made to these types of plans but benefits received from them are generally taxable when received.

Tax-deferred plans include registered pension plans, group sickness or accident plans, supplementary employment plans, deferred profit sharing plans, wage loss replacement plans, and certain employee trusts.

Minimizing Your Tax Withholdings. You may be familiar with the *TD1 Personal Tax Credit Return*. It's a form you'll complete every time you start a new job, to let your employer know how much income tax to withhold from your pay.

It is based on non-refundable tax credits you are entitled to, like your basic personal amount, spousal amount, amount for dependent children, caregiver amounts, tuition and education amounts, and special deductions like the deduction for Northern Residents. The purpose of the form is for you to direct your employer to recognize the increased tax deductions and credits you are entitled to and to take these into account when computing how much tax to withhold from your pay.

This form, however, won't take into account other tax deductible expenditures you may have; for example RRSP contributions, deductible spousal support, significant interest costs, rental losses, child care, commission sales or other expenses of employment, medical expenses or large charitable donations. If you're eligible for any of these deductions or credits, file *Form T1213 Request to Reduce Tax Deductions at Source* so that your employer can further reduce withholding taxes and increase your take-home pay.

Summary: Deductible Employment Expenses

- Accounting and legal fees, not including income tax preparation
- Advertising and promotion
- Motor vehicle expenses including Capital Cost Allowance (CCA), interest or leasing costs and operating costs like gas, oil and maintenance
- Travel expenses including rail, air, bus or other travel costs if away from the employer's home base at least 12 hours
- Parking costs (but generally not at the place of employment)
- Meals[4], tips and hotel costs providing the excursion is for at least 12 hours and away from the taxpayer's metropolitan area.
- Food, beverages and entertainment expenses[4]
- Supplies used up directly in the work (stationery, maps, etc.)
- Salaries paid to an assistant (including spouses or children if Fair Market Value is actually paid for work actually performed)
- Office rent or certain home office expenses
- Employed artists are allowed to claim the cost of supplies used up in their employment to a maximum of 20% of net income or $1,000, as explained later.

---

[4] Meals and tips are subject to a 50% restriction except for long-haul truck drivers whose deduction is higher, as described in a later chapter. Have on file a signed form T2200 *Declaration of Conditions of Employment.*

- Long distance truck drivers may claim the cost of meals and lodging according to specific rules while en route; certain forestry employees may claim the cost of operating their power saws
- Tradespersons may claim the cost of tools purchased if required by their employer for use in their employment (subject to claim maximums as described later).

Employment Commissions included in income may be offset by Employment Expenses on Line 229 and the GST/HST Rebate on Line 457 under certain conditions. See *Jacks on Tax* by Evelyn Jacks for a line-by-line guide and instructions for maximizing your deductions in these cases.

Grab the TD1 and T1213 forms off the internet, from your human resource department, your tax software or ask your tax or financial advisors to help you. Then use all these legal tax provisions to accumulate more wealth by reducing your tax withholdings. Less tax will be taken from your earnings—a wise move—especially if you prefer to use your hard-earned wages to pay off non-deductible credit card debt, your mortgage, or invest in a TFSA or RRSP.

Bring on the Perks. The next thing to do to build your own wealth faster when you are employed is to leverage the lower-taxed corporate dollars your employer's company may be subject to, in order to build your compensation. You can earn equity as well as employment income, with proper tax planning. That's the subject of the next chapter.

Tax Strategy

Be sure to negotiate for the opportunity to join private health care plans to mitigate risks to your earning capacity and earn perks even if they might be taxable, to leverage your employer's investment in the business. That might include an employer-provided auto, low-interest investment loans, stock options, employer-sponsored pension or matching RRSP contributions, and a variety of tax free perks.

CHAPTER 21

Tax-Free Benefits

When you receive tax-free benefits from your employer, you will have a lucrative opportunity to improve your lifestyle, your income-earning capacity and your personal net worth. Consider the following list before you go into any employment contract negotiation:

Employer-Paid Educational Costs. You are not taxed when training is paid for by your employer for courses taken primarily for the benefit of the employer. However, a taxable benefit arises when the training is primarily for your personal benefit. Amounts included in your income for tuition will be eligible for the tuition tax credit if they would have been eligible had they been paid by you personally.

Financial Counselling and Income Tax Return Preparation. Financial counselling services or income tax return preparation provided directly or indirectly by an employer normally produce a taxable benefit. However, financial counselling services in respect of your re-employment or retirement will not result in a taxable benefit. This is important during difficult financial times when employees are forced to accept an early retirement package or a layoff. Be sure to ask for these services.

Frequent Flyer Points. Up until 2009, CRA took the position that where you accumulate frequent flyer points while travelling on employer-paid business trips and used them to obtain air travel or other benefits for personal use by you or your family, the fair market value of such air travel or other benefits must be included in your income. For 2009 and subsequent years, the CRA no longer requires frequent flyer points earned why flying on business to be included in an employee's income, so long as:

• the points are not converted to cash,

- the plan or arrangement is not indicative of an alternate form of remuneration, and
- the plan or arrangement is not for tax avoidance purposes.

Where an employer controls the points (e.g., a company credit card is used), the employer will continue to be required to report the fair market value of any benefits received by the employee as income on the employee's T4 slip when the points are redeemed.

Non-Cash Gifts Under $500. A gift (either in cash or in kind) from your employer is an employment benefit. However non-cash gifts and non-cash awards to an arm's length employee, that is someone not related to the employer, regardless of the number of them, are non-taxable to the extent that the total aggregate value of all non-cash gifts and awards to that employee for the year is less than $500. The total value in excess of $500 annually will be taxable.

In addition, a separate non-cash long service/anniversary award may also qualify for non-taxable status to the extent its total value is $500 or less. The value in excess of $500 will be taxable. In order to qualify, the anniversary award cannot be for less than five years of service or for five years since the last long service award had been provided to the employee.

For the purposes of applying the $500 thresholds, the annual gifts and awards threshold and the long service/anniversary awards threshold are separate.

Items of an immaterial or nominal value, such as coffee, tea, T-shirts with employer logos, mugs, plaques, trophies, etc., will not be considered a taxable benefit to employees. There is no defined monetary threshold that determines an immaterial amount. Factors that may be taken into account include the value, frequency, and administrative practicability of accounting for nominal benefits.

Overtime Meals and Allowances. No taxable benefit will arise on overtime meal perks if:

- the value of the meal or meal allowance is reasonable (a value of up to $17 will generally be considered reasonable),
- the employee works two or more hours of overtime right before or right after his or her scheduled hours of work, and
- the overtime is infrequent and occasional in nature. Less than three times a week will generally be considered infrequent or occasional. This condition may also be met where the meal or allowance is provided three or more times per week on an occasional basis to meet workload demands such as major repairs or periodic financial reporting.

If overtime occurs on a frequent basis or becomes the norm, the CRA considers the overtime meal allowances to be a taxable benefit since they start taking on the characteristics of additional remuneration.

Vacations. Where an employer pays for a vacation for you or your family, the cost is considered to be a taxable benefit. In such cases, the benefit is equal to the fair market value of the travel and accommodation less any amount you repay to your employer. The taxable benefit may be reduced if there is conclusive evidence to show that you were involved in business activities for your employer during the vacation.

In a situation where your presence is required for business purposes and this function is the main purpose of the trip, no benefit will be associated with the travelling expenses necessary to accomplish the business objectives of the trip if the expenditures are reasonable in relation to the business function.

Where a business trip is extended to provide for a paid holiday or vacation, you are considered to have received a taxable benefit equal to the costs borne by the employer with respect to that extension.

Note that if your spouse accompanies you on a business trip the payment or reimbursement by the employer of the spouse's travelling expenses is a taxable benefit unless the spouse was, in fact, engaged primarily in business activities on behalf of the employer during the trip.

Relocation Costs. If your employer reimburses you for a loss suffered in selling the family home upon being required to move to another locality or upon retirement from employment in a remote area, only a portion of the reimbursement must be included in income as a taxable benefit.

Where the loss and reimbursement are both less than $15,000 no taxable benefit will accrue. Where the loss and reimbursement exceed $15,000 the benefit is one-half of the excess of the reimbursement over $15,000.

Employer-Paid Parking. Parking costs paid by your employer will generally be included as a taxable benefit, calculated at fair market value. Parking is excluded from the value of a stand-by charge, or auto operating expense benefits, or benefits for disabled employees. However, recent court challenges have found in favour of the taxpayer in establishing a non-taxable status for parking, when it was found to be in the employer's favour to offer parking to employees.

Employer-Paid Health Care Premiums. The tax status of premiums paid and benefits received from employer-sponsored group and non-group health plans can be confusing, but is very important in the overall scheme of compensation to the employee. These plans can provide important peace of mind when expensive health care costs arise.

Premiums will be taxable in two instances: where the employer pays or reimburses you for the employee portion of premiums to a provincial health care plan; or where the employer pays some or all of the premium under a non-group plan that is a wage loss replacement, sickness or accident insurance plan, a disability insurance plan, or an income maintenance insurance plan. However, payroll source deductions made for the payment of the premiums are considered to be payments made by you, not the employer.

If the wage loss replacement plan is a group plan, or if the health care plan is private, then the employer's portion of the premiums paid is not considered to be a taxable benefit.

If the plan was funded, in whole or in part, by the employer, then the benefits received are taxable, but you are entitled to a deduction for the lesser of the amount received from the plan and all premiums that you have paid since 1968 and not previously deducted. The deduction should be claimed on Line 229 of the tax return.

Using the Employer's Capital Pool. Employees should always strive to build capital—assets that can produce other sources of income or grow in value. One way to do so is to use your employer's money—at preferred low or no-interest rates. This however, will give rise to a taxable benefit.

For example, the employer may loan funds to you or your spouse. In either case, a taxable benefit would accrue to you, unless your spouse is also an employee of the same employer. The same rules will apply when you receive a loan from a third party, if the employer is involved in securing the loan for you.

If the employer-provided loan was used to acquire income-producing investments, the amount of the interest benefit shown on the T4 will be deductible as a carrying charge.

On a no-interest loan, the amount of the benefit is equal to:

- the interest on the loan at CRA's currently prescribed rate (see Part I for details for the current tax year), plus
- any payments made by the employer, less
- amounts of interest paid back by you to the employer either during the year or within 30 days after the end of the year.

This benefit is included in your income and will be reported on your T4. Now is a good time to take advantage of these prescribed rates, as they have rarely been lower.

If the loan bears interest, there is no taxable benefit where the interest rate on the loan is equal to or greater than a commercial rate so long as you actually pay the interest. Special rules apply to housing loans and home relocation loans, discussed later.

Note: The rules above apply to shareholders as well as to employees. The difference between a shareholder loan and an employee loan is that the benefit accrues to the employee, even if the loan is to someone else. However, the benefit accrues to the debtor if the loan is a shareholder loan.

This is because of a special anti-avoidance rule that prevents a shareholder from indefinitely postponing the recognition of income from a corporation by taking continuous shareholder loans. Professional help should be sought to report these transactions.

Where the employer-provided loan is forgiven or settled for an amount less than the amount outstanding, the forgiven amount must be included in your income.

Where the shareholder is also an employee, certain loans will be allowed the treatment given to any employee if it can be established that bona fide loan arrangements are made, the loan is repaid over a reasonable period of time and the loan is a direct result of the employer-employee relationship. This means that the company must make similar loans available to all employees.

Employee Stock Option Plans. Employees may be presented with an opportunity to purchase shares in the employer's corporation at some future date, but at a price set at the time the option was granted. This is known as the exercise price.

There are no tax consequences when an employee stock option is granted. But when you exercise these stock or security options a taxable benefit arises, equal to the difference between the market value of the shares purchased and the exercise price. When is this taxable? It depends on the type of corporation.

If the employer is a Canadian Controlled Private Corporation (CCPC), the taxable benefit is deemed to arise when you dispose of the shares. In the case of a public corporation, the taxable benefit arises when you exercise the option.

When the security options taxable benefit is included in income, you will also be eligible for the Security Options Deduction which is equal to one-half of the taxable benefit.

It is wise to get some professional help before stock options are exercised or the shares disposed of, as complicated new technical provisions must be observed. For example, if the shares acquired under such a stock option are donated to a registered charity or to a private foundation (after March 19, 2007), you may claim a deduction equal to the taxable benefit. In addition, be sure to get professional help if you previously deferred your stock option benefits; a provision no longer available for stock options exercised after March 4, 2010.

Tax Strategy

While employment income is usually taxable as received, a few special tax preferences exist to help the employee defer some compensation into the future. Tap into these wherever you can. But start with a good, long-term contract, a substantial perk package, and a "golden parachute" in case things don't work out.

CHAPTER 22

Accumulating Money

Cash flow and income are two different things, but to many people, the terms are interchangeable. What you really need to know is how much money you have to work with each month, after all source deductions and pension remittances have been deducted. The difference in the interpretation of cash flow and income, however is important. The money that ends up in your pocket is often created from many different sources, which co-mingle before and after tax.

Here's the tax secret > Your opportunity is to "blend" the taxable and tax-free sources, to get the financial results you want.

To accumulate more money in your savings accounts, you will benefit from an analysis of your after-tax cash flow. This will make the planning of a tax-efficient income structure easier; it will also help you build real bench strength in your savings pools and, as important, stay invested, to grow and preserve wealth.

Sources of Cash Flow

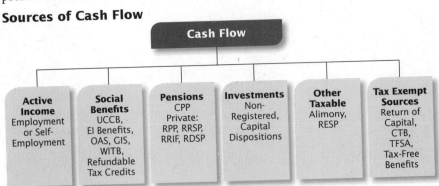

Cash Flow					
Active Income Employment or Self-Employment	**Social Benefits** UCCB, EI Benefits, OAS, GIS, WITB, Refundable Tax Credits	**Pensions** CPP Private: RPP, RRSP, RRIF, RDSP	**Investments** Non-Registered, Capital Dispositions	**Other Taxable** Alimony, RESP	**Tax Exempt Sources** Return of Capital, CTB, TFSA, Tax-Free Benefits

What are the Sources of Cash Flow? Cash flow is derived from a variety of sources:

- **Active Income:** Employment and/or self-employment
- **Social Benefits:** Universal Child Care Benefits (UCCB), Employment Insurance, and the Old Age Security (OAS) and Guaranteed Income Supplement (GIS) and the Working Income Tax Benefit are examples. These are income-tested. This category may include other federal and provincial tax credits.
- **Pensions:** These sources are contributory in nature—the taxpayer and/or an employer contribute to the fund. This can include public pensions—such as the Canada Pension Plan (CPP). It can also include taxable and exempt foreign pension receipts, or private pension benefits from employer-sponsored Registered Pension Plans (RPPs), Registered Retirement Savings Plans (RRSPs), Registered Retirement Income Funds (RRIFs), and annuities or from Registered Disability Savings Plans (RDSPs).
- **Non-Registered Investments:** Clients may have passive income sources from investments in non-registered accounts. Those earnings can include interest, dividends, net rental income and royalties; known as "income from property" in the *Income Tax Act*.
- **Capital Dispositions:** A capital gain or loss can occur when investors dispose of income-producing assets which have increased or decreased in value. This can include stocks, bonds, mutual fund units, other securities, personal residences, rental properties, shares in small business corporations, farming or fishing enterprises, and other personal properties, like family art or other heirlooms.
- *Other Taxable Amounts:* This can include taxable alimony, non-taxable child support or income from a Registered Education Savings Plan, for example.

Receipt of many the amounts above have tax consequences. However cash flow can also result from the following tax exempt sources:

- **Return of Capital:** These receipts represent a return of the original amount invested; therefore receipts are not considered taxable investment income until they exceed the original cost, or in the case of mutual funds, the original weighted average cost.
- **Refundable Tax Credits:** These are good sources of new capital, especially for families. They include the Child Tax Benefit or the Goods and Services Tax Credit available from the federal government and several provincial credits.

- **Tax Free Withdrawals From a TFSA:** These amounts can be used for any purpose and easily reinvested into investments that provide further tax efficiency.
- **Gifts or Inheritances:** These sources can be significant; they need to be identified to establish redundancy—those amounts that are not needed and can be saved for the future.
- **Insurance Proceeds:** Benefits from a life or certain wage loss and disability insurance policies are not taxable.

Once you have charted where all your income sources stem from, you can begin a formal "accumulation" process: figuring out how to deploy both income and your savings as efficiently as possible to maximize the amount of after-tax income available to use to invest into savings, real estate and even a business if that's a dream of yours. You'll also want to review your current savings pools to evaluate if you have the money in the right places.

When you think about how you will accumulate more money for lifestyle wants and future needs, think about the following:

How much money do I have and how do I use it? Find left over or "redundant income" for savings purposes and to manage your consumer debt. *That debt is not deductible and erodes your ability to make your money work for you.* Plan how you can pay it down.

Manage Time. Use the "time value of money" to your advantage: invest sooner, for longer. File tax returns on time. Use an RRSP to create instant tax savings you can reinvest.

Manage the Tax. Pay only the correct amount of tax on income, never more. Keep as much of the first dollar of income earned as long as you can before paying tax; never prepay taxes if you don't have to. Your big tax refund is actually a bad thing! Get your money working for you sooner—use more of the first dollar you earn to do so.

Manage Income with Tax Efficiency. To accumulate more, manage income. That is: a) make sure you are able to maximize the amount of after-tax income available to invest, b) add additional sources of income to average down overall tax rates and c) split income with the right people, in the right amounts and in the most efficient manner to enhance that effort.

Manage Behavioral Risks. Wealthy people are particularly good at investing money immediately into assets that grow in value over time. You too can develop a sense of urgency using the time value of money to your biggest advantage: this is especially important if you are young.

Younger people who invest larger pre-tax dollars and hold onto them the longest in tax deferred investment accounts, get richer. Yet, so many people miss maximizing their unused RRSP contribution room every year, and worse, their ability to fund their TFSA. If you're 18, get into the habit of saving $5,000 a year there. That's just over $100 a week… can you do this? Consider work schedules and savings habits to find out.

Wealthy people also know that the more you control choices regarding non-discretionary expenses (i.e.: food, clothing and shelter), the more you will have left over to allocate to investments, real estate and, potentially as a hedge against job loss, a small business. Your home may be your castle, but too much home, can set you back. We'll discuss this in a later chapter in this part of the book.

Can You, Too, Accumulate? The answer is yes, the odds are in your favour. Two thirds of Canadians are indeed wealthy, according to several recent studies.

The Wealth of Canadians: An Overview of the Results of the Survey of Financial Security from Statistics Canada in 2005, reported on family net worth three years before the global financial crisis. It reflected well on the outcomes of borrowing in a low interest rate environment: a 23% increase in family net wealth over 1999, after adjusting for inflation.

The majority (75%) of these borrowing were for the most significant asset comprising of family net worth: the principal residence. They represented an increase of 43.3% over a similar study completed in 1999. But the increase could be well explained by both the rise in cost to purchase a home and the increase in the number of families who owned their principal residence with a mortgage (+16.6%). The median value of mortgages in 2005 amounted to $93,000, up 17.0% from about $79,500 in 1999.

While the main contributor to the growth of assets was the market value of real estate, the second most important component of family net worth was the growth in participation in employer pensions, which increased net worth by 35%.

While Canadians are more indebted than ever in a prolonged low-interest environment, their net worth statements will continue to show growth as long as their primary asset—the principal residence—**retains** its value and debt is paid down before interest rates rise. It should not be the only significant asset though. Also important are the sources of retirement income you are putting into place today.

Overcoming Obstacles. In planning to minimize risk while accumulating wealth, the issues of concern for you are:

- historically low savings rates, particularly in some income sectors.
- the need to save for a couple more years to replace the OAS benefits now pushed back to 67 for some.
- the need for successful debt management at a time when income and capital eroders (taxes, the cost of acquiring and keeping capital and inflation) may be rising in the foreseeable future.
- the need to focus on long term trends for taxes; given provincial budget changes to the taxation of high incomes, often caused by the realization of private pension income sources.

Robert Ironside, ABD, Ph.D. and Knowledge Bureau Faculty Member and course author has the following comments with regard to risk management in accumulation strategies: "Many, many investors have moved significant portions of their portfolios into fixed income. In order to get yields above zero, many investors have started to lengthen out their maturities. If the securities have maturities beyond about five years, I think they are highly exposed to purchasing power risk (the loss of value due to inflation).

As to tax, that is a huge issue, because tax is levied on the nominal return, not the real return. Although investors should only be concerned with the real, after-tax return, most of them focus only on the nominal return. As inflation (and nominal returns) rise, the real, after-tax return falls in a linear fashion. It does not take much to produce a negative, real, after-tax return. The higher the nominal return, the more negative the real, after-tax return."

Tax Strategy

To effectively accumulate wealth over time, always look for ways to minimize taxes, control non-deductible expenses and the costs associated with consumer debt and split income with other family members in a lower tax bracket. And remember, not all income sources are taxed alike, nor will all investments stand the test of time in case of increasing taxes, interest rates and inflation Therefore those who diversify investments and income have the opportunity to average down taxes on all sources of wealth.

CHAPTER 23

The Costs of Accumulating Money

There are two significant obstacles to your accumulating capital today: taxes and the costs or fees of investing. In both cases you can make choices to increase your capital by decreasing these obstacles.

Decrease Taxes on Income and Capital as it Accumulates. Taxes can erode close to 50% of the accumulated wealth of Canadian high net worth families. The wealthier a family is, the more important tax efficiency becomes.

Here's the tax secret > Once you pay tax on income and capital (now or in the future) you are free to do with the money whatever you so choose. This is your tax-paid capital, and can be withdrawn as a "Return of Capital" with no further tax consequences. Return of tax-paid capital can "fill income gaps" over volatile economic cycles or when there is an interruption of income from actively earned sources. Your goal is to build that figure up as high as possible.

What is the Impact of Tax Over Time? It's important to keep track of how much tax you pay for two reasons:

- Over your lifetime tax will likely be your single largest expense.
- You need only pay the correct amount, not more, and by using legal and available tax planning techniques you can significantly reduce that number.

Understanding Taxes Payable. The line to take note of on the T1 tax return is Line 435—total taxes paid to federal and provincial governments. Circle it the next time to chat about taxes. To illustrate the importance of the taxation of income sources on after-tax cash flow planning from investment activities, see the table below.

Table 1: General Tax Consequences for a Variety of Investments

Investment	Tax Paid at Time of Investment (Accumulation)	Tax Paid on Growth	Tax Paid on Income	Tax Paid on Withdrawal or Disposition
RRSP or RPP Account	Invest Pre-Tax: A tax deduction is received for the principal invested	Deferred	Deferred	At Marginal Tax Rate at time of withdrawal; income splitting is possible beginning at 65.
TFSA	Invest with Post-Tax Funds	Zero	Zero	Zero
Non-Registered Account	Marginal Tax Rate as capital is earned	Marginal tax rate annual accrued interest earnings in compounding investments.	Marginal tax rate on income inclusion: 100% for interest; a percentage of dividends.	Marginal tax rate on 50% of the gain.
Principal Residence	Marginal Tax Rate as capital is earned	Zero	Rental income may be taxable, after allowable deductions	Zero, if capital cost allowance is not claimed

Understanding your lifetime tax obligation is important; too, because it will help you understand the magnitude of tax savings possible with effective planning. The chart below makes the average tax burden clearer—at a very general and high level—to taxpayers contemplating whether tax planning should be a more proactive activity in the family and with the inter-advisory team of professionals working with them.

Table 2: Computing Lifetime Tax Burdens for a Single in Ontario (Estimated)

Years	Annual Income	Total Lifetime Income	Approximate Annual Taxes	Total Lifetime Tax	Tax as a Percent of Taxable Income
30	$ 50,000	$1,500,000	$ 9,000	$270,000	18%
30	$ 75,000	$2,250,000	$17,000	$510,000	23%
30	$100,000	$3,000,000	$27,300	$819,000	27%

As personal taxable incomes grow, so does the percent of money paid in taxes. (You will recall, this is due to our progressive tax system.) During your active working years it is common that the first approximately 20% to 30% of income earned will disappear in personal income tax. This affects even low income earners, as individuals start paying taxes when incomes exceed the Basic Personal Amount—just below $11,000 at the time of writing.

- The amount of income tax paid by the average mid to high income earner in Canada therefore could easily exceed $500,000.
- A couple earning a similar income could easily pay in excess of $1 million in tax during their working years. Add in the taxes paid by an average family over three generations—20 to 45, 45 to 60, 60 to 85—and the amount is staggering.

Investors must also keep an eye on the future purchasing power of their savings, looking for ways to minimize taxes and fees such as interest costs and MERs, to protecting their income and capital against inflation, which is a type of tax. Inflation will be discussed in the next chapter.

Minimizing Fees. The second obstacle over which you have control is the "cost" of investing those redundant earnings which turn into investible capital.

Such costs vary with the type of investment chosen, as most readers will know. Investors don't always understand investment fee structures, though, nor do they understand the impact this has on their wealth management activities. Product selection that minimizes fees plays a large role in the executing the four elements of Real Wealth Management: accumulation, growth, preservation and transition of wealth, and therefore needs to come up in planning product selection decisions between you and your financial advisor. The extent to which these costs can be managed may help wealth to grow more significantly over time. Consider the following

The Impact of Investment Costs Over Time

The Facts	8% Gross Return	2% Management Fees	6% Net Return	Total Fees Paid Over 25 Years
RRSP	$10,000 invested per year for 25 years @ 8% return = $731,059.	The 2% management fee may represent as much as 25% of the total gain since the 2% in fees is 25% of the 8% return.	$10,000 invested per year for 25 years @ 6% return = $548,645.	Estimated Fees paid over 25 years = $182,414.

Source: Elements of Real Wealth Management Course, published by Knowledge Bureau.

Lower fees do offer a significant advantage right from day one, as illustrated below, a computation you should consider with your tax and financial advisors: the least expensive investment from a fee point of view increased wealth by 17% more over 5 years when compared to the most expensive investment.

Comparing Fees and Results on an Investment of $10,000

Investment	5 Year Compounded Return	Management Fee	Ending Value after 5 years
A	+5.7%	2.38%	$13,319.25
B	+9.2%	0.18%	$15,527.92
C	+3.0%	1.39%	$11,592.74
D	+4.9%	0.25%	$12,702.16

Source: Elements of Real Wealth Management Course, published by Knowledge Bureau.

The After-Tax Costs of Investing. Some fees can be written off on your tax return, thereby minimizing your net cost:

- **Management Fees.** The cost of a mutual fund or exchange traded funds is the management fee charged yearly, transactions costs, administration costs and sales tax on the fees. Management fees on mutual funds typically range from 1% to 3% of the value of the fund each year. Lower risk funds have lower fees while higher risk funds have higher fees. Alternatively, exchange traded funds have fees that range from 0.15% to 1%. The largest contributors to the difference in the fees are the distribution and commission costs paid to advisors. The mutual fund fees will typically include a commission to the advisor while the fees quoted for the exchange traded funds do not.

- **Brokerage Fees.** The transaction cost of trading stock could be a flat fee of $10 to $50 or it could be a percent of the size of the trade. The transaction commission percent will typically range from 1% and up depending often on the size of the trade as well as the price of the security. Managed accounts take a percentage of the capital.

- **Debt Instruments—Cost of Spreads.** The cost of investing in bonds, GICs or other interest-producing assets varies. In most cases the cost of purchasing a GIC is zero in that there is typically no transaction cost or commission expense incurred. However the management fee is the spread between what an institution will pay on its debt instruments vs. what it will charge its customers to borrow money. Alternatively, the price you pay for a specific bond will also have the commission and the transaction cost already built in. In some instances this will create a very low net return for the investor so you need to be aware of what these amounts are. The same will be true for most other interest-producing assets that are traded in the open market.

- **Investment Counsel.** The cost of investment counsel will typically be in the 1% range and will decline as the value of a portfolio rises beyond specific thresholds. The additional cost of investment council services will be administration, product and transaction fees. Total investment council fees from all sources typically range in the 1% to 2.5% range. In certain cases, investment council fees may be tax deductible.

- **Investment Loans.** The cost of borrowing to invest is your interest cost which may be tax deductible in the case of certain non-registered accounts or non-financial assets. If the investment is worth less than the loan at the end of the day, borrowing may be too expensive, even after tax: the chance that you may have to find new money to pay back the loan requires consideration at the time this decision is made. Interest costs are a deduction that can offset all other income of the year.

Tax Strategy

Always assess the after-tax cost of your fees for investing because you can indeed control your net tax outcomes. A higher return due to lower fees (as opposed to increased risk) can result in significantly more income in retirement and higher estate values.

CHAPTER 24

Growing Your Wealth

Investopedia[5] describes the time value of money as follows: "The idea that money available at the present time is worth more than the same amount in the future, due to its potential earning capacity. This core principle of finance holds that, provided money can earn interest, any amount of money is worth more the sooner it is received."

These days, of course, money is earning hardly any interest. Some would argue that investments in non-financial assets, particularly a tax exempt principal residence or other real estate may make more sense.

Nonetheless, to grow your wealth, understanding the time value of money is an important cornerstone, because it underscores how wrong it is to overpay your taxes and spend too much money on non-deductible debt.

Author Shauna Carter, makes a great point, succinctly describing why the time value of money is so important in making financial decisions:

"Why would any rational person defer receiving payment into the future when he or she could have the same amount of money now? For most of us, taking the money in the present is just plain instinctive. So at the most basic level, the time value of money demonstrates that, all things being equal, it is better to have money now rather than later... time literally is money—the value of the money you have now is not the same as it will be in the future and vice versa."

Here's the tax secret > Compounding, very simply, is the concept of earning interest on your interest. The longer the time horizon for investment, the more wealth is created. Therefore investing more money sooner, makes one richer; that includes your tax refunds.

---

[5] Investopedia.com; a Forbes Company, 2007

Value of $10,000 invested at a 3.5% rate of return before taxes

Years	Value	Increase in Principal
30	$28,000	180%
20	$19,900	99%
10	$14,100	41%
5	$11,900	19%

Invested longer, perhaps over multiple generations, at higher rates of return, capital will double and triple. Therefore, to build wealth efficiently over time focus needs to be on those investments that (a) pay interest or another type of income (b) allow for tax deferral along the way so that the compounded growth of earnings can be maximized without being interrupted by taxation and (c) minimize the cost related to borrowing or management fees.

Allowing too much erosion up front (before investing) and along the way reduces the opportunity to accumulate, grow, preserve and transition wealth and cripples the power of compounding. Keeping that important principle in mind, you'll want to grow your wealth in today's economic climate using eight important steps:

1. **Invest Consistently.** Growth of capital cannot take place without the regularly and systematic investment of income. This is also a positive way to average your investments into various economic cycles. Make regular contributions to registered and non-registered accounts according to age eligibility and contribution room, and stick to your pre-determined investment plans: monthly, quarterly, semi-annually, etc.

2. **Manage Debt.** Debt, in a potentially rising interest rate environment, could be disastrous for some, especially those over-leveraged with margin accounts or home ownership.

3. **Manage Risk With Tax Efficiency.** To better manage risk factors relating to the growth and preservation of portfolios, establish tax efficiency as a leading factor in growth planning. Invest in assets that generate tax-efficient income sources: dividends and capital gains, for example. But as it relates to managing capital, be sure to preserve documentation on prior capital losses which are valuable hedges against future taxation, because they will offset inflationary capital gains. *Capital loss balances are currently not indexed to inflation, but they perhaps should be.*

4. **Don't Prepay Taxes.** Pay only the correct amount of tax on your source deductions and quarterly instalment remittances.

5. **Manage Costs of Building Wealth.** Reduce the costs of both spending and saving money to maximize the time value of money: invest whole dollars, sooner. Then minimize the costs of fees on your investments, since this is one of the most significant eroders of wealth over time.

6. **Beat Inflation on Income.** Remember, unused RRSP and TFSA contribution room are not indexed to inflation. This means that that investors who maximize their savings sooner beat both tax and inflation erosion using these investments.

7. **Beat Inflation on Capital.** Likewise, adjusted cost bases on capital assets are not indexed to inflation. Therefore capital dispositions should be planned to minimize tax as a hedge. This can be done with timing (disposing assets over multiple tax years to reduce marginal tax rate spikes), by transferring assets into the hands of lower income earners (with resulting income being taxed at lower marginal tax rates) and by using options to earn exempt gains (by transferring qualifying securities to charity or selling tax exempt assets).

8. **Increase Net Worth: Assess Financial Stability Regularly.** Make sure personal net worth of each family member is growing. This requires management of spending and saving, asset and debt ratios.

The link between income and capital is important as you can see. The ability to accumulate savings as a priority over spending is one of the reasons why "the rich get richer" and consumers get poorer over time. In Canada today the wealthy have acquired net assets in a variety of categories:

- Private pensions
- Financial Assets
- Non-financial Assets
- Equity in Business

Private Pensions. Five common investments are available so serve a variety of purposes on a tax-assisted basis for retirement and/or a period of time when capital is required to fund a specific lifecycle change: (a) the RRSP, (b) the spousal RRSP, (c) the TFSA, (d) the RESP and (e) the RDSP.

While all of these investment options provide unique tax advantages, interest deductibility is not possible if capital is borrowed to make the investment. They all allow investments to grow on a tax-deferred basis over time, which is a primary opportunity and principle for accelerating growth: dollars invested on a tax sheltered basis grow faster than those subject to tax along the way.

Financial Assets: Building Quality Capital. To get the best results, ensure that every asset is performing consistently with the goals set for it: emergencies, retirement, education, vacation, disability, etc. If certain assets are under-performing, should certain assets be sold and others bought? What is the ultimate purpose on disposition or withdrawal? Consider how you are using current capital assets to build more wealth over time.

Non-Financial Assets and Business Equity. Including tangible assets like real estate and business assets into your asset mix can have lucrative results, as we will discuss in more detail in the next section, however, these are long term assets, not always easy to sell and you need to be prepared for that reality.

Therefore to help set your investment priorities for the growth of your money consider the following flowchart:

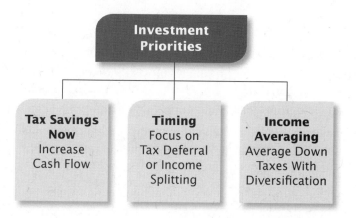

Measure Periodically. Measure progress regularly with a periodic review of the Personal Net Worth Statement. Timing can often be the difference between success and failure, especially when it comes to tax efficiency. Acting soon enough could be very beneficial (for example by maximizing RRSP and TFSA contributions within deadlines and investment milestones).

Tax Strategy

Always project forward the values of future income and capital taking into account taxes, fees and inflation and compare the projections to your future wants and needs. Make adjustments to the plan, as required, in consultation with your tax and financial advisors.

CHAPTER 25

Preserving What You've Built

Preserving your wealth is about managing risks. Unexpected life events might cause you to draw on your savings earlier—death, disability, critical illness or job loss can all force you to draw on your savings prematurely. Your income needs to be protected by insurance in these cases.

Financial events that require risk management may include a surprise tax audit that results in unexpected amounts payable. There may be a storm that causes great damage to your property. Perhaps a leveraged investment has gone bad. Having an emergency savings reserve is extremely important.

Economic events such as significant market corrections, above average inflation, rising interest rates or falling real estate values cannot easily be controlled. They can, however, significantly decrease your wealth.

Unfortunately, the first decade of the 2000s has not been kind to investors. Had a mythical investor invested another $10,000 in the S&P 500 on January 1, 2000, by December 31, 2010 the investment would have been worth a nominal $10,400, after growing at an annually compounded rate of 0.31% per year. Had we subtracted the loss of purchasing power due to inflation, the real purchasing power of our $10,000 investment would have fallen to $7,900[6].

Here's the tax secret > You can protect your wealth from life, financial and economic circumstances with three deliberate plans that require revisiting, however, all year long.

---

[6] Source: *Financial Recovery in a Fragile World*, by Al Emid, Robert Ironside and Evelyn Jacks

- **Protect Income** from taxes (by keeping more of the first dollar you earn, longer), debt-servicing (by eliminating consumer and non-deductible interest and fees), and inflation (by negotiating inflation-protected salaries and pensions).
- **Protect Capital: Financial and Non-Financial Assets.** Minimize and defer taxes, reduce the cost of borrowing and management fees, and reduce volatility in your financial portfolio. Also, strive for a rate of return that beats the inflation rate plus taxes.
- **Protect Lifestyle.** To what extent will you be able to keep your lifestyle in the event of a loss of job, a divorce, disability, illness or death? Protect you and your family from financial hardship, by avoiding the unnecessary encroachment of capital, and insure yourself against critical illness or death.

Most important today, because these circumstances can happen at any time, but always the worst possible time, it makes sense that your debt load is managed at all times. Because debt to disposable income ratios are at all-time highs in Canada today, this warrants a separate discussion.

Debt Management. Debt, in abundance, is your enemy. Just as long term compounding is effective in the accumulation and growth of wealth, long term compounding of interest costs on debt incurred to earn income, can be disastrous to your long term wealth accumulation plans. Tax deductibility will decrease that cost, however, for most people, non-deductible interest, like interest on credit card debt and the mortgage on the principal residence constitutes significant cash flow erosion and needs to be addressed in assessing financial stability on an ongoing basis.

Consider the debt on your home today. For many Canadians, this is the most significant asset. Home ownership has a number of advantages, not the least of which is a tax exemption on the gains accrued in the home used as the principal residence. Another advantage is the ability to leverage the equity in the home for other investment activities.

However, interest costs along the way are not generally deductible (unless the home is used as an income-producing asset, or to collateralize an investment loan). Therefore, the cost of home ownership, over time can have a significant impact on net worth, especially if the value of the property is not keeping pace with inflation and costs.

The longer the mortgage amortization period, the greater the non-deductible interest costs on the mortgage, **and the more after-tax dollars it will take to become debt-free.** The wealth erosion factor is doubled, because debt is paid with smaller after-tax dollars.

Consider the following comparisons based on a $200,000 mortgage financed at a rate of 5% for a $225,000 home. How much would you have to sell this house for after each ending year in the period to make up for the negative compound interest costs? The rate of return on your investment in the home would be the difference between the rising value of the home and the decreasing value of the mortgage. Therefore, the sooner you pay off the mortgage, the greater the long term average rate of return will be.

Year	Equity	Mortgage Balance	Accumulated Interest Cost	Sale Price to Recover Costs
0	$ 25,000	$200,000	$ 0	$225,000
1	$ 29,155	$195,845	$ 9,804	$234,804
2	$ 33,519	$191,481	$ 19,388	$244,388
3	$ 38,105	$186,895	$ 28,761	$253,761
4	$ 42,923	$182,077	$ 37,902	$262,902
5	$ 47,985	$177,015	$ 46,799	$271,799
...				
25	$225,000	$ –	$148,963	$373,963

The Long Term Costs of Negative Compound Interest ($200,000 Mortgage at 5%)

	Monthly Payment (after-tax dollars)	Total Payments	Total Interest
15 Years	$1,576.25	$283,726	$ 83,726
20 Years	$1,314.25	$315,420	$115,420
25 Years	$1,163.21	$348,963	$148,963

Source: Elements of Real Wealth Management Course, published by Knowledge Bureau.

By changing the amortization period from 15 to 25 years the monthly payment declines by 26% but the total interest costs over the life of the mortgage increase by 78%, or just over $65,000!

Why is this important? Remember that you pay your mortgage with after-tax dollars. At a 50% tax bracket, you'll have to earn $130,000 just to pay the extra interest on your mortgage over the 25 years. Very expensive. Plus there is a lost opportunity cost of investing elsewhere. Your investment is also at risk when interest rates rise.

The Cost of Higher Interest Rates: 7.5% per year ($200,000 Mortgage)

	Monthly Payment	Total Payments	Total Interest
15 Years	$1,841.03	$331,385	$131,385
20 Years	$1,597.20	$383,329	$183,329
25 Years	$1,463.11	$438,933	$238,933

Finally, consider this—any increase in interest costs on a mortgage does not necessarily correlate an increase in the appreciating value of the home, over the inflation rate. The opposite may happen.

Will you be able to preserve your wealth and be ready for retirement? Good news… most people will, according to recent studies, although lower income earners are at risk, and this is why a tax-efficient personal productivity strategy is important.

Mr. Jack M. Mintz, Research Director and Palmer Chair in Public Policy, School of Public Policy, The University of Calgary released a research paper in December 2009 to the Department of Finance which overviewed the adequacy of Canada's Retirement Income System. Amongst many findings, he concluded the following:

- **On the amount of savings required by Canadians.** Low-income Canadians need a higher level of replacement income to avoid poverty. Some middle- and high-income Canadians may even need less than 60 percent of their pre-retirement income to sustain an adequate standard of living (for example, the OECD suggests 50 percent for individuals with incomes over $90,000 in Canada, twice the median).
- **On availability of RPP vs. no RPP.** Contrary to the impression that individuals without private pensions are not saving enough in RRSPs, some very recent evidence has shown that Canadians with RPPs have somewhat less retirement income than those without RPPs because non-RPP holders tend to have other assets to support their retirement. As well, they are more likely work after the age of 65. *RPP holders therefore need more help in saving to expand wealth to draw on in retirement.*
- **On poverty and the adequacy of CPP/OAS/GIS.** Canada has one of the lowest poverty rates among elders in the OECD countries, and our public pension system, that is, OAS/GIS, CPP/QPP and provincial top-up programs are ensuring that low-income Canadians are able to achieve high income replacement rates, even exceeding 100

percent. Due to high replacement rates from public pensions, those earning $20,000 achieve a replacement rate of about 90 percent, even with low levels of RPP/RRSP savings. However, low income earners will require more money to avoid poverty in the future.

As we will discuss in the next part of the book, with recent changes to the OAS and CPP in 2012, which push the withdrawal of these income sources back, retirement income adequacy, particularly for lower income earners, will have to be reassessed, especially for those under 54 who will not receive their OAS until age 67. (Some phased in benefits will be allowed for those born in 1958 to 1962.)

Tax Strategy

You can preserve the wealth you have built by continuing to invest your money in privately held accounts—registered and non-registered—to expand your wealth. If you have capital accumulations, that money is a "business" that requires rules to grow by. The alternative, is the destruction of your hard-earned wealth by wealth eroders like taxes, inflation and fees.

Essential Tax Facts

Follow these simple rules to take charge:

Have a Plan for Tax-Efficient Income and Capital. People who become wealthy follow a consistent, purposeful process for thinking about their earning and savings activities.

Increase Personal Productivity. Employees should complete the TD1 *Personal Tax Credit Return* and its sister, Form T1213 *Request to Reduce Tax Deductions at Source*, to reduce withholding taxes or quarterly instalments to pay just right amount of tax all year long.

Earn Tax Free Benefits. Employees will mitigate risk with a variety of tax-free benefits, including:

- Premiums paid by the employer to private health care plans. Premiums paid under provincial hospitalization and medical care insurance plans are taxable.
- If you paid all of the premiums to a wage loss replacement plan, then periodic payments (or a lump sum paid in lieu of periodic payments) from the plan are tax-free and should not be reported on an information slip.
- Employees who use their company car less than 50% for business should discuss the reduction of standby charges with their payroll department.
- Employees can negotiate for a reimbursement of up to $15,000 of losses on the sale of your home may be tax-free, where the employer required the move.

Analyze Cash Flow. To begin accumulating wealth, investors will analyze cash flow and build out the "new money" from tax-exempt sources, social benefits and return of capital that can average down taxes and create new money for specific investments. This is also a good way to find money to reduce debt.

Invest in the Right Order. Because taxes can erode 50% of accumulated wealth over time, a focus on tax planning for the preservation of your capital is important. So is the right order of investing. To build purchasing power, returns must be higher than the rate of inflation annually, and eventually the rate of taxation.

Reduce Management Fees. That can make up for the cost of inflation erosion, too. Consult on which fees are tax deductible.

Plan Capital Encroachment Wisely. Time withdrawals to minimize taxes.

Manage Debt. Use the time value of money to your advantage, not that of your creditors. That means, by default, that you would reduce non-deductible debt and increase savings instead.

PART V

Tax Savvy Retirements

CHAPTER 26

Maximizing Your
Tax-Efficient Retirement

According to the Credit Suisse Global Wealth Report[7], wealth accumulates for three principal reasons:

1. **Precaution:** When people manage risks to their income and savings due to changing economic or life events,

2. **Readiness:** For the future, principally for retirement income needs and

3. **Intergenerational Transfers:** People wish to pass on their wealth, and in doing so, dispose of debt and protect their financial assets from ongoing financial erosion.

Done well, the money you save and protect throughout your lifetime will end up in the right financial "buckets," allowing you to maximize the purchasing power of your capital.

Here's the tax secret > These are important opportunities in the plans younger people make today, too, because retirement planning really begins with the first dollar you save for your future.

There are several recent "gifts" from the federal government that will help you to save preserve more money than the retirees that have come before us. Specifically, pension income splitting with your spouse (which was introduced in 2007), and the ability to save within a Tax-Free Savings Account (TFSA), introduced in 2008, are real winning strategies. But, since 2006 several other key tax changes have been introduced. Many of these affect

---

[7]   2nd Global Wealth Report, 2011 in collaboration with the Credit Suisse Research Institute and Professors Anthony Shorrocks and Jim Davies, Oxford University Press.

today's retirees, but many more will affect those under the age of 54. You may wish to speak with your professional advisors about the following if you think they may affect you and your investments:

- *OAS eligibility* has been changed to age 67 starting in 2023; the opportunity to postpone taking OAS until age 70 will be introduced in 2013. This will be discussed in more detail in the next chapter, also.
- *Funding and Pension Benefits from the CPP* has changed, starting in 2012. This is explained later in this chapter.
- A new *Family Caregiver Amount* will increase five different non-refundable tax credits in 2012.
- *The Age Credit Amount* was enhanced in 2006 by $1,000.
- *Indexing* has increased tax brackets, to ease the burden of tax on earnings. For 2012, for example, the inflation adjustment rate was set at 2.8%, meaning that the tax brackets and most of the personal amounts are increased by 2.8% over their 2011 levels.
- A new *Pooled Retirement Pension Plan (PRPP)* was introduced into federal law in 2012, awaiting provincial adaptation at the time of writing, to enable small businesses to establish an employer-provided pension to their employees.
- *Taxation of Dividends* changed. A reduction in the general corporate income tax rate was announced as of January 1, 2010 with further reductions in 2011 and 2012, which has affected dividend taxation for individuals.
- *Distributions from publicly traded income trusts and limited partnerships.* A new tax was announced in 2006, but became effective in 2011.

Factors in Planning. A well planned retirement involves carefully strategizing to withdraw your future taxable income from different sources, with a view to "averaging down" the taxes you pay in your combined retirement period—and taking into account the marginal tax brackets of two people in the case of spouses, not just one.

This is a unique distinction for the planning of modern retirements. In the past, one person generally brought most of the retirement assets to the table; this is not so today. Two spouses, each with significant pension savings in many cases, are challenged to be more tax savvy in order to achieve the kind of purchasing power required to hedge against rising prices for changing needs, like the cost of medical services and prescription drugs, for example, travel or maintaining several retirement homes.

The time value of money is also a critical factor. No longer do we think about retirement planning as ensuring each dollar is adequately spent before we die... very difficult to do as no one can really pinpoint the exact date for one thing! But for another, today, you may spend a long time in retirement, and according to the Global Wealth Report, your "age-wealth profile" will be higher if any one of three things happens: your life expectancy is longer, your retirement is earlier or your public pensions are lower.

We know that in Canada that latter circumstance is already happening—in the future, retirees will have to wait two years longer to collect their Old Age Security. Many organizations that carry employer-sponsored pension plans have also moved away from defined benefit to money purchase plans, or, have not offered a pension plan at all.

Your investment returns need to grow bigger as a result of your increasing self-reliance in retirement. However, this has been difficult to achieve in the recent economic environment. It therefore makes sense for you to be more deliberate about your potential for tax savings now and in the future. That's smart, because you will simply reserve for yourself more purchasing power, but more important, an eye on your tax returns can help you to minimize the risk you otherwise would have to take in your portfolio to get the type of returns you want on your investments.

Here's the tax secret > Planning for a tax-efficient retirement requires the management of both income structure and the continued growth and preservation of your capital accumulations. In short, taxes happen on both income and capital; pensioners are increasingly concerned with the later as they move through their retirement.

Transitioning. The closer you are to retirement, the bigger the argument for a deliberate and concerted interest and effort in understanding your retirement finances. Your relationship with your money will definitely change in retirement, and this could be especially challenging if you are an employee today.

In transitioning from work life to retirement, make sure you have the knowledge to leave your structured financial environment, where your employer took care of things like tax remittances, RRSP or Registered Pension Plan (RPP) contributions, your health care plans and in some cases, your employer-provided vehicle, communications devices and investment loans, too. It's quite possible that your new life in retirement will be the first time you will take care of many of those financial decisions on your own, and you need a plan around which to understand these new responsibilities. This section of the book can help.

For self-employed people, the thought of giving up control of their business interests, which have generated predictable income returns, can bring considerable financial stress, especially in volatile economic times. But these folks have a leg-up on their employed fellow taxpayers, because they already manage relationships with financial advisors and understand the importance of diversifying income sources, maximizing tax provisions and staying onside with CRA.

This is important, too, as a move from an active work life into an active retirement, brings a change in your relationship with the tax department. You will want to understand your new responsibilities to self-remit taxes on time, and benefit from new tax provisions available to reduce tax on your retirement income.

Three Stages and Ages. Most people will experience three retirement income planning stages, from a tax efficiency point of view:

- Pre-retirement
- Phased-in retirement
- Full retirement

Three distinct age groups typically correspond to these phases:

- **Pre-Age 60:** At the younger end you'll save for retirement, at the upper end; you may begin a phased-in retirement.
- **Age 60 to 64:** These are the "early retirement" years, before Old Age Security is received.
- **Age 65 and beyond:** Full retirement begins for the purposes of generating taxable income from the Old Age Security (age 65 to 70), Canada Pension Plan (it's mandatory at age 70) and the Registered Retirement Savings Plan (you must withdraw funds after age 71).

Getting the Right Help. With recent tax and pension reforms for seniors, there is lots of flexibility around planning for taxable income the later years—for example you can choose to postpone taking certain income sources, like CPP and OAS to age 70, in order to "melt down" other taxable income sources, like your RRSP accumulations sooner. Choosing the right advisor is important in this period of transition and you may wish to look for an MFA—Investment and Retirement Income Specialist[8] for these skills. The parameters to discuss include the following:

---

[8] The MFA designation is offered by Knowledge Bureau, who can put you in touch with graduates of the program.

1. *Retirement period.* What is your anticipated retirement period, based on your life expectancy, taking average retirement periods in Canada, average longevity factors and your own family health histories into account?

2. *Required Pension and Investment Income level.* What is the required income level for your vision for retirement? This requires budgeting and how to fund basic needs and lifestyle wants.

3. *Inter-Spousal Pension Income Planning.* Does your retirement vision match your spouse's? If not, this needs to be discussed to make decisions about income levels and capital preservation.

4. *Family Risk Management.* What expectations do you have for return on your investments in both the short and long term, and how much risk are you willing to take to achieve that?

5. *Anticipated Growth in Capital.* How much additional savings can you expect to create by taking a tax-efficient approach to the accumulation, growth, preservation and transition of your capital? Will preparing a new budget for anticipated needs and wants help? Can debt management help?

6. *Instalment Payments and Your Income Withdrawal Strategy.* What is the precise amount of withdrawal or capital encroachment you are prepared to make to fund needs or wants, and what are the rules for withdrawal in changing economic circumstances? This is important because withdrawing too much income can put you into a quarterly tax remittance profile, which you will definitely want to avoid if you didn't need the money in the first place.

Strategies for Achieving Results. A Real Wealth Management™[9] (RWM) strategy is a good one around which to think and plan your retirement income. It provides a consistent framework for strategic planning with your tax and financial advisors, focusing on the decisions required to continually accumulate, grow, preserve and transition wealth in the most tax and cost-efficient way.

When we apply these elements to retirement income planning, the following principles emerge:

---

[9] RWM is a trademark of Knowledge Bureau, which teaches this methodology to tax and financial advisors and their clients in order to accumulate, grow, preserve and transition sustainable family wealth.

Tax-Efficient Retirement Income Planning Guide
©Knowledge Bureau, Inc.

1. Categorizing Your Concerns	What are the trigger questions that require financial decision-making?	Stage Your Solutions
☐ Life Triggers	• I want to retire in 3 to 5 years. What should I be thinking about? • What do I need to do to retire today? • I wish to retire gradually. What's the most savvy way to do this?	☐ Pre-Age 60 ☐ Age 60 to 64 ☐ Age 65 plus
☐ Financial Triggers	• How should I save for my retirement: RRSP or TFSA? Something else? • When should I begin to encroach upon my investments? • Should I take CPP early at age 60? • How much can I receive in benefits from my employer-sponsored plan? • I have lost my job and will not be going back to work. What is the most tax-efficient way for me to carry on? • I have enough money, I have achieved my goals and will retire.	☐ Pre-Retirement ☐ Phased in Retirement ☐ Manage Unexpected Retirement ☐ Full Retirement

2. Probe for Detail	Questions to Discuss with Advisors	Document It
Who? What?	• Planning for one retirement or two? • Important Data: Family Member Details, Cash Flow Details, Assets, Liabilities, Tax Filing Profile	☐ Cash Flow: Income ☐ Expenses ☐ Net Worth Statement ☐ Tax Returns
Expectations	• What amount of monthly income, after tax, would provide you with peace of mind?	☐ Expectations for income ☐ Short term needs and wants: 1, 3 and 5 years from now. ☐ Long term: 10-20 years.

3. The Retirement Income Planning Process

Sources	Data	Analysis
Analyze Income and Capital	• List sources of income today: – Employment – Wage Loss replacement – Employment Insurance – Self-Employment – CPP, OAS Benefits – Superannuation, Private Periodic Pensions – Investment Income – Capital Gains and Losses – Other • List sources of future income sources: – RPPs, IPPs, RCAs – TFSAs, RRSPs, RRIFs, RDSPs – Non-Registered Pools of Money – Non-Financial Assets	• Tax status of income source: – Tax exempt – Taxable – Tax preferred – Tax deferred – Transfer to kids? • Personal Net Worth: Assets less debt... today and projected at the time of retirement. • Are there deficiencies in any capital pool —registered, non-registered, other? Investment fees too high?
Income Management	• How much from each source? • When? • From which source first? • Which taxpayer?	• At what income level is next tax bracket? • Can income be split? • Clawbacks minimized?
Portfolio Management	• Accumulation of Capital: – Which bucket first? • Growth of Capital – Inside or outside a registered account – Risk management – Insurance options? • Preservation: Tax-efficient savings/ withdrawal principles: – Pre-tax savings – Post-tax savings – Can we improve rates of return, yields? – Can we reduce risk exposure? – Should we insure against tax, health risk?	**Asset allocation:** • Are you protecting, growing or recreating capital? • Is the portfolio in sync with your risk profile? **Product selection:** • Tax exempt • Tax preferred • Tax deferred • Taxable

4. Decision-Making: Retirement Income Plan Recommendations		
	The Action Plan	**Benchmarks**
Tomorrow	• Income Plan: Layer in the income sources: – Employment: Full or part time – Public Pensions: CPP and OAS – Private Pensions: RPP, RRSP, Other – Investments: TFSA Interest-bearing Mutual Funds Stocks, Bonds Real Estate Business Interests Insurance Return of Capital only Blend: income/capital	• How does the income plan affect portfolio construction? – Capital Encroachment? – Redundant Income? – Risk and Return? – Asset Allocation – Taxes

Tax Strategy

When you have a consistent strategic plan that you review periodically with your tax and financial advisors, you will be able to accumulate, grow, preserve and eventually transition your wealth on a tax-efficient basis. This is all possible if you plan to layer in your pension income sources throughout your full retirement period in such a way as to avoid the top marginal tax brackets. The longer the retirement income period the more opportunities there are to "average down" taxes. Another is the opportunity to use two retirements—that of both spouses—to split income and tax.

CHAPTER 27

New Public Pensions:
The OAS and Canada Pension Plan

You have learned that retirement income planning involves staging both your savings and the withdrawal of your benefits throughout your lifetime. Age 65 is a particularly significant milestone in planning for retirement. There are three specific reasons:

1. Old Age Security (OAS) generally begins... although there are new options to postpone it.

2. New tax credits (like the Age Amount) and income splitting opportunities become available.

3. Most Canadians start drawing pension benefits from the Canada Pension Plan (CPP), which is a based on contributions from employment or self-employment.

The OAS. Cumulatively speaking, the OAS is lucrative. It could represent over $500 a month, $6,500 a year or, between spouses, in excess of $250,000 of income in retirement, if each spouse lives 20 years. The OAS is also indexed to inflation. It's therefore very important to preserve this income source from tax erosion.

While it is a universal payment, which means almost every Canadian resident receives it; unfortunately, the OAS can be "clawed back" at higher individual net income levels, beginning at approximately $69,000, and this must be managed by planning your income from other sources carefully.

The Old Age Security is also taxable each year. For those age 65 and over, a non-refundable tax credit known as the Age Amount is available to offset some of that tax erosion, and this is in addition to the Basic Personal Amount, found on Schedule 1 of the T1 return. Individual retirees will be able to earn over $17,000 completely tax-free each year.

However, in the case of the Age Amount, again there is a clawback for every dollar earned above a net income threshold; this time approximately $33,000. These clawback zones are indexed each year.

Here's the tax secret > Managing the clawback of the Old Age Security Benefit and the offsetting Age Amount is an important cornerstone of retirement income planning.

The New OAS Rules. Beginning in July 2013, taxpayers may elect to defer receiving their OAS pension for up to five years (to age 70). For those who elect to defer receiving their OAS pension, the amount they will receive will be increased by 0.6% for each month of deferral. The maximum increase in OAS (based on deferral to age 70) will be 0.6% x 60 months or 36%.

Taxpayers who would be subject to full clawback of OAS in the year they turn 65 should elect this option. Preliminary calculations indicate that the cumulative OAS benefits received will be maximized for taxpayers who defer one year for each year that they will live beyond age 79 (to a maximum of five years).

Further out on the timeline, the age eligibility for the OAS and GIS programs will be increased from age 65 to age 67 beginning in 2023 and will be completed by 2029. The eligibility for the (spouse's) Allowance and the Allowance for Survivors will also increase from age 60 to age 62 in the same time period. Those born before 1958 will not be affected. Those born after 1962 will not be eligible for OAS until they reach age 67. Those born in 1958 to 1962 will be eligible between ages 65 and 67.

Income Levels. Beyond this, tax-efficient retirement income planning with your OAS hinges on two things: what your tax bracket is, and at what marginal tax rate your income will be taxed above this. Therefore when making decisions about how much money to withdraw from your various capital pools (public or private pension accumulations or your investments) consider your income thresholds carefully before you act:

- Income levels beyond the OAS clawback zones: Do you have anything to lose by postponing receiving the OAS and taking other income sources instead
- Income levels up to the top of the OAS Clawback Zone
- Income levels up to the top of the Age Credit Clawback Zone

- Income levels up to the top of your current tax bracket

Structuring income around these income thresholds should be discussed with your advisors whenever you make investment decisions that will affect your income in retirement.

Dividends and the OAS. Dividend income withdrawals from non-registered accounts may have an unanticipated negative effect on your OAS pension. Actual dividend income earned is "grossed up" in value on the tax return, thereby increasing net income the figure used to determine the size of your OAS "clawback" plus the size of other refundable, or non-refundable tax credits. Those taxes on these grossed-up dividends are later offset by a corresponding dividend tax credit, which reduces taxes on income.

Therefore, while dividend income is widely considered to be a very tax-efficient source of investment income, it can cause erosion of your OAS, which is very expensive, especially if you could, in fact, plan your affairs differently.

With this in mind, it is also important to acknowledge that there are three types of tax treatments for dividend income. The dividend income you receive from a public company is taxed in one manner, whereas the dividend income received from a privately owned business is taxed at slightly higher levels, depending on which province you live in. Finally, the dividend income you receive from foreign (e.g. U.S.) public companies is fully taxed as income in Canada. There is no gross-up or offsetting credit for dividends received from non-Canadian companies.

Have your tax advisors work with your investment advisors to achieve the right dividend mix in planning retirement income withdrawals.

OAS and Non-Residents. Non-residents who receive OAS payments must submit an *Old Age Security Return of Income* (T4155) to determine whether a recovery tax for OAS clawback purposes is required. Age and years of residence in Canada determine eligibility. Those who live in Canada qualify for the OAS if they are 65 or older, living in Canada and are a Canadian citizen or a legal resident at the time your pension is approved. Also, those who lived in Canada for at least 10 years after reaching age 18 qualify.

When people living outside Canada want to receive the OAS, they also must be 65 or older, meet the citizenship/residency requirements described above and lastly, have lived in Canada for at least 20 years after reaching age 18.

The New Canada Pension Plan

The Canada Pension Plan is a mandatory, contributory pension plan to which employees and employers must contribute, in return for a variety of benefits. It is more than a retirement savings plan, for example, in that it provides some protection to contributors and their families against the loss of income due to retirement, disability and death. It features benefits for survivors and some indexing to inflation.

The Canada Pension Plan is governed by a separate Act (*Canada Pension Plan Act*) and is jointly administered by the Canada Revenue Agency and Service Canada. Benefits received under the Canada Pension Plan are reported on the recipient's T4A(P) *Statement of Canada Pension Plan Benefits* slip and must be reported on the recipient's tax return.

CPP retirement benefits are not eligible for the $2,000 Pension Income Amount. However, spouses may equalize the taxable CPP retirement benefits by assigning them equally for a better after-tax result.

Service Canada provides you with a *Canada Pension Plan Statement of Contributions* which shows how much your pension entitlement is. Your *Statement of Contributions* shows your pension entitlement as of age 65, the date most people elect to retire. You should review this annually as part of your planning process.

The maximum retirement benefit receivable, in return for your lifetime contributions is based on 25% of the average maximum pensionable earnings over the prior five years. It's close to $1,000 a month. (The maximum monthly benefit for 2012, for example, was $986.67.)

When calculating your CPP retirement benefits, the number of working years less a portion of nil or low-earnings years due to work interruptions such as job loss is taken into account. Under the Child Rearing Provision, the years in which the contributor left the work force to raise children, will also be removed.

Survivor Benefits. When one spouse dies, the surviving spouse may be eligible to receive a CPP survivor benefit if the deceased spouse had made contributions to CPP. If the surviving spouse was under age 35 at the time of death and there are no minor children, no survivor pension is paid until the surviving spouse reaches age 65. Otherwise, both the surviving spouse and minor children (or children up to age 25 who are attending post-secondary education) are likely eligible to receive a survivor benefit.

Note that once the surviving spouse begins to receive their CPP retirement benefit, the maximum benefit (retirement plus survivor benefits) is limited to the maximum monthly retirement benefit. For those who have earned the maximum pension through their own contributions, this effectively means that the survivor benefits may be lost, and this is an unpleasant surprise to those who have contributed their maximums to the CPP throughout their careers.

What's New with CPP Planning? Important changes, which will affect decisions about contributing and receiving CPP benefits in retirement, began in 2012, including:

- An increase in the number of low-earnings drop out years, used to calculate your benefits
- An elimination of the requirement to stop working before you can start receiving CPP early (that is before age 65).
- All CPP benefit recipients will be required to continue making CPP contributions if they go back to work in the "early retirement period" of 60-64.
- An election not to continue to contribute to the CPP can be made if you work between age 65 and 70. Continuing to contribute will increase your pension entitlements through a Post-Retirement Benefit (PRB).

Common questions pre-retirees have in relation to these changes include:

- When to begin to take benefits from the CPP—early or later?
- When to stop contributing to the CPP?
- What is the effect of these decisions on CPP benefits over your lifetime?
- What other income sources should I draw on if I delay benefits?

Expected longevity plays a role in assessing the cost-benefit ratio of contributing to the CPP, especially when deciding whether or not to draw your taxable retirement benefits early at age 60.

Example > Both Ivan's father and grandfather lived past age 90. Ivan who is 59 is trying to decide if he should take his CPP retirement pension at age 60, 65, or 70. His current Statement of Earnings indicates that he would be eligible to receive $900 per month at age 65.

Option 1: Early draw at age 60—Ivan will receive a reduced pension of $625 per month. If he lives to age 90, he will receive the pension for 30 years so, ignoring inflation adjustments, he will receive $225,000 in pension benefits.

Option 2: Begin at age 65—Ivan will receive $900 per month (ignoring inflation adjustments). If he lives to age 90, he will receive the pension for 25 years so he will receive a total of $270,000 in pension benefits.

Option 3: Late draw at age 70—Ivan will receive an enhanced pension of $1,163 per month. If he lives to age 90, he will receive the pension for 20 years so he will receive a total of $279,120 from CPP, again ignoring inflation adjustments).

Thus, if Ivan is confident that he will live to age 90, he should wait until he reaches 70 to apply for benefits because he will receive more from the plan. In fact, he will receive more if he lives beyond age 80 by waiting and receiving the enhanced benefit.

What are the Tax Implications? CPP benefits are fully taxable. There are also other tax implications to consider. For example, receiving a larger income from CPP may increase clawbacks of certain personal credits and/or Old Age Security benefits. Waiting to receive larger benefits from the CPP in the future, could also coincide with higher minimum payments from the Registered Retirement Income Fund (RRIF), causing a spike in marginal tax rates. However, do the math, because this may not be true in every case as RRIF value may be lower due to withdrawals that began earlier.

Also, tapping into other saving early, while you continue to pay into the CPP, may ultimately significantly reduce estate values, depending on the survivor benefits available to your spouse. So there are many things to consider in layering your retirement income properly.

Important CPP Milestones. How much you will receive on a monthly basis will depend on how much you contribute, how long you contribute and when you apply to receive benefits. Most people will apply to receive benefits at age 65; however, some can elect to start receiving the benefits early at age 60. Others may elect not to receive the CPP until age 70. After this, the receipt of the CPP retirement benefit is mandatory. A life events approach to managing your CPP is therefore important, as outlined in the chart on the next page:

CPP Planning Milestones

Milestone	Pre-Retirement	Early Retirement	Late Retirement	Mandatory Retirement
Age	18-59	60-64	65-70	71
Contributions	Required	Required	Optional	Not allowed
Regular Retirement Benefits	Maximum benefits available at 65; reduced at 60	Reduced; but PRB may increase	Increased	Benefits depend on when benefits began
Post-Retirement Benefits (PRB)	Regular benefits may be increased if working age 60-70	Mandatory Contribution to PRB*	Optional Contribution to PRB**	Contributions must cease

*Employer/Employee contributions mandatory
**Employers must contribute if employee chooses to contribute.

Tax Strategy

A tax-efficient approach to planning your entitlements to the CPP includes paying only the correct amount of premiums; claiming available non-refundable tax credits, deductions in the case of the self-employed and refunds of overpayments along the way. Then, minimize taxes by splitting benefits equally with your spouse and averaging in your benefits with other pension income sources.

CHAPTER 28

Withdrawing Private Pension Benefits

Imagine: you have spent much of your life accumulating money in your employer-sponsored pension plan (RPP) and your RRSP and now it is time to spend it! Believe it or not, that's a difficult concept for lifelong savers, who don't want to touch their precious accumulations. However, the purpose of your RPP and RRSP is to create a retirement pension, and if you do so over a longer period of time, you'll be able to average down tax erosion.

Let's discuss these in more depth now.

Here's the tax secret > The withdrawals received from your registered savings accounts—RPPs, RRSPs, IPPs, DPSPs[10]—are taxable in the year received. Structured as a periodic pension, the amounts may qualify for a $2,000 federal pension income amount and pension income splitting with your spouse.

Registered Pension Plans (RPPs). Commuting your employer-sponsored pension plans to provide a periodic pension plan also requires planning, and depending on the type of plan you have contributed to, may involve some withdrawal restrictions.

Particularly important however, is a feature that allows those age 55 or older, to begin a "phased-in retirement" under a defined benefit pension plan, available since 2008.

It's a triple win for some. Those living with a spouse or common-law spouse may split periodic income from an RPP by election when the tax return is

---

[10] IPP—Individual Pension Plans, DPSP—Deferred Profit Sharing Plans common to owner-managed business environments.

filed. This can be done at any age; providing an advantage over those with RRSP accumulations only, who must wait to age 65 to take advantage of pension income splitting, as you will learn later in this section.

No conditions are imposed on whether the employee works part- or full-time. However, this ability to draw a pension while continuing to accrue benefits will not be extended to designated plans (more commonly called "top-hat plans"), which are those that cover only one employee or a small group of highly compensated individuals. Check with your employer and tax advisor about your eligibility for this option.

Tax-free/direct transfers. When an employee changes employers, arrangements to move the accumulated amounts in the employee's pension plan are often made. The *Income Tax Act* provides details of the allowable tax-free rollovers of funds from one RPP to another or to the taxpayer's Registered Retirement Savings Plan (RRSP) or RRIF[11] or LIRA[12]. Such transfers must be made directly from one registered plan to the other without tax consequences.

Amounts that are received in the hands of the taxpayer as a lump sum will be considered to be taxable income, so it's best to avoid that and plan for periodic withdrawals instead to minimize marginal tax rate spikes.

Given the income splitting opportunities under the RPP, for taxpayers under age 65, it is likely more advantageous to structure periodic pension benefits from an RPP rather than through the transfer to an RRSP or RRIF or LIF[13] where you must wait to age 65 to split income with your spouse. Discuss with your advisors in advance.

Individual Pension Plans (IPP). If you are running an incorporated business you may be in financial position to supplement your RRSP with an IPP, which is a defined benefit pension plan. The IPP offers both maximum tax relief and a maximum retirement pension. To qualify for an IPP, you must:

- Have employment income reported on a T4;
- Be an employee of an incorporated company; and
- Own at least 10% of the shares of the company or be paid at least 2.5 times the maximum CPP pensionable earnings (i.e. $125,250 for 2012).

There are significant advantages including the following:

---

[11] RRIF—Registered Retirement Income Fund
[12] LIRA—Locked-in Retirement Account
[13] LIF—Life Income Fund

- IPP contributions and expenses are fully tax-deductible to the business. If you borrow money or amortize the past service cost, you can deduct the interest charges.
- Employees may enjoy an annual maximum contribution that is higher than the maximum contribution for an RRSP.
- Pension benefits are protected from creditors under pension legislation.
- Extended contribution period: A company has 120 days after its year end to make an IPP contribution.
- Ownership of plan assets: At retirement, the IPP member owns any actuarial surplus. It may be used to upgrade pension benefits or the plan holder may pass it on to his or her spouse, heirs, or estate.
- Guaranteed lifetime income to IPP member and their spouses: This pension plan offers a predictable retirement income. An actuary determines the current annual cost of the future retirement income. Spouse pension benefits may be upgraded to 100% when the member retires or dies. The company is on the hook for this money.
- Additional benefits: Full consumer price indexing, early retirement pension with no reduction, and bridge benefits can be structured to fortify gaps left by other retirement income pools like the CPP or OAS.
- Annual minimum withdrawal amounts will be required from IPPs once a plan member is 72. These amounts will be based on current RRIF rules.
- Contributions to an IPP related to past years of employment will have to come from RRSP or RPP assets or by reducing RRSP contribution room, before deductible contributions can be made. These provisions will apply to IPP past service contributions made after March 22, 2011.

Deferred Profit Sharing Plans (DPSPs). A deferred profit sharing plan (DPSP) provides for payments by an employer to a trustee, in trust, for the benefit of the employees or former employees, based on an employer's profits from the employer's business.

Employees may not contribute to a DPSP so there is no deduction available to the employee when contributions are made. Employer's contributions are deductible to the employer however. Members of a DPSP will be subject to a pension adjustment which means that contributions to an RRSP will be limited as a result of membership in the DPSP.

Direct transfers to another DPSP, RPP or RRSP. When the employee leaves the employer, vested DPSP funds may be transferred to another DPSP, RPP or RRSP or RRIF. The transfer must be a direct transfer, using form T2151 *Direct Transfer of a Single Amount Under Subsection 147(19) or Section 147.3* to recognize the transfer. On death of the DPSP plan member, the funds in the DPSP may be transferred tax-free to the surviving spouse or common-law partner's RPP, RRSP, DPSP or RRIF. Use Form T2151 *Direct Transfer of a Single Amount Under Subsection 147(19) or Section 147.3* to recognize the transfer.

Amounts received by the taxpayer out of a DPSP are taxable. Such amounts will be eligible for the Pension Income Amount if received by a taxpayer who is over 64. The DPSP must pay all amounts vested in the plan to the beneficiary no later than the end of the year in which the beneficiary turns 71. However, the DPSP may provide for the conversion of the plan funds to an annuity.

The RRSP. Making a contribution to a tax deductible registered plan, like your RRSP, is a good thing if you want to reduce the taxes you pay along the way and claim more non-refundable credits like medical expenses. That's because net income, the figure upon which these amounts is calculated, is reduced by making an RRSP contribution. A lower net family income will also increase federal refundable tax credits like the Child Tax Benefit, the Working Income Tax Benefit, or the GST/HST Credits. It all means more cash for you throughout the year.

When it comes to tax advantages, investing within a registered account essentially enables some double-dipping: new dollars are created for investment purposes with your tax deduction, while tax on investment earnings is deferred into the future.

But there is one catch: you will be restricted in the amounts you can sock away in your RRSP; for example only "earned income" sources qualify, and a maximum contribution rate and dollar limit exist. In addition you have to be under 72 to contribute (or have a spouse who is under 72).

Check your *Notice of Assessment* from the CRA for your *Unused RRSP Contribution Room*. If you have no available RRSP contribution room, be sure to contribute to a TFSA.

Understanding Contribution Room. The RRSP is an essential tool in building up your savings for retirement. So just how much can you contribute? RRSP contribution room is the lesser of:

- 18% of earned income from the prior tax year minus any net "Pension Adjustments" (PAs) for the current year, and

- the maximum RRSP "contribution limit" for the current year minus any net Pension Adjustments for the current year.

Let's define some of those terms. The "Pension Adjustment" is a measure of benefits accruing to you as a member of another tax-deferred plan at work, such as an RPP (Registered Pension Plan) or DPSP (Deferred Profit Sharing Plan).

The RRSP "contribution limit" is 18% of earned income to a dollar maximum of $23,820 for 2012. If you don't make the full allowable contribution to your RRSP, the unused RRSP contribution room carries forward for use in the future.

Figuring out how much you can contribute begins with looking for your Unused Contribution Room on your *Notice of Assessment or Reassessment* from the CRA.

The RRSP deduction is recorded on Schedule 7 and from there on Line 208 of the tax return. This deduction can include:

- RRSP contributions made in prior years and not deducted or refunded
- RRSP contributions made in the tax year
- RRSP contributions made in the first 60 days after the end of the tax year.

Age Eligibility. Note that there is no lower age limit for contributing to an RRSP. As long as CRA has the unused RRSP contribution room recorded, even a young adult can make a contribution. But, RRSPs must be collapsed by the end of the year in which you turn 71.

Spousal RRSPs. You may contribute to your own RRSPs based on available RRSP contribution room, and may also contribute some or all of the amounts to a spousal RRSP. This may provide for income splitting advantages on retirement and can help an age-ineligible taxpayer prolong the ability to use an RRSP deduction. Spousal RRSPs are not subject to the Attribution Rules; that is, you can contribute to a spousal RRSP and have the resulting income taxed in the spouse's hands... but there is a catch. Withdrawals from a spousal RRSP will taxed in the contributor's hands if the money is withdrawn within three years of the last contribution to any spousal plan.

Example > John has been making contributions every year to equalize pension accumulations. If his wife Sofi withdraws money from a spousal RRSP within three years of the last contribution by John to any spousal plan, the amount of the withdrawal that represents John's contributions in the prior three years will be taxed in John's hands.

An exception to this rule occurs when the spousal RRSP accumulations are transferred into a Registered Retirement Income Fund or RRIF. In that case only the amounts in excess of the minimum amount you are required to withdraw will be taxed in the hands of the contributor to the spousal RRSP.

If you are "age ineligible" you may still contribute to a spousal RRSP, based on your RRSP contribution room, if your spouse is under 72 years old.

If John in our example above had turned 72 this year, he could no longer contribute to his own RRSP even though he still has unused RRSP contribution room. His wife Sofi is 65, though. John can choose to make a spousal RRSP contribution, thereby depositing the money into Sofi's RRSP. He can then take the deduction on his return.

Pension Income Splitting. The pension income splitting rules may impact the amount of contributions some taxpayers make to the family's RRSPs. These rules will be discussed later. But remember, double-digit returns by way of tax savings will often result from an RRSP contribution; so it's good to weigh that in to every investment decision.

Any amounts contributed in the year and not deducted are considered to be "undeducted RRSP contributions." These amounts may be carried forward and deducted in future years if this is advantageous.

The point of all of this is, of course, to increase your wealth for use in retirement income planning.

Here's the tax secret > An RRSP deduction on Line 208 of the return creates new money for savings with an increased tax refund; you'll save more because tax on investment income is deferred, and you'll increase entitlements to refundable tax credits and reduce clawbacks of social benefits like the Old Age Security or Employment Insurance as a result of your reduced net income.

You can also save the RRSP deduction for a future year, perhaps when an unusual spike in income occurs.

Example > Terry is out of work and not taxable, but he has maximized his RRSP contribution every year. He knows that he does not need to take the tax deduction, but can save his "undeducted RRSP contributions" for next year, when he expects a taxable severance package of over $80,000. He will get a bigger bang for his RRSP buck that way.

It can really pay off in a big way to claim your RRSP deduction when your marginal tax advantage is highest. But suppose you just don't have any cash to contribute to an RRSP. Here's more good news: RRSP contributions may be made in cash or in kind. That is, you may transfer an eligible investment from your non-registered investments to your RRSP and may claim a deduction for the fair market value of the asset at the time of the transfer.

If the fair market value at the time of the transfer is higher than the cost of the asset, you will have to report the capital gain in income for the year. However, there's a trap: if the fair market value of the asset is less than its cost, then the loss will be deemed to be nil. That is, it will not be claimable. Therefore, if you want to transfer an asset which has decreased in value to your RRSP in order to create a tax deduction, it's best to sell the asset, contribute the proceeds to the RRSP and then have the RRSP repurchase the asset. This method allows you to deduct the capital loss on your tax return. Also, be aware that any income accrued prior to the transfer of assets, such as interest, must be reported on the tax return.

Note, there are other new rules to ensure the taxpayer does not receive an advantage when assets are swapped from a non-registered account to a registered one, so check with your tax advisor before transferring assets back and forth. Non-compliance can result in expensive penalties.

Withdrawing RRSP Accumulations. Your RRSP accumulations can be taken out in a lump sum; however this is not usually a good idea as the amounts will be taxed at the highest marginal rate at that time. You can also choose to create a periodic pension—monthly, quarterly, semi-annually, etc. This is important if you wish to qualify for the pension income amount and pension income splitting, which is possible once you have reached age 65 (or are receiving the amounts as a result of the spouse's death).

Withdrawals from an RRSP will be reported on a T4RSP slip, recorded as periodic income on Line 115 of your tax return if they represent a periodic pension withdrawal or otherwise, use Line 129. Withdrawals will be subject to withholding tax at the following rates (which will differ in Quebec):

Up to $5,000	10%
$5,000 to $15,000	20%
Above $15,000	30%

Especially when you take a lump sum from your RRSP, it is important for you to take this withholding tax into consideration before you make a withdrawal, to ensure you end up with the exact amount of funds you need for the purpose you have in mind.

Here's the tax secret > Tax withholdings can be minimized by taking several smaller withdrawals from your RRSP, rather than one large one. You might also consider, for example, taking them over two tax years for a better after-tax result.

Sometimes you'll want to withdraw money from an RRSP because you have undeducted contributions, or over-contributions. Such withdrawals are not taxable.

RRSP Over-Contributions and Excess Contributions. Over-contributions could happen, for example, when you instruct your employer to make RRSP contributions on your behalf through a payroll deduction plan, but forget to mention a change in your contribution room due to a tax reassessment. To cushion errors in contributions due to fluctuating RRSP room, an over-contribution limit of $2,000 is allowed without penalty, provided you are at least 18 in the preceding taxation year.

Many taxpayers, in fact, use this rule for tax planning purposes. They purposely contribute the amount allowed under their contribution room plus $2000. This is a great way to earn even more tax deferred income within your RRSP.

Example > Debbie has RRSP contribution room of $5,000, which she has contributed. But she is allowed to contribute a total of $7,000 without penalty, and decides to do so to earn tax-deferred investment income while the money is in the plan.

Avoid Making "Excess Contributions." Excess contributions are RRSP contributions which exceed your contribution room plus $2,000. If you make an excess contribution, you need to create contribution room or pay the penalty. That's important, because without the benefit of the RRSP contribution, leaving excess amounts in an RRSP will result in double taxation and expensive penalties.

Work with your tax and financial advisor. Discuss the following opportunities in managing your RRSP withdrawals with your tax and financial advisor:

- *Withdrawal of Undeducted Contributions.* Amounts contributed to your RRSP and not yet deducted may be withdrawn tax-free and with no withholding taxes by filing Form T3012A, *Tax Deduction Waiver on the Refund of Your Undeducted RRSP Contributions.* The amount withdrawn will be included on a T4RSP slip and must be reported as income. You may, however, claim an offsetting deduction on your tax return. Taxpayers who withdraw undeducted contributions without using Form T3012A will have tax withheld but may use Form T746 *Calculating Your Deduction for Refund of Unused RRSP Contributions* to calculate their allowable deduction on line 232.

- *Contributions in Excess of Overcontribution Limits.* Excess RRSP contributions are subject to a penalty tax of 1% per month. A complicated form called a T1-OVP *Individual Tax Return for RRSP Excess Contributions* must be completed in that case and the penalty must be paid by March 31 of the year following. Penalties will accrue until the excess contributions are withdrawn from the RRSP. You'll want to ask a professional to help you with this form.

Tax-Free Transfers to an RRSP. You have learned that tax efficiency in retirement includes moving money into the right "buckets" so that layering of income sources is planned to average down the overall taxes paid. The following capital sources may be transferred to your RRSP on a tax-free basis over and above the normal RRSP contribution limits plus the $2,000 allowable over-contribution:

- *Eligible Retiring Allowances.* Amounts received on job termination as a severance package may be rolled over into an RRSP on a tax-free basis depending on certain conditions. For service after 1995, no RRSP rollover is allowed. For service after 1988 and before 1996, a single limit of $2,000 per year of service can be rolled into an RRSP. And for service before 1989, it is possible to roll over $2,000 for each year of service plus another $1,500 for each year in which the employer's contributions to the company pension plan did not vest in you. The eligible amount will be shown on the T4A from the former employer. In applying these rules, a single day in a calendar year counts as a "year" of employment.
- *Funds From Another RRSP.* You may request a direct transfer of RRSP accumulations from one RRSP to another RRSP under which you are the annuitant. Form T2033 may be used to make the transfer.
- *Funds From a Spouse's RRSP.* On the breakdown of a marriage or common- law relationship, where the terms of a separation or divorce agreement require that the funds from one spouse's RRSP be transferred to the other, the funds may be transferred tax-free. Form T2220 must be used.
- *Registered Pension Plan (RPP) Amounts.* If you cease to belong to an employer-sponsored RPP, the funds from the RPP may be transferred to your RRSP. Form T2151 must be used.

- *Deferred Profit Sharing Plan (DPSP) Accumulations.* You may transfer funds from your DPSP to your RRSP. Form T2151 must be used.
- *Foreign pension receipts.* Lump sum amounts received from a foreign pension plan in respect of a period while you were a non-resident may be transferred to your RRSP. Amounts that are exempt from tax under a tax treaty with the foreign country may not be transferred.
- *Saskatchewan pension plan amounts.* A lump sum payment out of the Saskatchewan pension plan may be transferred to your RRSP tax-free.

Tax-Free Transfers From an RRSP. Funds from your RRSP may be transferred on a tax-free basis to:

- *A Registered Pension Plan* (only possible if the RPP terms allow this). Form T2033 may be used.
- *Another RRSP.*
- The *RRSP of a spouse or former spouse on breakdown of marriage* or common-law relationship.
- A *RRIF.* You may transfer funds from your RRSP to a RRIF under which you are the annuitant. Form T2033 must be used.
- The *RRIF of a spouse or former spouse on breakdown of marriage* or common-law relationship. Form T2220 must be used.
- *An annuity.* Amounts can be transferred from your RRSP to an annuity contract for your life or jointly for the life of you and your spouse or common-law partner with or without a guarantee period. If there is a guarantee period, it may not be for a period longer than until you (or spouse or common-law partner) are 90 years old.
- *RRSP of spouse or former spouse or dependant on death.*
- *RDSP of surviving child or grandchild.* Effective March 5, 2010 rollovers to an RDSP may be made on a tax-free basis if the surviving child or grandchild has sufficient RDSP contribution room.

Creating Your RRSP-Funded Pension. When it comes time to create your periodic pension withdrawals from an RRSP, the accumulations will generally be transferred into one of two investment vehicles that will enable a periodic taxable income that is properly blended for tax efficiency:

- an annuity (which provides for equal monthly payments over a period of time)
- a Registered Retirement Income Fund (RRIF), which provides for gradually increasing payments over time.

Under a RRIF, a minimum amount must be withdrawn according to a predetermined schedule based on your age. The payments are taxable in the year received. However you can withdraw more than this as required. As with RRSP payments, the amounts will qualify for the $2,000 pension income amount on Line 314 if you are over age 64 or receiving the amounts as the result of a spouse's death.

Here's the tax secret > Before you withdraw, speak to your tax advisors about planning your income sources, taking into account the following concepts:

- Equalizing income between spouses—who should withdraw first or most—the higher income earner or the lower?
- Can other income sources be split between spouses—Canada Pension Plan benefits for example?
- Should dividends be reported by the higher earner (a possibility only if a Spousal Amount is thereby created or increased)?
- Should one spouse be earning more or less interest, dividends or capital gains from non-registered sources to reduce family net income?
- How will the clawback of the Age Amount or Old Age Security be affected by your pension withdrawals?
- How will your quarterly instalment payments be affected by your RRSP withdrawals?
- If you will be in a higher marginal tax bracket at death, should you withdraw more during your lifetime?

Tax Strategy

Many people make the mistake of waiting too long to start drawing taxable income out of their registered pension plans. Your goal for couples is two equal incomes. Have you accomplished that? Your goal for singles is to average down tax over a longer period of time and then save any "redundant" or unneeded income in a registered account. This is especially important now that provincial governments are introducing high income surtaxes, which will effect accumulations in registered accounts on the death of the last surviving spouse or single.

CHAPTER 29

Foreign Pensions

Canadian residents may be subject to tax on foreign pension income sources, and tax treaties with foreign countries are put into place to help avoid double taxation. Even if your foreign pension income is deposited in an account offshore, know that because Canadian residents are taxed on world income in Canadian funds, all foreign pension income received—no matter where in the world—is taxable in Canada.

Here's the tax secret > A foreign tax credit may be claimed if the "source country" withholds taxes. In addition, certain tax exemptions are available to Canadian tax filers; of recent note:

Tax Exemption on U.S. Social Security. Recipients of U.S. Social Security will claim a 15% deduction on Line 256 of the Canadian tax return. U.S. Social Security benefits received after January, 2010, will be eligible for a 50% deduction, if the social security pension began prior to 1996. This change should be reviewed with executors of estates receiving qualifying benefits as well.

German Social Security. German social security benefits became taxable in Canada in 2003. For pensions which began in 2005 or earlier, the portion of the pension that is non-taxable is 50%. For pensions which begin after 2005, the percentage that is taxable in Canada is set in the year that the pension starts. The 50% rate for 2005 increases by 2% each year for the period 2006 to 2020, and then increases by 1% each year until the taxable percentage reaches 100%.

This percentage is used in the pension begins and in the subsequent year. For each year thereafter, the non-taxable portion is fixed at the amount (in Euro) that was non-taxable in the first full year that the pension is received.

Filing Requirements for Recipients of German Pensions. As a result of pension reform in Germany in 2005, Canadian residents who receive a pension from Germany are required to file a German tax return to report their pension income. For those who do not, the German government is sending automatic assessments for taxes owing for all years back to 2005. Where the pensioner's income is low enough, they be evaluated as "unrestricted" and be subject for a reduced tax or no tax at all. Be sure to consult a tax advisor who is familiar with the tax filing requirement for recipients of German pensions if you are receiving one.

Snowbirds. Canadians who live in the U.S. for the winter may have both Canadian and U.S. tax filing consequences, depending on whether they are considered to have resident alien status, which requires the filing of a U.S. tax return. A "closer connection" declaration must be made on June 15 every year to avoid this. Follow the Snowbird Tax Guide below to ensure you don't put yourself into an unintended tax filing position by overstaying your winter visit:

1. *What does it mean to be a U.S. resident or to have a U.S. resident alien status?* To avoid U.S. taxation on world-wide income, it is necessary for the snowbird to avoid U.S. resident alien status. This occurs when the "substantial presence test" is met.

2. *What is the "substantial presence test"?* This is a test to determine your U.S. filing status. In calculating the Substantial Presence Test, each day:

    *   in current year counts as a full day;
    *   last year counts as one-third of a day; and
    *   the year before that counts as one-sixth of a day.

    Add up the total number of days you were present in the U.S. in the last three years, multiplied by these factors. If your total is at least 183 days, you are considered a resident alien for U.S. filing purposes in the year. If your total is less than 183 days, you are considered a non-resident alien. Even if you a resident alien because you meet the substantial presence test, you can be considered a non-resident alien if:

    *   you were present in the U.S. for less than 183 days
    *   your tax home is in Canada; and
    *   you had a closer connection to Canada than to the U.S.

3. *Are there tax implications to renting our winter vacation home to others?* Rental income on a U.S. property owned by a Canadian will automatically have a 30%, non-refundable withholding tax applied on the income. To avoid this withholding tax the Canadian can file a U.S. tax return.

4. *What do U.S. estate taxes include and when would U.S. estate taxes be triggered?* U.S. estate taxes are first based on worldwide assets. If worldwide assets are significant, even if the U.S. assets are not, U.S. estate taxes could still be payable. U.S. estate taxes would be applied on real estate, U.S. securities or certain other property that is deemed to be situated in the United States (collectively referred to as "U.S. situs assets"). As estate tax rates and exemptions are expected to change in 2013, it is essential to get tax advice before buying U. S. property.

5. *What are gift taxes and why are they important?* If you "gift" a U.S. property to another family member, U.S. Gift Taxes could apply. These could be significant; again a reason to seek tax advice.

6. *If the intent is to break all ties with Canada, and become a non-resident, how does one go about doing this and what are the departure taxes?* If your intent is to break all ties with Canada and become a non-resident you will need to consider both the "primary" ties as well as the "secondary" ties, and the impact of departure taxes. CRA could still deem you as a Canadian resident and thus charge penalties and taxes if you have not clearly "broken" all of your ties with Canada. There are a number of assets and investments that are "deemed" to have been sold the day one breaks their ties with Canada: non-registered investments, certain rental, vacation properties and farmland to name a few. This could result in a significant capital gains tax paid on departure. However, provisions are in place to defer this tax under certain situations.

7. *How are CPP, OAS, RRSP and RRIF Income Payments impacted by departure from Canada?* Pensions, RRSP investments and Canadian real estate are not considered to have been disposed of for tax purposes upon departure from Canada.

Tax Strategy

If you receive foreign pension income or travel and stay abroad extensively it is essential to get tax help to comply with international rules and tax filing requirements. Be sure to speak to a tax advisor about claiming foreign tax credits and exemptions and also about any filing requirements for income during your lifetime and assets held at death.

CHAPTER 30

Pension Income Splitting

With our progressive tax system, the more evenly you can spread your household income amongst family members, the more likely it is that you'll pay the least amount of income tax as a family. During the active earning years, the opportunities for splitting earned income are limited, but several opportunities exist to split retirement income and thereby reduce your total tax bill.

How is Pension Income Splitting Accomplished? There are a variety of methods; for example you can plan to assign half your CPP benefits to your spouse. You can accumulate your RRSP savings to ensure each spouse has equal amounts of money in their own RRSP; or you can use a spousal RRSP, which your spouse draws from, regardless of age, as required.

When you reach age 65, you can split your RRSP accumulations by election with your spouse. And when you retire with a periodic pension from an employer-sponsored plan, at any age, you can split that income with your spouse, too.

Splitting of Canada Pension Plan benefits is beneficial if one spouse receives significantly more CPP benefits than the other. You can split CPP pension benefits when both spouses have turned at least age 60. Through a simple application to Service Canada, CPP benefits earned while the couple was together may be split between them. Be sure to review Chapter 27 of this book for upcoming changes to the CPP which may affect seniors who wish to continue working after age 60 while drawing benefits.

RRSPs. There are two possible ways to draw down RRSP portfolios in a tax-efficient manner. Each option may require the client to take on more risk than what they should at this stage in their life.

- **Split Income with Spouse.** If you have not yet attained age 65, and therefore cannot yet make an election to split up to 50% of retirement income from an RRSP or RRIF with your spouse (see below), you could have the lower earning spouse withdraw taxable funds from his/her own RRSP first; depleting that source if necessary while keeping the higher earner's RRSP intact. Alternatively (or in addition), withdrawals from a spousal RRSP can be made.

  Spousal RRSPs have been available for some time. When one spouse has higher earned income than the other, the spousal RRSP provides an opportunity for both the self-employed and employees who will not be receiving a pension income to split RRSP income in retirement with their spouse. The spouse with the higher earned income claims the RRSP deduction, thereby reducing their income tax bill but the spouse (in whose name the contribution is made) will report the RRSP income when it is withdrawn as retirement income. However, there are "three year holding rules" to keep in mind.

Example > Otto operated a small business for many years and his wife Johanna worked in the family business. Otto was not able to set up a pension plan for Johanna or for himself so instead he contributed half his RRSP contribution limit to his own RRSP and the other half to an RRSP for Johanna. Otto sold the business and retired at age 60.

In retirement, Otto can withdraw funds from his own RRSP to provide income. Any withdrawals that Johanna makes from her RRSP will be taxable to Otto to the extent that he made contributions in the year of withdrawal or the prior three years. Beyond that, any withdrawals that Johanna makes from her RRSP will be included in her income. The couple can the each report retirement income even though all of the contributions were made by Otto.

Where neither spouse belongs to a Registered Pension Plan (RPP), the spousal RRSP may, however, be the only way to split pension income before age 65.

Alternatively, where the spouses are different ages, another strategy is to use a spousal plan to defer the time when the RRSP retirement income is taken until the year that younger spouse turns 71. A spousal plan can therefore provide a longer tax-free accumulation period, between the two spouses, which is a way to increase the earnings on capital for the household overall. This might also provide the opportunity for one spouse to generate taxable income from an RRSP, while the other taps into exempt or lower-taxed income sources, and preserves capital and earnings within the tax sheltered environment of the RRSP account. See the next chapter for a discussion of retirement income layering.

- **Withdraw up to Bracket Strategy.** Another important approach is to make additional RRSP withdrawals, in retirement, up to the next highest tax bracket or clawback zone. This income is going to be taxed at this same level at some point in time, so it may be prudent to withdraw the money now and reinvest it more tax-efficiently going forward. Further, accumulations may be taxed at higher marginal tax rate when the second surviving spouse dies.

Example > Michelle is a widow. She is 78 and requires $60,000 to live on and withdraws just enough from her RRIF each year to meet those requirements. She currently has $300,000 in her RRIF.

Michelle's current marginal tax rate is 31.15%. Her current federal bracket ends at $85,414 and her current provincial bracket ends at $78,043. When Michelle dies, her remaining RRIF balance will be included in her income and will take her into the highest income tax bracket (43.41%). To minimize taxes on her RRIF in her lifetime, she should withdraw as much as possible so that her rate remains at 31.15%. She should boost her income to the lowest of $69,562 (start of OAS clawback zone), $78,043 (top of provincial bracket) and $85,414 (top of federal bracket). By withdrawing an additional $9,650 each year, she will pay taxes on her remaining RRIF funds at 31.15% rather than 43.41% at death saving 12% or approximately $1,200 per year in taxes over her remaining lifetime. The additional withdrawal after tax (about $6,500) should be deposited into a TFSA if Michelle has enough contribution room, otherwise it should be invested in another non-registered account.

Here's the tax secret > Once you have reached the age of 65, RRSP accumulations in your own plan can be split with your spouse as "eligible pension income" discussed below. RRSP accumulations must be collapsed into a RRIF or annuity or both prior to age 72. Discuss the timing of taxable income under these options with your retirement income planner. After this try to maximize TFSA savings as a tax shelter.

Splitting Eligible Pension Income. This lucrative tax provision became possible for retirees starting in 2007. Essentially, income that qualifies for the $2,000 pension income amount qualifies for pension income splitting. Up to one-half of such pension income received can be reported by the recipient's spouse by making an annual election to do so.

What is the Pension Income Credit? The Pension Income Credit is a $2,000 tax credit that is claimed on Schedule 1 of the taxpayer's income tax return. This credit is multiplied by 15% on the federal tax return and therefore can reduce taxes payable by $300 each year for each spouse. A similar credit is available on the provincial return and its value varies by province.

To receive the pension income credit, you must first be receiving eligible pension income. To maximize the benefit of this credit, it is extremely important and valuable to split at least $2,000 to a spouse's tax return so that this benefit could be doubled for the family, each and every year.

Therefore, by first creating sources of income that would qualify for pension income splitting, and then by ensuring that at least $2,000 of the eligible pension income is shared each and every year between spouses, taxpayers can create significant tax savings in retirement.

> *Here's the tax secret* > "Eligible" pension income—that which can be split—is pension income that qualifies for the pension income credit, a $2,000 amount found on Schedule 1 of the tax return. The eligible income must be regular and systematic income.

This income generally falls into two qualifying categories:

(a) **For those under 65:** periodic pension receipts of a life annuity from a registered pension fund or superannuation, or the amounts in (b) below if received as a result of a spouse's death.

(b) **For those age 65 or over:** periodic annuity payments from an RRSP, RRIF, LIF, LRIF, PRIF, spousal RRIF, registered annuity or non-registered annuity and/or GIC income from an insurance company investment.

A good example of this is a government worker who retires at 45 with an employer-sponsored pension benefit. Up to 50% of pension income received could be split for tax purposes with the spouse, regardless of the age of the pensioner or their spouse. However, the rules for the other sources of income in (b) are different. The income can only be split once the annuitant reaches age 65.

Not Eligible. Specifically excluded from the definitions of pension and qualified pension income are:

- Old Age Security,
- Canada or Quebec Pension Plan Benefits,
- a death benefit
- foreign pension income which qualifies for a deduction or exemption (example: the exempt portion of U.S. Social Security)
- a payment received out of or under a salary deferral arrangement, a retirement compensation arrangement, an employee benefit plan, an employee trust or the Saskatchewan Pension Plan.

Splitting of pension income between spouses can be beneficial but not for all taxpayers. The following should be taken into account when planning for splitting of retirement income:

- the effect on the Age Amount and OAS clawback on both the transferor and the transferee (could be detrimental);
- the effect on total non-refundable credits available to the family unit, considering specifically the Age Amount, the Pension Amount, the Spousal Amount and other credits transferable;
- the potential for moving the transferor to a lower bracket and the impact of potentially moving the transferee to a higher bracket, together with requirements to make quarterly tax instalment payments.

How to Split Eligible Pension Income. The election to split pension income is made by each spouse filing form T1032 *Joint Election to Split Pension Income* with their tax returns. When filing electronically, the actual election forms are not submitted but should be maintained with the spouse's tax returns. The amount to be split is specified on the form and the pensioner takes a deduction on line 210 of their tax return and the recipient spouse includes the same amount in income on line 116 of their tax return. The best results are generally achieved by electing the amount needed to equalize taxable income although there are exceptions.

Tax Strategy

Pension income splitting with your spouse could save you thousands of dollars over your retirement years. It is a gift from government that can help you preserve and transition more wealth from all sources. Be sure to speak to your tax and financial advisors to optimize your opportunities.

CHAPTER 31

Retirement Income Layering

From our discussion so far, you can see that drawdown strategies from various public and registered accumulations can be complicated and ineffective if not done well. The goals is to reduce taxes on the timing of the withdrawal, and to average down taxes over a period of years, while income splitting with your spouse.

Here's the tax secret > Income layering of all your income sources in retirement can help you get a better after-tax result, and help you preserve your capital for the future too.

Non-Registered Investments. Review the output of income-producing assets available for pre-retirement and retirement planning with your tax and financial advisors when assets are held outside an RRSP. Some options include:

- **Debt instruments, generating interest:** Interest, in general, is not tax-efficient when held outside an RRSP; 100% of accrued earnings are added and there are no offsetting tax credits. Also, in the case of compounding investments, you must pay the tax on accrued investments before you get the earnings. This means you dip into your own pocket to pay the tax first. Therefore, interest should be earned within a TFSA or a registered account if possible.
- **Dividends from preferred and common shareholdings:** Dividends can be more tax efficient, depending on your province of residence; dividends can even offset taxes payable on other income of the year, depending on your marginal tax bracket. However, be careful; an overweighting in dividend income can cause a clawback of Old Age Security benefits and other tax credits, as discussed.

- **Accrued gains in income-producing assets:** Very tax efficient, as those gains will not be taxed until disposition. At that time, they will then be offset by capital losses of the year, and after this only 50% of the net amount is added to taxable income. Additional planning with charitable donations can render capital gains on certain securities completely tax-free.
- **TSWP mutual funds:** This income can be tax efficient as it is made up of a combination of tax paid capital and earnings. You will be able to receive the monthly cash flow you need, while also minimizing the tax paid. However, a capital gain may occur in the future, as capital withdrawals reduce the cost base of your assets.
- **Mutual fund distributions:** Regular distributions from the fund—capital gains, interest and dividends—have a variety of tax consequences. Generally you'll want to buy these investments at the beginning rather than the end of the previous year to avoid receiving all the distributions for the year over a short ownership period.
- **Corporate class mutual funds:** The capital class structure will allow you to protect against declining markets or buy into emerging markets by shifting capital into another class of shares of the corporation without triggering a capital gain.

Don't forget the TFSA. Significant protection against inflation and taxation can be achieved when you take advantage of investment opportunities in a Tax-Free Savings Account, especially if all other tax deferral opportunities have expired. Otherwise, the return of your tax-paid capital can supplement taxable income, as discussed above, but at the expense of a diminishing balance on which to earn future income.

Following is a summary of income sources and their tax attributes, which can help you to plan your cash flow more tax-effectively in retirement:

Retirement Income Layering Summary

Source	Tax Status	Tax Reporting
Employment	Taxable	Report on Line 101.
Old Age Security	Taxable to recipient. Clawed back when individual's net income on Line 236 exceeds indexed income thresholds.	Call 1-800-277-9914 to apply. Report income on Line 113 from T4A(OAS) slip. Report income tax deducted on Line 437.
Guaranteed Income Supplement & Allowance	Report as income (line 146) for purposes of reducing tax credits—these sources increase individual net income.	Deduct on Line 250 so that income is not taxable.

Source	Tax Status	Tax Reporting
Canada Pension Plan	Taxable to recipient (except survivors benefits paid to minors, which are received by widow/widower but taxed to child).	Report on Line 114 from T4A(P) slip, remember to take into account the ability to split income with spouse through a benefit assignment.
Retiring Allowances (Severance Pay)	Taxable but portions may qualify for tax free rollover to an RRSP or Registered Pension Plan (RPP).	Report amounts from T4 or T3 slips. Amounts in Box 66 of T4 can be transferred to an RRSP or RPP on a tax-free basis. Qualifying amounts on T3 slip are in Box 47.
Superannuation (Periodic Pension Benefits)	Taxable but up to 50% of income may be split with spouse.	Report amounts from T4A or T3 on Line 115; to split income complete form T1032 and follow reporting instructions.
Foreign Pension Income	Taxable in Canadian funds, however some are non-taxable due to a tax treaty.	Report gross amounts on Line 115, but take treaty deductions available on Line 256. Most taxable periodic pensions qualify for the pension income amount, too.
Annuity payments	Amounts from general annuities, Deferred Profit Sharing Plans (DPSPs) are taxable.	Depending on age some of these amounts may qualify for the offsetting pension income amount and income splitting.
Retroactive Lump Sums	Taxable if received for years after 1977, but may qualify for lump sum averaging. Includes employment income, certain damages, wage loss replacement, support from a spouse, RPP benefits, EI.	Attach form T1198 *Statement of Qualifying Retroactive Lump-Sum Payments.*
Interest Income	From bank accounts, term deposits, GICs, etc. are taxable on an annual accrual basis.	Report on Line 121. Note that in the case of bonds or T-Bills, a capital gain or loss may occur on disposition before maturity.
Capital Gains and Losses	Partially taxable. Income from the disposition of capital property is included at 50%.	Report on Line 127 if gains exceed losses for the year. Carry losses back 3 years or forward to offset capital gains in the future.

Source	Tax Status	Tax Reporting
Dividend Income	Taxable. Income can be received from "eligible" or "other than eligible" dividends; the latter coming from small business corps that qualify for the small business deduction.	The actual dividend is grossed up by 25% in the case of ineligible dividends and 38% in the case of eligible dividends on Line 120. Then an offsetting dividend tax credit is taken in the amount of 13.33% and 15.02% respectively on Schedule 1.
RRSPs	Taxable. Both principal and earnings are taxable but qualify for pension income amount if taxpayer is at least age 65 or receiving amounts due to death of spouse	Report on Line 129; if not eligible for the pension income amount on Line 314; otherwise report on Line 115. Amounts that qualify for the pension income amount also qualify for pension income splitting.
Spousal RRSP	Taxable in hands of contributor if holding period of 3 years from last spousal RRSP contribution is not met.	As above. Pay attention to designation of benefits at death; tax free transfers on marriage breakdown.
RRIF	Taxable in hands of recipient.	As above. Note in case of spousal plan, transfers of RRSP accumulations to a RRIF results in minimum payments that are taxable to the annuitant. Amounts over this are taxed to spouse until holding period is over.
Self-Employment	Proprietors are taxed on net business income and must make CPP contributions at least to age 65. Optional between 65 and 70 if receiving benefits.	File a Business Income Statement. Incorporated taxpayers lose CPP pension building opportunity if drawing dividends only.
Retirement Compensation Arrangements (RCA)	When making a withdrawal from an RCA the income is fully taxable. The income comes from two parts: refundable tax from CRA and the RCA investment itself.	Income reported on a T4A-RCA slip is reported on line 130 of the recipient's return. This income is classed as "other income" not eligible for any off-setting deductions or credits. RCA income is not eligible for pension income splitting.
Individual Pension Plans (IPP)	Taxable based on same rules followed for RRSP and RRIF.	See RRSP information regarding pension income splitting.

Insurance. In the event you have one of more of the following insurance policies additional income may be available in times of need:

Disability Income	If premiums were paid by the employee, the income received is tax free. Any amount paid by the employer, renders the entire income taxable. Disability income plans, whether they are group or individual, pay to a maximum of age 65.	Report only taxable amounts on line 104 (other employment income). Deduct premiums paid by employee if the amount is taxable.
Long Term Care Income	The income received is as a monthly tax-free benefit. The benefit is paid in the event the insured is unable to complete one or more "daily activities" as defined by the policy. Can be used for any purpose, based on home or facility care expenses.	Form T2201 Disability Tax Credit may assist with eligibility.
Critical Illness Insurance	These plans can be available up to the insured's age 75 or 80. A lump sum tax-free benefit would be received in the event the insured was diagnosed of having a critical illness.	The conditions covered under each plan vary, the three conditions found under all plans relate to heart attack, stroke or cancer.
Life Insurance Policies	Many life insurance plans accumulate cash on a tax-free basis, which can be withdrawn at any time. The tax implications at the time of the withdrawal will depend on the amount withdrawn and the "adjusted cost basis" of the contract.	As a general rule, the cost base will decline to zero, making the cash withdrawal 100% taxable. Report taxable amounts on line 130 (Other Income). Amounts do not qualify for pension income splitting.
Line of Credit	A line of credit can often be secured for up to 75% of the cash value of a life insurance policy. This income is tax free; it is considered to be a loan.	No tax implications

A Simple Retirement Income Plan. To illustrate the power of retirement income planning, consider a typical senior, Jonathan age 65 and his wife, Diana, age 55, who are retiring this year and planning their retirement income over the next five years. Shown below is a tax-efficient income layering plan given their income sources: OAS, CPP, superannuation, RRSP accumulations, TFSAs and Jonathan's dividends from his small business. Diana was a stay at home mom, then worked as a nurse and is now fully retired.

Over the next five years, the couple will require $60,000 after-tax income (indexed) which will be composed of:

- Jonathan's OAS, CPP, RPP (split with Diana for tax purposes), and small business dividends.
- Diana's TFSA withdrawals to top up to the required income levels. By year 5, Diana's TFSA will be depleted and funds may be withdrawn from Jonathan's.

RRSP balances will be preserved in the near term to ensure Diana has sufficient funds should Jonathan pass away as his pension will cease on his death. Assuming 2% inflation adjustments, year 1 and 5 of the plan are as follows:

2012:	Jonathan	Diana	2017:	Jonathan	Diana
Age:	65	55		70	60
OAS	$6,510			$7,045	
CPP	$9,800			$10,605	
RPP (split)	$15,700	$15,700		$16,993	$16,993
RRSP					
Dividends	$12,000			$12,987	
TFSA		$5,500			$6,000
Total Income	$44,010	$21,200		$47,630	$22,933
– Income Tax	$4,518	$684		$4,884	$864
After-tax income	$39,492	$20,516		$42,746	$22,129

Because the couple is able to split Jonathan's pension income, the couple saves $2,800 in income taxes each year—at total of $14,000 over the five-year period.

Tax Strategy

A proper retirement income layering plan can provide significant tax savings. Multiplied over an average retirement period of 20 years for each taxpayer the saving can run into the tens of thousands of dollars.

CHAPTER 32

Minimizing Tax Instalments

Seniors often must make quarterly tax instalment remittances: due on the 15th of March, June, September and December. Farmers do so once by December 31, based on their net income for the year.

Instalment Payment Threshold. Starting in 2008 and subsequent years, the quarterly instalment threshold, used to determine whether instalments are payable by individuals was increased from taxes owing of $2,000 ($1,200 for Quebec filers) to taxes owing in excess of $3,000 ($1,800 for Quebec filers) in the current or either of the two immediately preceding tax years. Therefore, if you expect your income will drop this year over prior years, change your quarterly remittances.

Here's the tax secret > It is not mandatory to follow the instalment notices sent by CRA. You can request to change your payments based on your prior year results or an estimation of current year income.

There are three methods by which CRA will accept those tax remittances from you. These are:

- The current-year method: You can pay your estimated taxes for the current year by paying 25% of that amount on each of the instalment due dates.
- The prior-year method: You can pay one-quarter of the taxes due in the prior year on each of the instalment dates.
- The no-calculation option: Use the instalment notices that CRA sends out and pay the amount specified. CRA calculates the mount due for the first two instalments as one-quarter of the taxes payable in the

second prior year and the last two instalments as one-half of taxes payable in the prior year less the first two instalment payments.

Example > Gertrude's income consists of Old Age Security, CPP and investment income. Her taxes due in 2010 were $4,400. In 2011 her taxes due were $4,000. Per the CRA instalment notices she her instalments were:

- March and June: $1,100
- September and December: $900

Gertrude made her first there instalments as required (total $3,100) and found in December that her investment income for the year had dropped so that her balance due for 2012 would only be $3,500. Since she has already paid $3,100, she can reduce her December instalment to $400.

You can also reduce your withholding for the Old Age Security Recovery Tax (your clawback) with a T1213 (OAS) *Request To Reduce Old Age Security Recovery Tax at Source.*

Tax Strategy

Don't take money out of your investments to make quarterly tax instalment payments you don't need to make.

Essential Tax Facts

Follow these simple rules to take charge:

Save Well to Maximize Economic Power in Retirement. Tax-efficient retirement income planning begins with the first dollar you save. That makes retirement planning important for everyone. Plan to put together a variety of retirement income "buckets" for each spouse, including access to public and private pensions and non-registered investment pools.

Withdraw Money with Tax Efficiency. A tax focus can help you withdraw only the right amount of pension income for cash flow purposes, and this will ensure that you don't over-encroach on other savings, especially when your investment returns are low.

Know How Your Withdrawals Affect Your Tax Bracket. The withdrawals you make from your registered savings accounts—RPPs, RRSPs, IPPs, DPSPs—are taxable in the year received. Structured as a periodic pension, the amounts may qualify for a $2,000 federal pension income amount and pension income splitting with your spouse. However, your age may be a factor with some of these plans.

Make Sure You Take Advantage of Pension Income Splitting. You may split income with your spouse no matter your age at retirement, when you have an employer-sponsored RPP. Therefore, it is likely more advantageous not to the transfer these amounts to an RRSP or RRIF or LIF, where you must wait to age 65 to split income with your spouse. Discuss this with your advisors in advance before you commute your pension at work.

Employer-Sponsored Plans Offer Great Tax Benefits. Members of some RPPs may choose to work on a part time basis, drawing up to 60% of the benefits that have otherwise accrued and at the same time continue with contributions to an RPP. Speak to your HR department and your tax advisors about this, too.

Plan Your CPP Pensions Wisely. CPP retirement benefits are not eligible for the $2,000 Pension Income Amount. However, spouses may equalize the taxable CPP retirement benefits by assigning them equally for a better after-tax result. Decide whether you want to continue to contribute to the CPP if you work after age 64. However, remember you must "opt out" to stop contributing.

Put RRSP Accumulations in the Hands of Your Younger Spouse. Retirement can continue to be an accumulation period in your household, especially if you have a younger spouse, who does not have equal pension savings. Your unused RRSP contribution room carries forward for use in the future, but a taxpayer must be under 72 years of age to contribute to an RRSP, unless there is a younger spouse. If you are "age ineligible" you may still contribute to a spousal RRSP, based on your RRSP contribution room, if your spouse is under 72 years old.

Avoid Making "Excess Contributions." These are RRSP contributions which exceed your contribution room plus $2,000. If you do, you need to create contribution room or pay the penalty. Penalties for excess contributions are 1% of the excess for each month that the funds remain in your RRSP to withdraw them as soon as you discover that you've made an excess contribution.

You Don't Need to Take Your RRSP Deduction this Year. Any amounts contributed in the year and not deducted are considered to be "undeducted RRSP contributions." These amounts may be carried forward and deducted in future years if this is advantageous. You can also save the RRSP deduction for a future year, perhaps when an unusual spike in income occurs. An example might be a large retirement income withdrawal to take a trip.

Don't Flip Losing Shares into Your RRSP. When RRSP contributions are made by transferring capital property into the account, you are deemed to have disposed of the property at the time of the transfer. Report accrued gains in the year of transfer. Investments that have declined in value should not be transferred to an RRSP as the loss in value will not be deductible.

Manage RRSP Withdrawals. If you need to take funds from your RRSP, consider taking them over two tax years for a better after-tax result.

Always Plan to Consider the Time Value of Money. A dollar in your pocket today is more valuable than a dollar to be received in the future. Don't over-remit or overpay your taxes in retirement. Try to keep your money invested.

PART VI

Tax Savvy Investing

CHAPTER 33

What is Tax-Efficient Investing?

N ow that you better understand the end game—how your savings will be withdrawn and taxed in retirement—you can be more purposeful in your investment activities along the way, including how you choose your investments. Your future retirement income security, after all, is dependent on the investment decisions you make when you are young.

Here's the tax secret > Retirement income planning begins with the
first dollars you invest. Tax efficiency will make your money grow
faster, and last longer in retirement, too.

Saving money consistently, and in a variety of different investment accounts or "buckets" will help you put away more money when you are younger, avoid paying tax on investment earnings along the way, and then pay the least "average tax" within a retirement period. In other words, your object is to try to save on a pre-tax, tax deferred basis, and then withdraw your taxable savings in such a way as to pay the very least amount of taxes possible in retirement.

According to Statistics Canada, the average age of your retirement will likely be 62, and the average length of retirement will be 15 years for men and 19 years for women. Depending on how healthy you will be in your future, you can, in fact, determine what is "enough" for retirement by keeping your eye on funding at least 15 to 19 years for your golden years, now.

It's a good strategy to think about those years your first priority with a tax-efficient accumulation and growth strategy; then learn how to preserve your capital in retirement to make it last longer, so it's available if you live longer. There is a methodology you can follow, that really works.

The researchers at the Department of Finance, for example, tell us that retirement income adequacy[14] "critically" depends on:

- the tax assistance for savings (TFSA, RRSP plus tax-efficient non–registered income sources),
- the timing of your investments and
- the type of investment you make.

Using tax-assisted savings accounts, starting to contribute to them early and then choosing the right investment products to get the returns you need all count towards your solution. When you get that, and you get started, this three-pronged approach will allow more time to have fun with your savings, rather than worrying about whether they will last. That's the ultimate reward of tax-efficient investing.

What is Tax-Efficient Investing? Technically speaking, tax-efficient investing is the process of selecting investments with the most appropriate tax "preferences" for your age, family status and income, so you can exercise your rights to arrange your affairs within the framework of the law to pay the least amount of taxes on both income and capital.

To help you make decisions on paying the least amount of taxes, thereby accumulating more throughout your lifetime, know your marginal tax bracket and rate and how to avoid spiking your income into the next tax bracket or expose your income to a high income surtax.

Understanding Marginal Tax Rates. Your decision-making can be greatly improved when you know the marginal tax rates your investment income will be subject to—now and in the future. The marginal tax rate is the rate of tax paid on the next dollar earned. Income type and income level both factor into your MTR, as shown in the chart below. We have indicated the top marginal rates here.

Marginal Tax Rates in Canada
(2012 Income $133,000 to $500,000)

Province	Ordinary Income	Capital Gains	Eligible Dividends	Ineligible Dividends
Alberta	39.00%	19.50%	19.29%	27.71%
British Columbia	43.70%	21.85%	25.78%	33.71%
Ontario	46.41%	23.20%	29.54%	32.57%

Source: Knowledge Bureau, Inc.

---

[14] *Investment Performance and Costs of Pension and Other Retirement Savings Funds in Canada: Implications on Wealth Accumulation and Retirement*, Dr. Vijay Jog, December 2, 2009

You can see that the marginal tax rate will depend on the type of income you earn and how much other income you have. Most types of capital gains attract one-half of the marginal tax rate for interest income, for example. The MTR for dividend income is not as easily calculated, as the dividend gross up and dividend tax credit vary with the type of dividend, and there are variations in the dividend tax credits by province.

Generally, however, dividends attract a lower MTR than interest, business or property income. The effect the gross up has on clawbacks of tax credits and other government benefits must be taken into account though.

Example > Thomas, who lives in BC has an employment income of $55,000, two children and a spouse who does not work outside the home. He expects to earn $25,000 in capital gains this year. What is his marginal tax rate when his tax credits are taken into account?

Without taking into account his tax credits, his marginal tax rate on ordinary income is 31.15%. Taking into account his Child Tax Benefit, his marginal tax rate is 35.15% on ordinary income. On capital gains, it's half that or 17.58%.

The MTR is an effective tool in helping us make decisions about what to invest in first, second, third and so on. In this section, you'll learn more about each of these investment income sources.

Growing Your Net Worth. When we look at the scope of tax assistance available for financial assets – inside and outside of a registered account—as well as non-financial assets like real estate, it helps us to develop a checklist of criteria to look for before making an investment so we can get to a point of evaluation in our investment activities. How well are we doing, year over year?

The object is to increase personal net worth. There are two things to know about this:

- Your personal net worth is your total assets, less total liabilities.
- The sustainability of your net wealth—that is, the purchasing power of your money in the future—is your net worth, adjusted for taxes and inflation.

Making decisions that are tax-effective enhances the performance of your money and increases net worth more quickly. It also makes sure your money has purchasing power when you need it.

Those are the strategic goals. The process used to help you get there involves eight specific priorities in making decisions about your investments. You will want to ask eight questions in making your investment product selections:

1. **Avoid Tax:** Can I avoid tax now and in the future?
2. **Defer Tax:** Can I defer tax into the future?
3. **Reduce Tax:** How can I earn tax-preferred income—that is income subject to low MTRs?
4. **Control Tax:** Is it possible to control the taxes I pay on withdrawals from savings?
5. **Average Down Tax:** Can I blend income and capital for a more tax-efficient cash flow?
6. **Preserve Income and Benefits:** Can I avoid increasing clawbacks?
7. **Shift Income:** Can I shift taxable income to lower earners or alternate tax structures?
8. **Split Income:** Can I use income splitting to minimize tax on capital withdrawals?

Some of the important tax attributes of your investment choices have already been discussed in this book, but now let's embellish on a couple more of them, so you can have a deeper discussion about your investment choices with your professional advisors around the concepts and questions above.

Avoiding and Deferring Tax. Whenever you can avoid or defer paying tax today, you should, to take advantage of the time value of money. Your money grows faster when invested on a tax free or tax-deferred basis. A common way to do so is to invest in "registered" accounts.

Only the TFSA features tax free compounding and tax free accumulation of value. No tax is paid on any earnings, but note that the TFSA must be funded by tax-paid dollars… capital that has already been stripped by taxation.

The most common of the other registered investments, the Registered Retirement Savings Plan (RRSP), and for employees who belong to an employer-sponsored plan, or Registered Pension Plan (RPP), both provide for a tax deduction when principal is invested. In this way "whole dollars" are invested, and these bigger pre-tax dollars will obviously grow more quickly.

Example > Registered vs. Non-Registered Investment over 40 years, 30% tax bracket

If you had $5,000 to invest every year over a 40-year period, you would have deposited more than $200,000 into your savings.

If those funds were in a registered account (such as a TFSA or RRSP), the balance in the account at the end of the 40-year period would be **$494,133**, if you averaged a 4% return on your investment.

If you deposited the money into a non-registered account instead, and paid the 30% taxes due on the earnings each year, the balance at the end of the 40-year period would only be **$370,454**. That's *$123,679* less because the income is taxed as it is earned.

There's more to consider too. If you had deposited the money to an RRSP or RPP, you would have received a deduction. This deduction reduces net income on the T1 Return. This in turn can increase social benefits and refundable tax credits, as previously described, as well as reducing your taxes for the year. The combined amounts—increased social benefits and credits and the tax savings themselves—can generate new capital for investments, like a TFSA. This is a great way to leverage one investment into another to build even more wealth.

Example > **Your average tax refund of $1,660 is reinvested in a TFSA every year for 40 years.**

If you contributed your tax refund of $1,660 every year for 40 years into a TFSA which earned 4% interest, the balance in your TFSA one year after the last deposit would be $164,052. You can see that the power of creating a tax refund in a tax deferred account and then reinvesting it into a tax free account can make you hundreds of thousands of dollars richer.

When you multiply that wealth within the family—each adult being tax savvy in this way—it can be worth millions of dollars to your family net worth. This is a simple but effective way for you to hedge your financial results against the wealth eroders you have no control over, like inflation.

When you invest in a **registered savings account**, there is no taxable income inclusion on the investment earned along the way. However, depending on the type of account, (other than a TFSA, of course) there will tax consequences when you withdraw the money.

In the case of the RRSP and RPP, withdrawals of both the principal and the earnings will result in a full income inclusion in the year of withdrawal. That's because when you contributed to these accounts, the principal was invested on a pre-tax basis.

Some registered investments defer tax without the benefit of a deduction up front for capital invested but attract government grants and bonds as part of the returns. These "tax sweeteners" can help you grow your money for specific purposes faster.

This includes the Registered Education Savings Plan (RESP) and the Registered Disability Savings Plan (RDSP). For details check out Chapters 17 and 18.

These investment vehicles allow taxpayers to choose the best time to generate the income subject to tax, and in the hands of beneficiaries who are generally taxed at very low marginal tax rates, if at all. In some cases, income can be transferred to other family members, or split between family members.

In summary, your registered investment accounts will feature the following tax consequences, which can make you richer, if you know how to arrange your affairs in an optimal way to get the tax results you want:

- Principal and earnings taxed on withdrawal: RRSP, RRIF, RPP
- Earnings only taxed on withdrawal: RESP, RDSP

Preserving Your Savings. Astutely timed, your accumulated savings in these accounts will be withdrawn when you are in a lower tax bracket (for example, upon retirement). But what happens if you are now fabulously rich, because you did all the right things when you were young, and now you are in a higher tax bracket than you ever imagined you would be?

Here's the tax secret > You can reduce taxes payable on the lifecycle of your investment with the power of income splitting with your spouse. If you are single, you will have to plan farther ahead: the key is to withdraw your taxable income over longer periods of time and use a strategy to "top up your income" to the top of your current tax bracket to improve your tax efficiency quotient over the lifecycle of your investment.

This brings up another important question. Is there an optimal level of accumulations in a registered account? The correct answer is "it depends."

Single people will have to work harder to average down taxes, with income diversification strategies, and the timing of their withdrawals.

If you are married or live with a common-law spouse, the income splitting strategies that were discussed in the last section of this book, and be very effective in reducing the taxes on your registered accumulations. You will want to test for tax efficiency throughout your lifetime, and that of spouse.

Test for Tax Efficiency. The eight principles for tax-efficient investing, can therefore help you reach that retirement income adequacy that is critically affected by your use of tax assistance, timing and investment product selection. You will be able to consider important decisions with a better process so you can decide what should I invest in first: an RRSP or a TFSA.

Remember the strategic goal is to keep your eye on four things when you make decisions about your investments: the most tax-efficient way to accumulate, grow, preserve and transition the most sustainable wealth for the family over your lifetime.

Making investment decisions that are tax efficient will help you to build a series of capital pools with different tax attributes, now and in the future. The objective is to average down the taxes paid on over time by planning to "realize" income for tax purposes at the lowest possible marginal tax rates over the lifecycle of the investment.

The Lifecycle of the Investment. With every dollar you invest, consider the net return you'll receive within the lifecycle of the investment. There are typically three tax milestones to consider:

- Tax assistance for initial savings: whether you invest with dollars that are smaller because they have already been taxed,
- Taxation of investment income: how your earnings are taxed in your investment account, and
- Taxation of income and capital on withdrawal in the future.

It is that final rate of return, at the end of an investing lifecycle that really counts. If you were to think about this in an equation, you might call this *your tax efficiency quotient*:

Total net earnings (after taxes)
over the net principle invested (after taxes)

Example > Net earnings: $1,000/Net Invested: $20,000 = 5%

Example > Consider the following "average" Canadian employees who are about to retire at age 65. Both George and Henry saved $5,000 faithfully every year starting at age 25 to age 65. George chose to save by making RRSP contributions and Henry chose to save in a non-registered account. Each made the same investments and over the 40-year accumulation period earned an average of 6% per year.

Each year, Henry reduced his savings in order to pay the income taxes on the earnings (20% in early years, 30% in later years). George enjoyed larger tax refunds of $1,000 in the early years and $1,500 in later years). The results of their savings are as follows after 40 years:

	George	Henry
Account Balance	$820,238	$565,505

Now, in retirement, both George and Henry have $15,000 in pension benefits annually from OAS and CPP and will add the maximum amount they can from their savings, assuming 4% annual return on capital, 2.7% inflation adjustment and a 20-year retirement. The results are as follows:

	George	Henry
CPP and OAS	$15,000	$15,000
Starting Annual Pension	$48,000 (all taxable)	$33,000 (taxable $22,620)
Annual Income	$63,000	$48,000
Taxable Income	$63,000	$37,620
Average Tax Rate	20.5%	14.5%
Net After Tax	$50,085	$47,555

George has a higher taxable income and is paying tax at a higher rate because the full amount of his RRSP income is taxable whereas only the income portion of Henry's withdrawals are taxable. However, in spite of the tax difference, George realizes $2,530 more after-tax in the first year of retirement and even more in subsequent years due to indexing of their pensions.

The most compelling reason for the difference is that the taxes during the accumulation period in the non-registered account are higher (30% for the majority of the accumulation period) whereas taxes during retirement on the RRSP income are only 20.5%.

Should George and Henry have another source of income in retirement, such as an RPP, the tax rate in retirement would be higher and if the rate in retirement exceeds the rate in the accumulation years, the situation could be reversed—Henry could end up with more after-tax income than George.

Tax Strategy

When we plan for net lifetime returns on our investments, we can better consider the value of your money when you need it—its purchasing power after taxes, fees and inflation at the time of investment, as the money works to earn a return on investment and upon withdrawal. The goal is to keep taxes and fees to a minimum along the way and to hedge against inflation by increasing performance: the after-tax rate of return earned in relation to your lifetime marginal tax rates. These are the things we think about in making sound decisions about tax-efficient investing.

CHAPTER 34

Earning Investment Income

We know that growing money in a tax-assisted and tax-sheltered plan will make us richer over time, but there is a place for non-registered investment accounts, especially if we have taken advantage of all age- and income-eligible investing opportunities, or maximized deposit restricted opportunities, for example in the TFSA, RESP or RDSP.

We are therefore now going to move into a discussion of investments held outside of your registered investment accounts. There are three broad classifications of taxable income these investment accounts will generate:

- income from property: interest, dividends, rents, royalties
- real property and
- capital gains and losses, which occur on the sale or deemed disposition of several "categories" of assets.

Here's the tax secret > Realizing income for tax purposes in your non-registered accounts requires planning, too. You will want to plan to earn income sources which attract the least amount of tax, time the realization of that tax and where possible, split investment income with other family members to pay the least taxes possible as an economic unit.

Your investment product selections will help you to diversify and time your income accordingly. Earning interest is often the result of parking your money in a "safe haven," but it may not be the most advantageous place for growth, as discussed below.

Earning Interest. Interest income is common to most investors. It can often accrue on a compounding basis (that is, interest is reinvested rather than paid out to the investor during the term of the contract). The following are examples of "debt obligations" which are investment contracts that pay interest income:

- A *Guaranteed Investment Certificate (GIC)* which features a fixed interest rate for a term spanning generally one to five years.
- A *Canada Savings Bond (CSB)*.
- A *treasury bill* or *zero coupon bond* which provides no stated interest, but is sold at a discount to its maturity value.
- A *strip bond* or coupon.
- A Guaranteed Investment Certificate offering interest rates that rise as time goes on. These are also known as *deferred interest obligations*.
- An *income bond* or debenture where the interest paid is linked to a corporation's profit or cash flow.
- An *indexed debt obligation instrument* that is linked to inflation rates, such as Government of Canada Real Return Bonds.

Interest reporting follows two basic tax rules:

1. You must report the interest in the taxation year when it is actually received or receivable.

2. Compounding investments allow you to earn interest on interest during the term of the contract, paying out the income at the end of the term. However, you must report all interest income that accrues on an annual basis, in the year ending on the debt's anniversary date. An issue date in November of one year, for example, does not require interest reporting until the following year. In other words, the accrual of interest for the period November to December 31 is not required.

These reporting rules stemmed from a tax reform back in the early 80s. For investments acquired in the period 1981 up to and including 1989, a three-year reporting cycle was required, but you could switch to annual accrual reporting if desired. After 1989, investors must report accrued interest annually.

Although you pay tax on income you have not yet actually received with money from other sources, you have effectively reinvested the whole amount of the earnings generated. But, because you are tapping out other income sources to pay the tax on your interest-bearing investments, these are not the most tax-efficient investment vehicles.

Things get a little trickier when investment contracts have unique features:

- they may be non-interest bearing and sold at a discount to their maturity value
- the interest rates may be adjusted for inflation over time
- the rate of interest may increase as the term progresses
- interest payments may vary with the debtor's cash flows or profits
- where the instrument is transferred before the end of the term, a reconciliation of interest earnings must take place.

Here are some examples:

Coupon Bonds. Regular government or corporate bonds can also be called "coupon bonds" and pay a stated rate of interest. If the interest is from a Canadian source it will be reported on a T5 slip and entered on the tax return in the calendar year received in the normal manner. If from a foreign source, interest is reported annually in Canadian funds on Schedule 4 and may generate a foreign tax credit if taxes have been withheld at source in the foreign country.

Further complications arise when the bond or coupon is sold before maturity. In that case, the new investor receives interest on the next payment date, as usual, even though some of the interest may have accrued prior to the purchase. An adjustment must be made to ensure each bond owner reports the correct amount of interest up to the date of ownership change. In addition, a capital gain or loss might arise on the disposition.

Treasury Bills. These are short-term government debt obligations, generally available in three, six or twelve month terms. If the T-Bill's term exceeds one year, the normal annual interest accrual rules would apply.

T-Bills are similar to strip bonds (discussed below) because they are acquired at a discount to their maturity value and have no stated interest rate. On maturity you will receive their face value, which will include the accrued interest amount. This is generally reported on a T5008 slip. If you sell the T-Bill before maturity, a capital gain or loss could result however because of the short term, T-Bill are seldom traded.

Strip Bonds. These are also known as zero-coupon bonds as they do not pay interest during the period of ownership. They are purchased at a discount and if held to term will yield a future value that is higher. The difference between the present and future value is considered to be the interest paid over the period to maturity. The resulting interest must be reported annually on the anniversary date of the bond's issue date each year.

If a strip bond is sold prior to its maturity date, a capital gain or loss may result. The Adjusted Cost Base (ACB) used in the calculation of the gain or loss will be the original amount paid for the strip bond plus the interest accrued from the date of purchase to the date of disposition.

Indexed Debt Obligations. These investments include, in addition to interest paid on the amount invested, a payment (or deduction) on maturity that represents the decrease (or increase) in the purchasing power of the investment during the term of the investment. This additional payment is reported according to the normal annual accrual rules. If in the year of disposition or maturity it is determined that interest has been over-accrued, the over-accrued amount can be deducted as a carrying charge on Schedule 4.

Income Bonds and Income Debentures. A special type of bond or debenture may be issued with a term of up to five years by corporations that are in financial difficulty and under the control of a receiver or trustee in bankruptcy. A return on such an income bond is paid only if the issuing corporation earns a profit from its operations. Such amounts paid or received by the investor are then treated as a dividend for tax purposes.

Exchanges of Debentures for Securities. When a bond or debenture is exchanged for shares of a corporation, the exchange is not considered to be a disposition for tax purposes, providing that the share is received directly from the corporation which issued it. Therefore there are no tax consequences. This is also true when one debenture is exchanged for another bond or debenture, providing that the principal amount is the same.

Planning with Interest Income. Recently, worried investors have flown out of the stock market to what they consider to be "safe" havens: Guaranteed Investment Certificates (GICs) and other interest-bearing debt obligations, like Canada Savings Bonds. The guaranteed return of principal is attractive to many, but with interest rates of half of one percent, the returns are dismal.

Here's the tax secret > Interest income reporting is often obvious: you will receive a T5, T3 or T600 slip, depending on the investment. But, you must report interest income earned even if you did not receive a T-slip. Due to low interest rates, many taxpayers have forgotten to report some of their interest earnings. An adjustment to prior filed returns can be made to avoid interest or penalties in those cases.

Where to park your money as you wait for the right investment opportunities does have expensive tax consequences if you wait too long. Canada Savings Bonds, for example, do not have many of the characteristics of the other bonds we have discussed, but they are a good interest-bearing invest-ment to talk about in planning with interest income because they are well known to many millions.

They are issued by the Government of Canada, are non-marketable and redeemable on demand. After the first three months, they pay interest up to the end of the month prior to cashing; otherwise interest is paid on November 1 each year, in the case of regular bonds. Compound bonds are also available, where interest accrues but is only paid on redemption.

Unfortunately, the tax efficiency rating on this investment is poor, and that's why we often try to earn interest within registered accounts, where the income is sheltered from tax until withdrawal. When you take taxes and inflation into account, most investors will actually lose principal and purchasing power on an investment like CSBs because it is neither tax efficient nor inflation-proof, as demonstrated below:

Real After-Tax Return of $1,000 Compounding CSB*

Year	Interest Earned	Taxes	Inflation Adjustment	Principal and Earnings Left**	Real After-Tax Return
Principal	$1,000.00				
0	Plus:	Less:	Less:		
1	$5.00	−$1.55	−$20.00	$983.45	−1.66%
2	$5.03	−$1.56	−$20.10	$966.82	−1.69%
3	$5.05	−$1.57	−$20.20	$950.10	−1.73%
4	$5.08	−$1.57	−$20.30	$933.30	−1.77%
5	$5.10	−$1.58	−$20.40	$916.42	−1.81%
6	$5.13	−$1.59	−$20.51	$899.45	−1.85%
7	$5.15	−$1.60	−$20.61	$882.40	−1.90%
8	$5.18	−$1.61	−$20.71	$865.26	−1.94%
9	$5.20	−$1.61	−$20.81	$848.04	−1.99%
10	$5.23	−$1.62	−$20.92	$830.73	−2.04%
Total	$1,051.14	−$15.85	−$204.56	$830.73	−18.37%

*Assumes 0.5% interest rate, inflation at 2% and a 10-year hold period Taxpayer is in 31% tax bracket.

**Amounts shown in current-year dollars (i.e. adjusted for inflation from year 0).

Your return after taxes and inflation, after 10 years is actually a loss of 18.37% in real dollar terms. Therefore timing and investment type—two of the three important criteria for building sound futures—are off on this investment in this environment.

Using a TFSA with Interest-bearing Investments. One way to improve tax efficiency for interest-bearing investments is to hold them in a registered account such as a TFSA. Will the CSB fare better here? Consider the following:

Real After-Tax Return of $1000 Compounding CSB in a TFSA*

Year	Interest Earned	Taxes	Inflation Adjustment	Principal and Earnings Left**	Real After-Tax Return
Principal	$1,000.00				
0	Plus:	Less:	Less:		
1	$ 5.00	$0	−$20.00	$985.00	−1.50%
2	$ 5.03	$0	−$20.10	$969.93	−1.53%
3	$ 5.05	$0	−$20.20	$954.77	−1.56%
4	$ 5.08	$0	−$20.30	$939.55	−1.59%
5	$ 5.10	$0	−$20.40	$924.25	−1.63%
6	$ 5.13	$0	−$20.51	$908.87	−1.66%
7	$ 5.15	$0	−$20.61	$893.41	−1.70%
8	$ 5.18	$0	−$20.71	$877.88	−1.74%
9	$ 5.20	$0	−$20.81	$862.27	−1.78%
10	$ 5.23	$0	−$20.92	$846.58	−1.82%
Total	$1,051.14	$0	−$204.56	$846.58	−16.52%

* Assumes 0.5% interest rate, inflation at 2% and a 10-year hold period. Taxpayer is in 31% tax bracket.
** Amounts shown in current-year dollars (i.e. adjusted for inflation from year 0)

Because the less-than-1% return does not exceed the inflation rate of 2%, your capital will be eroded, even in the TFSA, but because the income is earned tax-free, you save the $15.85 in taxes paid in the previous example.

Your money's purchasing power is only eroded by 16.52%. Your net after-tax return, therefore, is 1.85% more if the CSB is held within the TFSA.

Tax Strategy

Planning for interest income could become more significant in the future if interest rates rise. Consider whether this income source should be earned inside a registered account to get the best tax efficiencies and hedge against inflation.

CHAPTER 35

Earning Dividends

A more tax-efficient way to invest is to look for an excellent quality stock that pays a regular dividend. This is the return of the after-tax profits of a corporation to its shareholders. Dividends received by individuals from Canadian corporations are subject to special rules, as an adjustment must be made to compensate for the taxes already paid by the corporation.

The adjustment is in the form of a "gross-up" of actual dividends paid to an individual, offset by a "dividend tax credit" when calculating taxes payable. The actual net after-tax result varies depending on the rate of tax the corporation paid on the income from which dividend is paid, and the taxpayer's province of residence.

If the dividend is paid from income that attracted a high rate of corporate tax, generally from a public corporation or a large private corporation, the dividend is called an "eligible dividend" and is grossed up by 38% for 2012 and later years. The dividend tax credit is 15.02% of the grossed-up amount.

If the dividend is paid from income that attracted a low rate of tax (generally within a private, Canadian-controlled small business corporation), the dividend is grossed up by 25% and the dividend tax credit is 13.33% of the grossed-up amount. These dividends are sometimes called "ineligible dividends" or "other than eligible dividends."

Here's the tax secret > The grossed-up dividend generates a "dividend tax credit," both federally and provincially. These credits reduce taxes otherwise payable, and could generate a "negative income tax" which offsets taxes on other income sources at certain tax brackets, making dividends a very tax-efficient form of investment income.

Earning Tax-Free Dividend Income. A taxpayer can earn a significant amount of eligible dividends on a tax-free basis, depending on the province of residence. This is an example of a tax-efficient income source for some taxpayers, for example, business owners, who might be tempted to forgo employment income sources in favor of dividends from the investment in their business.

Example > Small business owners can pay themselves up to $42,600 in dividends before they begin to pay any federal taxes. Provincial taxes begin at lower income levels.

Maggie operates a small business in BC. She could pay herself up to $27,700 dividends from her corporation in 2012 and still not pay any income tax. The marginal tax rate on small business dividends above that amount starts at only 4.16%.

Trevor operates a small business in Ontario. He could pay himself up to $39,400 without paying any income taxes (other than the Ontario Health Premium).

However, on the downside, business owners will want to be careful to create some "earned income" for the purposes of creating pensions from the CPP and RRSP. Speak to your tax advisor if you have these options.

Planning Reduced Taxes With Dividends. Keep your eye on the marginal tax rates attributed to the earning of dividends. The dividend tax credit will give dividend income a preferred marginal tax rate. In fact, depending on where you live, it is possible to offset other income in the year as well. This is particularly true in the province of BC, as illustrated below.

	Taxable Income Range	Ordinary Income	Capital Gains	Small Bus. Corp. Div.	Eligible Div.
BC	Up to $10,822	0%	0%	0%	0%
	$10,823 to $11,354	15.00%	7.50%	2.08%	−2.03%
	$11,355 to $37,013	20.06%	10.03%	4.16%	−6.84%
	$37,014 to $42,707	22.70%	11.35%	7.46%	−3.20%
	$42,708 to $74,028	29.70%	14.85%	16.21%	6.46%
	$74,029 to $84,993	32.50%	16.25%	19.71%	10.32%
	$84,994 to $85.414	34.29%	17.15%	21.95%	12.79%
	$85,415 to $103,205	38.29%	19.15%	26.95%	18.31%
	$103,206 to $132,406	40.70%	20.35%	29.96%	21.64%
	Over $132,406	43.70%	21.85%	33.71%	25.78%

Example > Tristan has a taxable income of $35,000 which includes $1,000 of eligible dividends. These dividends are grossed up to $1,380 and added to his taxable income. His federal tax on the dividends is 15% x $1,380 = $207. His provincial tax on the dividends is $1,380 x 5.06% = $69.83. His federal dividend tax credit is $1,380 x 15.02% = $207.27. His provincial dividend tax credit is $1,380 x 10% = $138.00.

The net result of the dividend income is $207.00 + $69.83 – $207.27 – $138.00 = –$68.44. There is a "negative tax" because the dividend tax credit exceeds the taxes payable on the dividends. This negative tax reduces taxes on other income of the year making these dividends at this tax bracket extremely tax efficient.

At first glance, astute retirees might plan a move to BC to earn out dividends in retirement from their small businesses or their significant investments in the marketplace. However, the dividend gross up might have other effects—increasing clawbacks on tax credits and social benefits could raise your MTRs and this needs to be taken into account, too. In real life, one would take cost of living and other relevant personal factors into account, as well.

Reduced Social Benefits. You have learned that because the dividend "gross up" artificially increases net income, it may reduce your refundable or non-refundable tax credits, such as:

- The Canada Child Tax Benefit
- The GST/HST Credit
- The Working Income Tax Benefit
- Provincial refundable tax credits
- The Age Amount
- The Spousal Amount
- Amount for Eligible Dependant
- Medical expenses
- Amounts for Other Adult Dependants.

It may also negatively affect other financial transactions that are dependent upon the size of net income on the tax return:

- Old Age Security Clawbacks
- Employment Insurance Clawbacks
- Guaranteed Income Supplements
- Provincial per diem rates for nursing homes
- Certain provincial medical/prescription plans.

If your income is high enough that you are not eligible for these tax credits and you are already fully clawed back, eligible dividends attract a lower rate of tax. If you can claim the credits or are subject to clawback, eligible dividends will attract a fairly high overall MTR although still less than the MTR on interest. On the other hand, the MTR on eligible dividends for lower income taxpayers is often negative (because the dividend tax credit exceeds the taxes owing on the dividend income).

Therefore income planning around investment options is important, especially for seniors, and should take into account all these rules.

Example > Roger is a senior Manitoba resident with taxable income of $70,000. If Roger earns and additional $1,000 of interest income, he will be subject to taxes at 39.40% plus a clawback of $150 (15% x $1,000) of his Old Age Security. The tax on the interest income is therefore $394 + $150 = $544 or 54.4%.

If that extra income was received as eligible dividends, then $1,380 would be added to Roger's income and this would attract tax at 22.6% plus a clawback of $207 ($15% x $1,380). The tax on the dividends income would then be $226 + $207 = $433 or 43.3%.

There is a significant win for this taxpayer if the source of his retirement income has changed from interest to dividends.

Other Types of Dividends. You should be aware of the tax consequences of the following types of dividends:

- **Capital Dividends.** Sometimes a shareholder in a private corporation may receive a Capital Dividend. Such dividends are not taxable. To qualify as a Capital Dividend, the dividend must be paid out of the Capital Dividend Account (CDA) of a private Canadian corporation. This account is set up to accumulate the non-taxable (50%) portion of any capital gains realized by the corporation, capital dividends received from other corporations, untaxed portions of gains realized on the disposition of eligible capital property, and life insurance proceeds received by the corporation.
- **Capital Gains Dividends.** These are dividends received from a mutual fund company. They are reported on a T5 Slip and Schedule 3. Capital gains dividends are considered to be capital gains and not dividends (that is, they are taxed at 50%, are not grossed up and are not eligible for the dividend tax credit).

- **Stock Dividends.** This type of dividend arises when a corporation decides to issue additional shares to its existing shareholders, instead of paying a cash dividend. Like regular dividends, stock dividends must be included in income, and are subject to gross-up, and the dividend tax credit. The amount of the dividend is the amount that the corporation adds to its capital accounts on issuing the share. Where the stock dividend is paid by a public company, this is usually the fair market value of the shares issued.

Tax Strategy

Earning dividends can be an effective way to reduce your marginal tax rates, however some unintended results may occur when the gross-up reduces either social benefits or refundable and non-refundable tax credits. For these reasons, see a tax advisor, particularly if planning dividends from a corporation you own is part of your tax-efficient investment income planning.

CHAPTER 36

Revenue Properties

Many investors recently have increased their personal net worth by investing in real property. If that investment is in a principal residence, a tax-free gain on the sale of your home is possible. This is so even if you earn income from that tax exempt residence—by renting out a room or rooms, for example, or by running a business from your home. We'll dig deeper into the tax consequences of primary and secondary residences or rental properties later, but our mandate in this chapter is to discuss revenue properties held for investment purposes.

Here's the tax secret > Rental properties are often audited so a good place to start in assessing whether revenue property ownership is right for you is to consider the increased tax compliance issues you'll need to account for when you become a real estate investor.

Those who collect rental income from a property rented to tenants will have tax consequences in operating the property and usually upon the disposition of the property as well. In the first year, it is important to set up the tax reporting for a revenue property properly:

- A *Statement of Real Estate Rentals* (Form T776) must be completed.
- Income and expenses will be reported on a calendar year basis. Technically, a landlord is supposed to use accrual accounting in reporting revenues and expenses. As a practical matter, there are generally few major differences between cash and accrual accounting for individual landlords, and most individuals report rental income on a cash basis. The CRA will accept cash accounting so long as the cash income does not differ significantly from accrual income.

- Gross rental income must be reported. It is best to open a separate bank account to keep this in. If you rent to someone you are related to, you must report fair market value rents if you rent for less.
- Advance payments of rent can be included in income according to the years they relate to.
- Lease cancellation payments received are included in rental income.
- In order to deduct operating expenses from rental income, there must be a profit motive (i.e. you must be renting to make a profit).
- Fully deductible operating expenses include maintenance, repairs, supplies, interest, taxes.
- Partially deductible expenses could include the business portion of auto expenses and meal and entertainment expenses incurred (but generally only if you have a number of rental properties).
- Expenditures for asset acquisition or improvement cannot be deducted in full. Rather Capital Cost Allowance (CCA) schedules must be set up to account for depreciation expense. If an expenditure extends the useful life of the property or improves upon the original condition of the property, then the expenditure is capital in nature and not 100% deductible.
- As land is not a depreciable asset, it is necessary to separate the cost of land and buildings on the CCA schedule. A rental loss cannot be created or increased with a CCA claim.
- Not deductible are any expenses that relate to personal living expenses of the owner, or any expenses that relate to the cost of the land or principal portions of loans taken to acquire or maintain the property.

Rentals to Family Members. Rentals to family members can be tricky and often fail audit tests. When you rent a portion of your home to a family member for a nominal rent you may not claim a rental loss, as there is no profit motive. But in this case, you need not include the rent in income.

Example > Will and Emily rent out their basement (30% if the living space in their home) to Emily's brother who recently lost his job. They charge him $300 per month. Similar accommodations in town normally rent for $500 to $600 per month. After property taxes, mortgage interest and utilities for the home the rental statement shows a loss of $2,700. Because there is no profit motive in this arrangement and the rent is below market value, the $2,700 loss cannot be claimed. However, since the expenses exceed the income, it is not necessary to include the rent collected in income.

Deductible expenses. Expenses are usually deducted on a cash basis as paid, so long as this does not result in a material difference from accrual basis accounting. If you account on an accrual basis, expenses are to be matched with the revenue to which they relate, so that expenses prepaid in one year are not deducted then but in the later year to which they relate. Common deductible operating expenses include:

- **Advertising**—Amounts paid to advertise the availability of the rental property.
- **Condominium fees**—Amounts applicable to the period when the rental condo was available for rent may be deducted.
- **Insurance**—If the insurance is prepaid for future years, claim only the portion that applies to the rental year, unless you are using cash basis accounting.
- **Landscaping costs** may be deducted in the year paid.
- **Legal, accounting and other professional fees**—There are unique rules to consider in deducting fees paid to professionals:
  - Legal fees to prepare leases or to collect rent are deductible.
  - Legal fees to acquire the property form part of the cost of the property.
  - Legal fees on the sale of the property are outlays and expenses which will reduce any capital gain on the sale.
  - Accounting fees to prepare statements, keep books, or prepare the tax return are deductible.
- **Maintenance and repairs**—Costs of regular maintenance and minor repairs are deductible. For major repairs, it must be determined if the cost is a current expense or capital in nature.
- **Management and administration fees**—If you pay a third party to manage or otherwise look after some aspect of the property, the amount paid is deductible. Note that if a caretaker is given a suite in an apartment block as compensation for caretaking, a T4 Slip must be issued to report the fair market value of the rent as employment income.
- **Mortgage interest**—Interest on a mortgage to purchase the property plus any interest on additional loans to improve the rental property may be deducted.
- **Motor vehicle expenses**—Travelling expenses are generally considered to be personal living expenses of the landlord. And, if you own only one rental property, then motor vehicle expenses to collect rent are not deductible. However, if you personally travel to make repairs

to the property, then the cost of transporting tools and materials to the property may be deducted.

- **Office and office supplies**—Office and other supplies used up in earning rental income are deductible as are home office expenses in situations where you use the office to keep books or serve tenants.
- **Property taxes**—These are deductible.
- **Renovations for the disabled**—Costs incurred to make the rental property accessible to individuals with a mobility impairment may be fully deducted.
- **Utilities**—If costs are paid by the landlord and not reimbursed by the tenant, they will be deductible. Costs charged to tenants are deductible if amounts collected are included in rental income.

Multiple owners. When two or more taxpayers jointly own a revenue property, it is necessary to determine whether they own the property as co-owners or as partners in a partnership. If a partnership exists, CCA is claimed before the partnership income is allocated to the partners. In effect, all the partners are subject to the same CCA claim. If a co-ownership exists, each owner can claim CCA individually on their share of the capital costs. The next chapter covers the consequences of revenue property dispositions.

Tax Strategy

The acquisition of a revenue property is often a good way to increase net worth. Rental income is considered to be income from property and will be subject to ongoing tax audit to ensure expenses—in particularly—maintenance and repairs are properly reported. Taxpayers are most often caught when improvements to the property are fully expensed, rather than depreciated on the Capital Cost Allowance schedule. Losses on rentals to family members can also be disallowed when there is no reasonable expectation of profits.

CHAPTER 37

Reporting Capital Gains and Losses

Wealthy people invest their money to build new wealth on a tax-exempt, pre-tax or tax-deferred basis, and then pay tax at the lowest marginal rates on the increases in values of their assets. *The Income Tax Act* supports this because when you invest you take risk, and you put your own money on the line first, before you earn any income.

Here's the tax secret > There is no immediate tax on the increase in value of your capital assets. However, when an income-producing asset is disposed of for an amount greater than its cost base on acquisition, a capital gain will arise. Fifty per cent of that gain is taxable.

On the flip side, if an asset is disposed of for less than its cost base, a capital loss is the result. That loss will offset capital gains of the year, and if unabsorbed, can be used again in "carry over" periods, which we will explain below.

Although it is usually income-producing assets like stocks, bonds and real estate that fall within the capital gains provisions, certain personal items may also be subject to capital gains tax. This can include second homes, coins, and rare jewelry.

Specifically, the amount of a capital gain (or loss) is the difference between the proceeds from disposing of the asset and the adjusted cost base (ACB) of that asset, less any outlays and expenses. These terms are foreign to most, but are important, so that you can understand how to transfer assets back and forth between family members and maximize your tax advantages, too. Use this equation to compute your capital gains or losses:

$$\text{Proceeds of Disposition} - \text{Adjusted Cost Base} - \text{Outlays and Expenses} = \text{Capital Gain or Loss}$$

Proceeds of Disposition. The proceeds of disposition will normally be the actual sales price received. But proceeds can also be a "deemed" amount (usually the fair market value) in cases where there is a taxable disposition but no money changes hands—on death, gifting or emigration, for example. Those deemed events are often involuntary and require planning. One might want to transfer capital assets to a spouse or adult child for example. Please see the Attribution Rules discussed in Chapter 15 for special restrictive rules.

Adjusted Cost Base. The adjusted cost base starts with the cost of an income-producing asset when acquired. This could be the cash outlay, or in the case of acquisition by way of a transfer by gift, inheritance, etc., the fair market value at the time of transfer. The ACB may also be increased or decreased by certain adjustments: the cost of improvements to the asset, for example, or in the case of land, non-deductible interest or property taxes.

Example > Jonas buys shares for $100 plus $10 commission and sells them six months later for $200 less $20 commission.

- The "Adjusted Cost Base" of the shares is $110 (price paid, including commissions).
- The "Proceeds of Disposition" are $200.
- The $20 commission on sale is an "outlay and expense" of sale.
- The "Capital Gain" is $200 – $110 – $20 = $70.

Capital Gains Inclusion Rate. The amount of capital gain that is included in income is called the "taxable gain" and this is determined by the capital gains inclusion rate. This has changed a number of times since the introduction of capital gains taxes in 1972, but currently is 50% of the net gain, after capital losses are accounted for.

Working With Losses. Capital losses may only be used to reduce capital gains in the current year. If losses exceed gains in the current year they may be carried back to reduce capital gains in any of the previous three years or in any future tax year.

Losses at Death. When the taxpayer dies, unused capital losses can no longer be carried forward so the unused capital losses (reduced by any capital gains deduction previously claimed) may be used to offset other types of income in the year of death or the immediately preceding year. Capital loss deductibility can be a very important part of estate preservation, so be sure to keep records of these important transactions.

Limited Partnership Losses. A special rule applies when investors lose money on disposition of (units in) a limited partnership. Limited partnership losses up to the partner's "at-risk amount" may be deducted against other income. However, when losses exceed the at-risk amount, they cannot be used to offset other income or be carried back. Instead, they must be carried forward until the taxpayer reports income from that limited partnership. In that year, limited partnership losses of other years are deducted on Line 251 of the tax return.

Limited partnership losses not claimed at death will expire; again something important to keep in mind as you plan your investments for the four elements of Real Wealth Management: accumulation, growth, preservation and transition of your wealth on an after-tax basis.

Trading Your Securities. Shares in public companies or units in a mutual fund that have identical rights and which cannot be distinguished one from the other, must be grouped together for tax purposes to properly calculate gains and losses. The cost of all identical shares in the group must be determined and then dividend the sum by the number of shares held to determine the average cost per share. This makes tax season difficult for disorganized taxpayers who cannot find the right documentation.

Example > Derek is a fairly active trader. Last year he purchased shares of XYZ Corporation and traded them as follows:

- June 28: Purchased 1,000 shares at $8.00 per share
- July 5: Sold 1,000 shares at $8.30 per share
- Aug 2: Purchased 3,000 shares at $7.00 per share
- Oct 1: Purchased 4,000 shares at $8.00 per share
- Oct 23: Sold 5,000 shares at $7.50 per share

The brokerage fee on each transaction was $25

The July 5 sale showed a gain of ($8.30 x 1,000) – ($8.00 x 1,000 + $25) – $25 = $8,300 – $8,025 – $25 = $250.

The October 23 sale resulted in a capital loss (negative gain) of ($7.50 x 5,000) – [($7.00 x 3,000 + $25) + ($8.00 x 4,000 + $25)] x 5,000/7,000 – $25 = $37,500 – $37,892.86 – $25 = –$417.86.

Therefore the net result of these transactions on his tax return is a net capital loss of $167.86 which can be used to offset any other gains in the year.

Without adequate records of the dates, purchase and sale prices and the fees charged, it would be impossible to determine the correct amount of income to report.

Superficial losses. There is a special rule to take note of when capital properties are acquired after a loss transaction. If such assets are purchased within 30 days prior to the disposition, or within 30 days after the disposition, this "superficial loss" will be disallowed and is generally added to the Adjusted Cost Base of the replacement property.

Example > Katherine owned shares of XYZ Corp which had an ACB of $12.00 per share. When they fell to $10.00 per share, she sold them. Since they recovered quickly, she repurchased the shares the following week for $11.00 per share. The $2.00 per share loss is deemed to be a superficial loss and cannot be claimed. The ACB of the repurchased shares is $11.00 + $2.00 = $13.00 per share.

A similar result can also occur when assets held in a non-registered account are transferred into a registered account. The loss on such a transfer is deemed to be nil and it is therefore recommended that shares that have decreased in value not be transferred to a registered account but rather sold and the proceeds contributed to the account.

Example > Jason wants to make an RRSP contribution but he does not have the cash to make the contribution. He has $10,000 worth of shares but these shares have an ACB of $12,000. If Jason transfers the shares to his RRSP, he will receive an RRSP contribution receipt for the fair market value of the shares ($10,000) but his loss on the deemed disposition will be nil. Jason should sell the shares for $10,000, claim the $2,000 capital loss and then make his RRSP contribution with the $10,000 cash proceeds.

Avoiding Capital Gains. In certain cases, when you dispose of capital assets, you may not have to include the capital gain in your income at all. That's maximizing tax efficiency! For example, when you donate publicly traded shares to a registered charity or private foundation, your capital gains inclusion rate is deemed to be zero—you get a donation credit for the value of the shares but you don't have to pay any tax on the gain!

Example > Diana purchased shares for $5,000 several years ago. The shares have done well and are now worth $15,000. If she donates the shares to a registered charity, she will receive a donation receipt for $15,000 and will not have to pay taxes on the $10,000 capital gain. If she were to sell the shares and donate the proceeds, she would still receive a donation receipt for $15,000 but she would also have to report and pay tax on a $5,000 taxable capital gain.

Replacement Properties. In cases where you dispose of a capital asset that is being used in a business and replace the asset with another, you may be able to defer any capital gains on the original asset until the replacement is disposed of. This rule does not apply to investment or rental properties.

Example > Peter's company owned a storage lot which has become too small for the company's needs. The lot was purchased for $75,000 and is currently worth $200,000. The company sold the lot and purchased another nearby for $300,000. Rather than pay the taxes on the $125,000 capital gain on the sale, the company may elect to adjust the ACB of the replacement lot by the capital gain. If this election is made, no capital gain is reported and the ACB of the replacement lot reduced by $125,000 to $175,000. The capital gain on the disposition of the old lot will thus be deferred until the replacement property is sold.

Mutual Funds. Mutual funds are common investments but can often cause some tax confusion, particularly because investors don't understand their real returns from these investments, after fees and taxes.

Here's the tax secret > In some cases, there are unintended results that can push investors into a higher tax bracket than expected at the end of a tax year and make quarterly instalment remittances, and often interest payments for under-remitting, necessary. You will want to speak to your tax and financial advisors before making an investment near the end of the year.

This is because mutual fund companies are required to distribute all interest, dividends, other income and net capital gains to their unit holders at least once every year. With the exception of any return of capital, these distributions are taxable. In the year you acquire a mutual fund, you will usually receive a full annual distribution, even if you invested late in the year. You may wish to hold over your purchase, therefore, to the new year.

In addition, rarely is this income received in cash, so your earnings will not help with the tax bill. Rather, the income is used to buy more units in the fund and those reinvested amounts are added to the Adjusted Cost Base. This makes the reporting of sales or deemed dispositions of mutual funds a more difficult undertaking at tax time, because you will need to have kept track of your ACB. Most mutual fund companies can help you with this.

Switches and Exchanges. In general, when you exchange an investment in one fund for another (e.g. from an equity fund to a balanced fund), a taxable disposition is considered to have occurred, with normal tax consequences— if your investment is in a mutual fund trust. There are no tax consequences when you switch from one class or series to another class or series of funds— if the investment is in corporate class funds.

Tax Consequences Upon Disposition of the Units. Mutual fund units or shares are classified as "identical properties" for tax purposes. As you have learned previously, the average cost of the shares/units must be calculated each time there is a purchase by dividing total units owned into the adjusted cost of the units/shares including all reinvested earnings, as illustrated above. This provides you with the cost per unit required to calculate the capital gains or losses properly. Note that dispositions do not affect the adjusted cost base of the remaining units.

Example > Scott purchased 1,000 units in an equity fund in 2011. The cost of the units was $12.40 per unit. He received a T3 slip for 2011 showing that income of $254 was allocated to him. Rather than receiving the $245 in cash, he received 20.32 additional units in the fund.

In 2012 he decided to move his investment into a bond fund with the same company. The 1,020.32 units of the equity fund were exchanged for 539.96 units in a bond fund with an ACB of $12,662.17. The ACB of the bond fund units at the time of the transaction will be the deemed proceeds of disposition of the equity fund units.

The ACB of the equity fund units is $12,400 (original cost) + $254 (income allocated to Scott in 2011). Scott will report a capital gain of $12,662.17 – ($12,400 + $254) = $8.17.

Segregated funds. A segregated fund is similar to a mutual fund in that it is a pooled investment, but it tends to have more advantageous tax attributes. It is established by an insurance company and the funds invested are segregated from the rest of the capital of the company. The main difference between a segregated and a mutual fund is that most segregated funds include a guarantee—that a minimum amount will always be returned to the investor regardless of the performance of the fund over time.

In addition, however, a segregated fund can allocate a loss to the unitholder (while a mutual fund may not). This can be used to offset other capital gains of the year, or the carry-over years. Segregated funds may also offer maturity and death guarantees on the capital invested and, specifically, reset guarantees—which is the ability to lock in market gains. This can be a very attractive feature of this investment type. The tax consequences are as follows:

- *Guarantee at Maturity.* If at maturity the value of the fund has dropped, the insurer must top up the fund by contributing additional assets to bring the value up to the guaranteed amount. There are no tax implications at the time of top up. However, there will be when the taxpayer disposes of the fund. This will be the difference between the ACB (which includes allocations of income over time) and the proceeds received.
- *Guarantee at Death.* The unitholder is deemed to have disposed of the contract at its fair market value at time of a deemed disposition— death or emigration for example. If the value of the assets in the fund increases, the gain will be taxable to the unitholder when the policy matures or to his estate if the policy owner dies.
- If the value of the assets in the fund decreases, and a guarantee is in place the taxpayer is deemed to have acquired additional notional units in the fund so that their proceeds are not less than the guaranteed amount. A capital loss may occur if the guaranteed value is less than 100% of the investment.

Investors may own other capital assets that have special tax consequences on disposition. The tax consequences of assets like your principal residence—a personal-use property discussed in Chapter 39. Other properties, like listed personal properties and the disposition of small business shares are discussed in more detail in *Jacks on Tax*, an online filing guide by Evelyn Jacks.

Tax Strategy

Adding capital assets to your investments will help you to accrue value on a tax deferred basis until there is an actual or deemed disposition of the property. When the assets produce income— dividends, rents, royalties or interest, for example, those income sources may have special tax attributes that help you to average down the taxes you pay throughout your lifetime. Capital losses, too, can be lucrative as they can offset current year gains or if there are none, be carried back three years or carried forward indefinitely to offset future capital gains. Therefore sound tax help is important before you buy and sell.

CHAPTER 38

Deductions for Investors

The difference between good and bad debt often lies in its tax deductibility. Those who leverage their assets as part of their strategic plan to build wealth, will often do so successfully by earning more income and increasing their net worth. However, in a world awash in debt, claiming tax deductible interest is often the only consolation for the eroding effect that the costs of debt can have on personal wealth.

Here's the tax secret > Carrying charges, such as safety deposit box fees and interest expenses may be deducted when there is a potential for income. In the case of investments, that means income from property: interest, dividends, rents and royalties. Capital gains are specifically excluded from this list however. Interest is not deductible unless you acquire an asset with the potential to earn income from property.

Borrowing to Invest in Registered Accounts. When you incur expenses to invest your money, a tax deduction is only allowed if the potential to earn income is in a non-registered environment. That means interest on loans used for the purposes of investing in an RRSP, TFSA, RESP or RDSP is not deductible. Nor is interest paid on a tax exempt property, like your principal residence, unless there is an expectation rental income will be earned.

Eligible carrying charges are all claimed on Schedule 4 of your federal tax return —*Statement of Investment Income.* The total carrying charges are then deducted on Line 221 and serve to offset all other income of the year, so they can be an important way to reduce overall tax burdens and increase eligibility for social benefits and credits.

But for this reason, these expenses are often audited. You must be prepared to trace all interest you have claimed back to a non-registered investment that has the potential to earn income.

Consider the following list of deductible amounts carefully to be sure you haven't missed any:

- *The safety deposit box...* which, believe it or not, is one of the most missed tax deductions on the return. If you have missed it, be sure to request an adjustment to prior filed returns. This can produce an additional refund of a couple of hundred dollars.
- *Accounting fees* relating to the preparation of tax schedules for investment income reporting.
- *Investment counsel fees.* These do not include commissions paid on buying or selling investments. These commissions form part of the adjusted cost base of the investment or reduce proceeds of disposition from the investment.
- *Taxable benefits reported on the T4 Slip for employer-provided loans* that were used for investment purposes. (Again, often missed: ask your tax practitioner about this if you have been fortunate enough to receive this perk of employment)
- *Canada Savings Bonds payroll deduction charge.*
- *Life insurance policy interest costs* if an investment loan was taken against cash values.
- *Management or safe custody fees.*
- *Interest paid on investment loans* if there is a reasonable expectation of income from the investment, even if the value of the investment has diminished.

Leveraging to Invest. Now that you know what can be deducted, know this: many investors wonder if they should leverage existing capital assets in order to invest more into the marketplace. Often they are approached to consider different leveraged loan arrangements, particularly if they believe they have not saved enough for retirement.

Be sure to crunch the numbers over the life of the loan. The potential for investment income must be present, not just from a tax point of view, but also in order for you to pay off your interest (before tax). You will need cash flow to do this. The investment must be able to pay real dollars on a guaranteed basis before your risk can be properly assessed. Otherwise you will have to dip into other funds to pay your loans. You need to assess those possibilities with your financial advisor, so that you can sleep at night.

Have your assets diminished in value since you acquired them with a loan? Will your interest still be deductible in that case? The answer is yes. You can continue to deduct the interest until the loan is fully repaid, even if you sell the assets. If you did not use the proceeds to pay down the loan, then you can deduct only the portion of interest that would have been paid had you done so.

Tax Strategy

Borrowing to invest, particularly in a low interest rate environment will help you to build wealth. However, it's important not to let the tax tail wag the dog. You must be able to pay back the loan, even if your assets diminish in value. In addition, borrowing costs to invest in a registered account, like an RRSP or a TFSA will not be deductible. Remember that one of the ways to increase the returns on your investment is to be vigilant about interest costs and management fees. If you must pay them, be sure they are tax deductible.

CHAPTER 39

Your Principal Residences

The ownership of a principal residence is a very important part of building your net worth and there are significant tax advantages for doing so, too.

Under current rules, each household (that is, an adult taxpayer and spouse if they have one) can designate one principal residence to be tax exempt on sale. But, a principal residence is classified to be "personal-use property," which means that any losses on disposition are deemed to be nil (that's right--not claimable on the tax return).

Here's the tax secret > A principal residence can include a house, cottage, condo, duplex, apartment, or trailer that is ordinarily inhabited by you or some family member at some time during the year. There is no minimum number of days for this purpose, either.

There is more good news. Except where the principal residence is a share in a co-operative housing corporation, the principal residence also includes the land immediately subjacent to the housing unit and up to one-half hectare of subjacent property that contributes to the use of the housing unit as a residence. If the lot size exceeds one-half hectare, it may be included in the principal residence if it can be shown to be necessary for the use of the housing unit.

For tax compliance purposes, if you have had only one principal residence, used solely for personal use in the entire period you have owned it, no tax reporting is required at the time of disposition, even if a capital gain results. That gain is yours—completely tax free.

More Than One Residence. Where more than one property is owned, and the family uses both residences at some time during the year, the calculation of the principal residence exemption becomes slightly more difficult when one property is disposed of. This is because, starting in 1982, only one property per year can be designated as a principal residence for the family.

If you owned your properties for a long period of time, as is the case with many family cottages, for example, know that for periods including 1971 to 1981, each spouse could declare one of the properties as their principal residence. This allowed for the sheltering of any capital gain that accrued in this period provided that each property was owned by a different spouse.

As you can imagine, these rules can be quite confusing to most taxpayers. Fortunately, it is all sorted out on *Form T2091—Designation of a Property as a Principal Residence by an Individual.* This form helps you to calculate the exempt portion of any capital gain when you sell one of two or more principal residences in the family. Do get some professional tax filing help with this, however.

It's also very important also for anyone who made a capital gains election on capital assets in 1994 to keep a copy of *Form T664 Capital Gains Election* with their will so that executors can take that 1994 valuation into account on the disposition of assets on the final return.

Mixed Use of Principal Residence. When you start using a principal residence for income-producing purposes, for example as a rental or home office, "change of use" rules must be observed for tax purposes. The fair market value of the property must be assessed in this case, because you are deemed to have disposed of the property and immediately reacquired it at the same fair market value, changing its classification from a personal-use property to an income-producing property.

An election can be made not to recognize the change in use of the property. Generally recognition of the change in use will be delayed until the time of sale of the property or when you rescind the election. Any capital gain will then be accounted for. But the capital gain is considered to be nil if the home is designated in each year as your principal residence. Use Form T2091 if you owned another property designated as principal residence in the same period.

In the meantime, if you rent a portion of your property; simply report rental income as usual. If you use it as a home workspace, claim the expenses in the appropriate manner described in an earlier chapter. However, it's very important that while your property is used for income-producing purposes of any kind, no Capital Cost Allowance (CCA) is used as a deduction, even for a small portion. This will compromise the principal residence exemption on that portion of the property.

If, at some time in the future, there is a change in use again, for example, if the property is used solely as a principal residence, the same FMV assessment must be made, as you are deemed to have disposed of and reacquired the property for this new use. Again an election is made so that the tax consequences are accounted for on actual disposition of the property in the future.

Flipping Principal Residences. During a real estate boom, the disposition of real property can be very lucrative, especially if you can earn one tax exempt gain after another with your principal residence. But, how often can you do that before it raises eyebrows at the CRA?

If you buy and sell real estate too often, CRA may disallow your claim for the principal residence exemption. Even worse, they could disallow the capital gains treatment that comes with a 50% inclusion rate and require reporting of 100% of the gain as a gross profit if they think you are in the business of buying and selling homes. The more closely your business or occupation is related to commercial real estate transactions, for example, if you are a real estate broker or builder, the more likely it is that any gain realized from such a transaction will not qualify for the principal residence exemption at all and be considered business income rather than a capital gain.

The courts have considered some of the following criteria on a case-by-case basis to guide us in assessing the right tax filing requirements:

- the taxpayer's intention with respect to the real estate at the time of its purchase,
- feasibility of the taxpayer's intention,
- geographical location and zoned use of the real estate acquired,
- extent to which these intentions were carried out by the taxpayer,
- evidence that the taxpayer's intention changed after purchase of the real estate,
- the nature of the business, profession, calling or trade of the taxpayer and associates,
- the extent to which borrowed money was used to finance the real estate acquisition and the terms of the financing, if any, arranged,
- the length of time throughout which the real estate was held by the taxpayer,
- factors which motivated the sale of the real estate, and
- evidence that the taxpayer and/or associates had dealt extensively in real estate.

Employer-Required Moves. When your employer requires you to move at least 40 kilometers closer to your place of employment and you keep your principal residence but rent out your home while you are gone, it is possible to elect no change in use and designate that property as your principal residence while you are gone. For the election to be valid, you must move back into the home before the end of the year in which your employment terminates.

Where the move is required by the employer and you sell your home at a loss, it is possible to receive a tax free reimbursement of those losses, in amounts up to $15,000, should your employer choose to assist you. Speak to your tax advisor about this.

In other cases, you may have to move and have to leave a vacant residence behind while you try to sell it. You may claim up to a maximum of $5,000 as a moving expense on your tax return for the costs incurred in the meantime, including mortgage interest, property taxes, insurance and utilities. Be sure to keep those receipts and speak to your tax advisor about all of these circumstances before filing your return. Your claims may be subject to audit.

Tax Strategy

Your principal residence can be a great investment if you can use the principal residence exemption to pocket your accrued gains in the future. If your intention is to earn income from the sale of your principal residence, your principal residence exemption may be at risk if you don't follow proper tax filing procedures. And if you flip your principal residences often enough, the gains may be fully or partially included in income. Therefore guard your access to the exemption well—it can significantly increase your net worth—by knowing the tax rules around your real estate transactions.

Essential Tax Facts

Follow these simple rules to take charge:

Exercise Your Investing Rights. Tax-efficient investing is the process of taking advantage of tax law to arrange your affairs to pay the least amount of taxes on your income and capital.

Look for Tax Efficiency Throughout the Lifecycle of Your Investments. You have the opportunity to select tax-efficient investments throughout your lifetime to get the best net results, throughout the lifecycle of the investment. Both lifecycles are important factors in your selections.

Grow Personal Wealth—On a Tax-Exempt Basis First. Your investing strategies should include a tax exempt principal residence and an investment in a TFSA, because your resulting growth will be tax exempt. However, for many taxpayers the path to the investment funds themselves begins with an RRSP, which increases your tax refund, tax credits and social benefits and can provide for a tax free distribution to use to buy a home under the Home Buyers' Plan.

Earn Interest in Registered Accounts. The full amount of accrued interest income must be reported annually if earned outside of an RRSP or a TFSA—so you must pay tax on compounding earnings before you receive them. For this reason, taxpayers often plan to earn interest income inside registered accounts.

Understand the Tax and Inflation Risk in Bonds. Over time, fluctuations in the rate of interest will affect the value of bonds. In general when interest rates rise, the value of a bond or debenture paying a fixed rate of interest will decrease, and vice versa. In those cases, a capital gain or loss may result on disposition. It may be difficult to achieve any gains, in fact, should interest rates rise in the future. But in addition, if interest rates don't keep pace with both tax and inflation, your money suffers a real erosion in purchasing power.

Write off Your Carrying Costs. Many Canadians buy CSBs on a payroll deduction plan. In that case, be sure to claim the interest you pay in financing the purchase on Line 221 as a carrying charge.

Dividends Can Be Very Tax Efficient. Aside from the lower marginal tax rates they attract, dividends can be used in family income splitting, especially if you follow the Attribution Rules to properly document transfers. Each taxpayer can earn a significant amount of dividends on a tax-free basis, depending on the level of other income sources and the province of residence.

Transfer Dividends to Spouse. A special rule allows the transfer of dividends from one spouse to another if by doing so a Spousal Amount is created or increased. The dividend income is left off the lower-income spouse's tax return and is reported by the higher-income spouse, who can then use the offsetting dividend tax credit.

Capital Gains Can Be Tax Free. When you transfer your winning shares to your favorite charity you can avoid paying tax on your capital gains entirely. In addition, generating capital gains when you have income under your personal amounts will render them tax free. That's a great result that comes from planning your investment strategies with lower earners in the family.

Plan to Use Your Principal Residence Exemption. One tax exempt principal residence can be owned per household. However, you will need to be careful to properly report dispositions when more than one personal residence exists, or there is a "mixed" personal and business use for the home.

Rental Properties can Attract Audit Activities. Revenue property owners often make the mistake of writing off in full the expenses they have incurred to improve the useful life of the property, thinking this is allowed as a maintenance expense. In addition, flipping principal residences for tax exempt gains too often can attract tax, when the status is changed by CRA to an investment property.

Trace Interest Costs to Your Investments. Your tax deductible interest charges can reduce your net income and taxes on other income sources. But you must trace that interest to investment or business use, especially important when your line of credit is also used for personal reasons.

Report and Preserve Your Capital Losses. These can be used to offset capital gains of the current year; carried back to offset capital gains of the past three years or carried forward indefinitely to reduce your taxes on capital gains in the future. As part of the reporting on your terminal tax return, capital losses can also reduce other income.

Claim Your Safety Deposit Box. It's one of the most missed tax deductions on the T1 Return.

PART VII

Taxes During
Life Changing Events

CHAPTER 40

Your Most Important Relationships

The most important relationships in your life are those you have with family and the extent to which your family income can be maintained in your old age will, according to a study by Statistics Canada, determine whether you live in greater or lesser splendor.

The impact of divorce or widowhood on income replacement in retirement is more significant for women; as is the ability to maintain the same level of family income as people age. It appears that women who remained married had a median family income at age 78 to 80 that was 83% of their family income at the age of 54 to 56. Yet women who became widowed after age 55 had a median income of 79% and those who became divorced had a median income of just 73%—10% less than the married women[15].

That makes a return to singlehood very costly and one of the most important family wealth eroders. How seniors fare in retirement is very much dependent upon their "potential income," defined by Statistics Canada as the sum of realized income from active and passive sources and the potential income from the sale of owned assets—both financial and non-financial such as real estate.

Here's the tax secret > It is the annuitized value of your net wealth that will determine how adequate your income will be in retirement, and your financial activities and calculations using after-tax rather than before-tax income will give you both a greater understanding and improvement in your relative position to others in your older years.

---

[15] June 20, 2012, Study: Impact of widowhood and divorce on income replacement among seniors, 1983 to 2007, Statistics Canada.

The primary purpose of this book has been to help you with that better understanding of managing your financial affairs towards a surer "potential income" in the future. This will come about because of your personal productivity and the investment decisions you make along the way. We hope you have gained more knowledge, skills and confidence in attaching an after-tax focus to those activities.

As you get older, your financial priorities will shift from income generation and capital accumulation to the growth and preservation of your wealth. Things will also change as you pass through various life events. Departure from an existing lifecycle, can give rise to a capital disposition, which you need to plan for including:

- separation or divorce or
- death of a loved one

In each case there is a deemed disposition of capital assets. However, in both cases when there is a transfer of assets to the spouse or former spouse, a tax-free rollover is possible.

Separation or Divorce. When spouses or common-law partners have lived apart for a period of at least 90 days because of a breakdown of their conjugal relationship, then from the beginning of that 90-day period they are no longer treated as spouses.

In the year of such a breakdown, there are numerous significant tax rules to observe including:

- the division of assets
- the divisions of spousal or individually held RRSPs
- the claiming of child care expenses
- support payments made and received
- legal fees paid
- federal non-refundable credits such as claims for dependent children under the dependent child amount and the amount for eligible dependants and refundable credits including the Child Tax Benefit, Universal Child Care Benefit, and the Working Income Tax Benefit, and
- the effect of relationship breakdown on provincial tax credits.

Division of Assets. On the breakdown of a marriage or common-law relationship, where the terms of a separation or divorce agreement require that the funds from one spouse's DPSP, RESP, RPP, PRPP, RRSP, or RRIF be transferred to the other, the funds may be transferred on a tax-free basis.

Spousal RRSPs. Withdrawals from spousal or common-law partner RRSPs made by the annuitant are generally reportable by the contributing spouse if any RRSP contribution has been made in the current year or the previous two years. However, this rule is waived for separating/divorcing couples. The minimum holding period requirement does not apply to spousal RRSPs when the taxpayers are living apart for the required period of time due to a breakdown in their relationship.

Depreciable Assets. The transfer of depreciable property (such as a rental house) between spouses as a result of a relationship breakdown takes place at the *Undepreciated Capital Cost (UCC)* of the property. As a result, no recapture, terminal loss, or capital gain is incurred on the transfer.

Other Financial and Non-Financial Assets. For other capital property, the transfer takes place at the *Adjusted Cost Base (ACB)* of the assets, so again no capital gains or losses are triggered.

Attribution Rules. When one spouse transfers assets to the other, the Attribution Rules generally attribute any income earned by the transferred assets back to the transferor. However the Attribution Rules do not apply to income earned during the period when the former spouses are living apart because of a breakdown in the relationship. Capital gains or losses, however, continue to attribute back unless the spouses elect otherwise.

Child Care Expenses. Child care expenses must normally be claimed by the lower-income spouse but may be claimed by the higher-income spouse during a period where the taxpayer was separated from the other supporting person due to a breakdown in their relationship for a period of at least 90 days as long as they were reconciled within the first 60 days after the taxation year.

If the taxpayers were not reconciled within 60 days after the taxation year, then each spouse may claim any child care expenses they paid during the year with no adjustment for child care expenses claimed by the other taxpayer.

Alimony, Support and Legal Fees on Separation or Divorce. Alimony or support payments made to a spouse or common-law partner are taxable to the recipient and deductible by the payor. In the year of separation or divorce, however, the payer may claim either the deduction for support or the spousal amount, but not both.

Legal fees to obtain a divorce or separation agreement are normally not deductible.

However, as of October 10, 2002, CRA considers legal costs incurred to obtain spousal support relating specifically to the care of children (not the spouse) under the *Divorce Act* or under provincial legislation, as well as the costs incurred to obtain an increase in support or to make child support non-taxable, to be deductible.

Federal Refundable Tax Credits. The federal Canada Child Tax Benefit (CCTB) and Goods and Services/Harmonized Sales Tax Credit are received as a redistribution of income for the purpose of assistance with the current expenses of mid- and low-income earners in the next "benefit year"—July to June, but they are calculated based on net family income from the prior tax year.

When a family breakdown occurs, CRA should be notified so that the calculation of the credits for the next CCTB or GST/HST Credit payment may be made without including the estranged spouse or common-law partner's net income.

While most taxpayers in this situation will want to immediately supplement their cash flow with these credits, especially in the case of the monthly CCTB, remember that since a separation is not recognized until 90 days after it begins, you should not notify CRA of your separation until you have been separated for a continuous period of 90 days. However, if you marry or divorce, you must notify CRA immediately. Also, because the statute of limitations for recovery of missed or underpaid credits is generally only 11 months, it's important to notify CRA immediately after you have met the rules. Some leniency in the time frames may be available.

The *Income Tax Act* assumes that the eligible CTB recipient is the female parent. However, "prescribed factors" will be considered in determining what constitutes care and upbringing and who is fulfilling that responsibility.

For example, where, after the breakdown of a conjugal relationship, the single parent and child returns to live with his or her parents, the single parent will continue to be presumed to be the supporting individual unless they too are under 18 years old. In that case, the grandparents may claim the Canada Child Tax Benefit for both their child and their grandchild.

Where both parents share custody of a child, CRA now allows the parents to share the CCTB and GST/HST Credit.

Provincial Tax Credits. Many provinces have tax reductions or refundable credits that are based on family net income. In most cases, in the year of separation, it is not necessary to include the estranged spouse or common-law partner's income in the family income calculation and normally no credits or reductions on behalf of the estranged spouse or common-law partner will be allowed. Each partner will claim the credits or reductions to which he or she is entitled based on their own income.

Issues to Discuss With Your Professional Advisors. Remember that a couple need not be legally or formally separated for their tax status to change. A couple is considered to be separated if they cease co-habitation for a period of at least 90 days. When a couple separates a series of financial events will occur; use the checklist that follows as a guide in developing your separation agreement, which is the basis for the tax consequences and your audit-proofing requirements, as well.

Tax Efficiency Checklist for Separating or Divorcing Couples

☐ *Where are the asset deeds and the safety deposit boxes and keys located?*

☐ *What is the estimated personal tax liability at the end of the first year of separation and each subsequent year based on your new income level?* Each person will be taxed as an individual after the separation and will be responsible for their own tax remittances. This must be carefully understood to properly manage any instalment remittance requirements and negotiate the right net cash flow required to manage family finances.

☐ *What are the individual net incomes?* Refundable and non-refundable tax credits will be allocated based on individual, not family, net income levels.

☐ *What is your unused RRSP contribution room?* Spousal RRSP contributions will no longer be allowed. Are you prepared to make your own contribution?

☐ *Are there new opportunities for family income splitting?* Income attribution becomes a non-issue, except for transfers to minor children or a new spouse.

☐ *Are there family trust structures or shares in corporate companies involved?* If so, review those structures and any change requirements with your professional advisory team. This will asset with income planning and income splitting.

☐ *Have all the transfer forms for private pension accumulations in RPPs, RRSPs, RRIFs, PRPP's, etc. been completed?* These accumulations can be split when the parties are living apart if the payments follow a written separation agreement, court order, decree or judgment. The transfer must be made directly between the plans of the two spouses and one spouse cannot be disqualified because of age (over age 71).

☐ *Have you transferred the TFSA?* TFSA accumulations can also be split on a tax-free basis. The funds from one party's TFSA may be transferred tax-free to the other party's TFSA. This will have no effect on the contribution room of either of the parties.

☐ *How will Canada Pension Plan accumulations be divided and when?*

☐ *Are there inheritances to consider?* Property brought into the marriage by one of the spouses will be considered owned by that person. Generally the property is assigned to that person during the negotiation of the separation agreement. Have the transfer forms been completed?

☐ *Is a designation of principal residence required?* After separation, CRA recognizes two family units, and therefore it is possible for each to own one tax-exempt principal residence. Who will own each of those residences and what are their valuations?

☐ *Have valuations been completed for the transfer of other property?* Property can be transferred on relationship dissolution at its Adjusted Cost Base, or Undepreciated Capital Cost in the case of depreciable property so that there are no tax consequences at the time of transfer. These rules effectively transfer any accrued gains on the property to the transferee.

By special election, assets may be transferred at their Fair Market Value. This could result in significant tax savings if, for example, the transferor had unused capital losses to apply to gains on the transferred property. Have the valuations been completed?

Where this election is made, the transferee receives a significant tax benefit in that future capital gains will be calculated based on the FMV at the time of transfer. Further, if the FMV of the property is less than its ACB, it may be advantageous to trigger the capital loss. This would allow the transferor to offset other capital gains of the year, the previous three years or capital gains realized in the future.

Also remember to take into account any capital gains election the individuals may have made in February 1994 and apply the increased adjusted cost base in calculating the tax consequences of property transfers resulting from the relationship breakdown. Do you have a copy of the T664 election form?

This checklist should help you to avoid expensive and unchangeable surprises at tax time and beyond when your most important relationships unravel due to separation and divorce.

Death of a Taxpayer. To everything there is a season, and for many, under-standing the tax consequences of death on personal and family net worth is a crowning achievement that allows for a powerful wealth transition. This type of preparedness, unfortunately, is rare.

While no personal wealth management plan can be completed without a plan for transferring assets to the next generation, the majority of Canadians are reluctant to discuss the transfer of their assets with family members and many don't have a will. But to paraphrase Benjamin Franklin, death and taxes are perhaps the only two constants we can count on from the moment of birth… and it pays well to be prepared for the inevitable.

Here's the tax secret > You can plan to transfer your assets on a
tax-efficient basis throughout your lifetime, to take advantage of
the highs and lows in economic cycles, and to preserve most of your
wealth at your death. Without those plans, however, you could lose
half of it.

A lifetime of complicated personal relationships makes the transition of wealth more difficult. That's why we look to significant legal documents—your will, power of attorney, and health care directives as well as your signifi-cant financial documents—the personal net worth statement, tax returns and your financial plans, for guidance.

Whether you are already alone or preparing to be alone, protecting your assets at the time of death is an important obligation to your family as well as society. Consider the following checklist for starting an estate plan:

Objectives for Starting an Estate Plan

☐ *Identify financial institutions.* Where are your assets held? Include key contacts.

☐ *Identify advisors.* Who are your professional advisors including banker, accountant, lawyer, stockbroker, insurance agent and what is their contact info?

☐ *Identify proxies.* Who will exercise Power of Attorney if you become disabled or cannot direct your own personal affairs?

☐ *Identify heirs.* List exact contact information, as well as their relation-ship to you. In the case of singles, these heirs could include your favorite charity. Discuss options for the transfer of assets and funds during your lifetime and at death.

☐ *Identify gifts.* Sketch out what you wish for each of your heirs to receive.

☐ *Identify needs.* Will any of your heirs require assistance with ongoing income?

☐ *Identify executors.* Prepare a list of possible executor(s) and make approaches.

☐ *Identify guardians.* Prepare a list of those to whom you would trust the care of your minor children, as well as those who should not have that responsibility.

☐ *Identify business succession plans.* How should your business interests be distributed, and who should step in to run the show?

☐ *Plan for probate fees and capital gains taxes at death.* Review life insurance policies that may be used for those purposes.

☐ *Identify capital assets and their fair market value annually.*

☐ *Identify asset transfer instructions.* Which assets should be transferred during your lifetime, and which should be transferred only upon your death?

☐ *Make plans for safekeeping.* Keep all important documents in a safety deposit box and identify the location.

☐ *Deal with debt.* Cleaning up spilled milk is no fun for anyone... especially if it's been there for a while. List debt obligations and the order they should be repaid. Make a list of ongoing financial obligations that should be cancelled on death.

☐ *Draw up your will.* Tell your lawyer where it is to be kept.

Tax Filing Deadlines at Time of Death. When someone dies, one mandatory final return must filed for the period January 1 to date of death, and this return must be filed by the later of:

- April 30 of the year immediately following the year of death
- six months after date of death

There are several "elective returns" that can be filed on death, which will allow you to claim against certain personal amounts, to result in a substantial tax benefit.

Note, however, the final return from January to date of death is usually the only one most taxpayers will file. On that return, income earned up to date of death is reported. Certain income sources may have to be "prorated" to the date of death, including interest, rents, royalties, or annuity income. Offsetting expenses are accrued to date of death in a similar fashion.

By far, however, the most significant transaction on the final return could revolve around the disposition of capital assets. That's because a deemed disposition of your assets is considered to have taken place immediately before your death.

When you die, you are deemed to have disposed of your assets immediately before death, usually at Fair Market Value (FMV). However, the value of the deemed disposition can vary, depending on who will acquire the assets… your spouse (including common-law partner), child or another. Transfers to children or others are generally made at the property's FMV; transfers to spouse can be at the asset's adjusted cost base (or UCC in the case of depreciable assets) or FMV.

The use of "tax-free rollovers." The deemed disposition rules on death of the taxpayer therefore override the Attribution Rules that apply while living. That is, capital property transferred to the spouse on your death will not be taxed until your spouse disposes of the property. The spouse will use your adjusted cost base, and pay tax on the full gain from the time you acquired the asset, thereby completely postponing the tax consequences at the time of your death until your spouse dies or sells the property.

Depending on your taxable income at the time of your death, your executor may wish to roll over assets to the spouse on a tax-free basis, or have them transfer at fair market value. Fair value may make sense if your income in the year of death is low or if you have unused capital losses from the past that have been carried forward. Such balances can often be used to offset income created by the higher valuations that have accrued to the date of death. It will also provide your surviving spouse with the opportunity to start with a higher adjusted cost base on the acquisition of your assets, which will save them money down the line as well.

Be sure to provide your executor with a copy of the 1994 tax return and in particular Form T664 *Capital Gains Election* upon which a capital gains election may have been made to use up your $100,000 Capital Gains Exemption. This will affect the calculation of the deemed disposition of capital properties on the final return.

In the absence of those plans, capital gains or losses resulting from the deemed disposition of your assets on death must be reported, together with any recapture or terminal loss on depreciable assets, with the resulting tax payable (if any) on that return.

RRSPs and other pensions. Didn't spend it all? What happens when you die and leave unspent accumulations in your RRSP, PRPP or RRIF?

You are deemed to have received the fair market value of all assets in those plans immediately prior to death. If there is a surviving spouse or common-law partner the assets may be transferred tax-free to that person's registered plan. In certain circumstances, the accumulations can be transferred to a financially dependent child or grandchild, even when there is a surviving spouse. Speak to your tax advisors about these options.

If there is no surviving spouse or common-law partner, the assets are trans-ferred to the estate and the full value of the RRSP or RRIF is included in income on the final return. Since 2009, any decrease in value of RRSP assets while held in the estate may be used to decrease the income reported on the deceased's final return. Similar rules will apply to accumulations in PRPPs.

Starting in 2011 and 2012, we have also seen several surtaxes added to new provincial tax brackets designed to "tax the rich." Unfortunately those brackets also seem to catch the unspent accumulations in registered plans such as RRSPs and RRIFs and therefore represent a new estate tax. Be sure you plan your withdrawals carefully throughout your lifetime to generate your taxes on these accumulations at the lower tax brackets or risk losing half the amounts above the high income bracket levels.

Example > Wilhelm was a widower, living in Ontario. When he passed away in May 2012, the value of his RRSP assets was $400,000. In addition, he owned a rental property with an accrued capital gain of $100,000 and had income for the year of $35,000. Because Wilhelm had no spouse, the value of his RRSP assets plus the capital gain on his rental property are added to his other income for the year. The result is a taxable income of $535,000. Beginning in July 2012, Ontario implemented a new tax bracket designed to "tax the rich." This bracket begins at taxable income of $500,000 so Wilhelm will be subject to this new tax on $35,000 of his income.

Tax-Free Savings Accounts. Accumulated earnings in your TFSA are not taxable, but earnings after death no longer accumulate tax-free. However the assets may be rolled over to the TFSA of a surviving spouse or common-law partner.

Life Insurance Policies. Death generates numerous tax consequences which can be expensive, particularly for single taxpayers. To preserve wealth, however, the acquisition of a life insurance policy can make some sense and can lead to numerous tax advantages, especially if deemed dispositions of capital assets result in a hefty tax bill.

Note, when an individual buys an insurance policy, the premium is not deductible. But, subsequent benefits or proceeds paid out to beneficiaries are tax exempt.

Income earned within whole life or universal life insurance policies will generally accumulate on a tax exempt basis provided that the policies have a limitation on the size of the investment component. These features should be discussed with your insurance advisor. The proceeds from a life insurance policy can help to pay the taxes which arise on the deemed disposition of taxable assets as at the date of death.

Tax Strategy

Your most important relationships can be complicated from a tax point of view when there is a change due to life events. It makes sense to prepare early for your terminal wealth at the time of divorce or death by assessing the value of your assets and tax consequences when life changes. At the end of the day, this is about the financial well-being of your economic units and a collaborative, strategic approach can help you remove emotion to get the results you will need and want for your future.

Be sure to see your tax, financial, and legal advisors for help with this. Don't hesitate to see a grief counselor when you lose the ones you've loved, and find yourself single again. It may ultimately be very expensive if acting on your own brings unintended tax results.

Essential Tax Facts

Follow these simple rules to take charge:

Transfer RRSP or Other Registered Assets to Your Spouse Tax-Free. Either at death, or through a court-ordered transfer, registered accounts can be transferred to a former spouse on a tax-free basis.

Transfer Your Spouse's TFSA Assets to Your Own TFSA. Either at death or on separation or divorce, TFSA assets received from your spouse that are not needed immediately may be transferred to your own TFSA even if you don't have TFSA contribution room.

Transfer Capital Assets to Your Spouse Tax-Free. While most asset transfers result in a deemed disposition at fair market value and result in a taxable capital gain, court-ordered transfers and transfers to your spouse at death may be made on a tax-free basis.

Use Your Deceased Spouse's Tax Free Zone and Any Loss Carryforwards by triggering capital gains on asset transfers. This will reduce your capital gains tax when you actually dispose of the assets (or when you die).

Minimize Tax on Asset Transfers to Your Children. Transfer of capital assets to your children will result in a deemed disposition and a resulting capital gain as the transfer will be at the fair market value of the assets. Where possible, time transfers to minimize the gain by transferring when market values are depressed or, if values are increasing, transfer in life rather than at death when the value will be higher.

Minimize Capital Gains Tax at Death by Donating Publicly Traded Securities. The capital gains inclusion rate for donated public securities is zero so if you're making a bequest, be sure to donate stocks rather than cash to avoid capital gains tax on the donated shares.

Use Life Insurance to Provide a Tax-Free Inheritance to Your Children. There is no tax on life insurance proceeds. Be sure to have enough life insurance to at least pay the taxes on your final return so that your assets do not have to be sold to pay the taxes. In some cases taxes can be deferred until the sale of assets has occurred however; speak to your tax advisor about this option.

Concluding Thoughts

Half a century ago, Finance Minister Edgar Benson, responding to a report by a royal commission and the public debate it generated, introduced a framework and guiding principles for a tax system we still follow. It was ground-breaking for its time, as it introduced, amongst other things, a tax on capital gains and other measures that would redistribute the tax burden and along the way raise 5% more revenues in the first five years.

The ideals of this new tax system, importantly, set standards for fairness and equity[16] and a goal for greater simplification, which, as we all know, is the great and illusive challenge when it comes to anything tax-related. They included the following goals:

- Fairness in taxation implies that people in similar circumstances should carry similar shares of the tax load.
- People with higher incomes should be expected to pay a larger share of their incomes than those with lower incomes.
- "Ability to pay" is embodied mainly in personal income tax as a progressive graduated tax.
- The tax system should be simple enough for the vast majority of taxpayers to willingly comply with the law, and understand it, while trusting an efficient and impartial tax department to administer it.
- The tax system should not interfere seriously with economic growth and productivity... while taxes cannot promote all economic goals, they should not interfere with incentives to work and invest.

Since then, successive governments have indeed used the tax system to promote economic and social goals, as well as raise and collect taxes, and

---

[16] Proposals for Tax Reform, Hon. E. J. Benson Minister of Finance 1969.

redistribute income. The by-product of all this fairness and equity, unfortunately, is complexity.

There are indeed lots of tactical tax secrets and essential tax facts when it comes to tax preparation. And, unfortunately, managing how big your tax refund will be is all about the small stuff. Whether or not you prepare your own tax return, you do need to know about the seemingly endless and obscure deductions and credits that change continuously.

Why? Because while governments use tax policy in reaction to economic and demographic change, and their own needs to fund the social policies of the day, your responsibility as a taxpayer is that of self-assessment and the payment of the resulting taxes on time.

But your responsibility to your family is to arrange your affairs within the framework of the law to pay the least taxes possible and benefit the most from available income redistribution opportunities in the form of tax credits and social benefits. By doing so, you will be successful at building sustainable wealth with purchasing power, which will allow you and your family members to take charge and be self-reliant.

We live in the best country in the world and it is a privilege to contribute by paying our fair share of taxes. But it's by paying the correct amount—no more—that we can enjoy the power of the time value of money. Tax efficiency helps families put more money to work in their investments sooner, so they can thrive even in the worst of personal, financial and economic events, and help each other out as a strong community, when that is needed.

That's been the key take away for me, as I have studied taxation over the years.

I sincerely hope this book has helped you seize new financial opportunities, understand how to build more tax-efficient capital, and ask better questions of the tax and financial professionals you are working with so you can better manage what counts: the financial results that enable you to live a rich, full and meaningful life in the way you want to lead it.

Yours in tax savings,
Evelyn Jacks

Appendices

Appendix 1. What's New in Tax?

The following tax changes should be taken into account when taking charge of your tax filings and also tax planning activities with your advisors.

Changes for Employees

There are several changes relating to the reporting of benefits at work and statutory deductions:

CPP Contributions. The basic exemption for CPP remains at $3,500 which means you don't have to make CPP contributions on the first $3,500 of earnings you make.

Above that, in 2012, you'll have to contribute to CPP 4.95% of your earnings, to a maximum of $2,306.70 (based on pensionable earnings of up to $50,100). Your employer will match your contribution.

If you're self-employed, you'll have to contribute 9.9% of your earnings, to a maximum of $4,613.40 to CPP.

Employment Insurance Rates. If you earn less than $2,000, you are not required to pay EI premiums (unchanged). However, if you earn more in 2012, you be required to pay premiums of 1.83%[17] of your earnings to a maximum of $839.97 (based on insurable earnings of $45,900). Your employer will have to pay 140% of your premiums so the maximum employer premium for 2012 is $1,175.96.

---

[17] Rates for Quebec employees vary. The Quebec premium rate is 1.47% for 2012.

EI Benefit Clawback. If you become unemployed, you may be collecting EI Benefits and those are reportable on Line 119 from the information on a T4E slip. A clawback of regular benefits reported is possible when net income exceeds $57,375 in 2012. This is deducted on Line 235 and added to taxes on line 422.

Group Sickness and Accident Insurance Plans. Employer contributions made to a plan after March 28, 2012 to a plan that relate to coverage after 2012 will now be taxable to you and included in income in 2013. However, contributions to a wage-loss replacement benefit payable on a periodic basis will continue to be a tax-free benefit. This will apply however to premiums paid for critical illness or dismembership insurance where benefits are provided in a lump sum.

Lumps Sums in Lieu of Health/Dental Coverage. As of 2012, lump sum amounts received in lieu of health and/or dental coverage will no longer be considered to be a tax-free reimbursement of future medical expenses and will be taxable when received. These will be reported to you on a T4A slip. However, if your employer became insolvent prior to 2012 and these lump sum payments are received in a later year, the amounts paid to you will remain non-taxable even though they are received after 2011.

Employee Profit Sharing Plans (EPSPs). A special tax at the top marginal rate will be charge to a "specified employee" for contributions to an employee profit sharing plan if that the contribution exceeds 20% of the employee's salary received in the year. A "specified employee" is an employee who has a significant equity interest in the employer or who does not deal "at arm's length" with the employer. These would generally be family members who are shareholders in and employees of a private corporation. Where this tax is applied, a deduction will be allowed for the excess EPSP contribution so that it is not taxed twice.

Phase Out of Overseas Employment Tax Credit (OETC). This is a credit of 80% of an employee's tax on qualifying income to a maximum of $80,000, but it will be phased out from 2013 to 2016, so anyone negotiating a contract to work on an oil rig, for example, needs to know about this in advance to properly determine source deductions. To qualify for the OETC, the individual Canadian resident must be working abroad for at least six consecutive months for a specified employer on a construction, installation, agricultural, engineering or resource-based contract. For 2013, 60% of the tax on qualifying income up to $60,000 will be claimed; in 2014 the figures are 40% on $40,000 and in 2015 they are 20% on $20,000. Use form T626 to do these calculations. This will not affect 2012 returns or contracts which were committed to in writing by March 29, 2012.

Changes for Students

There are several important recent tax issues for students:

Exam Fees. Students can now claim certain exam fees if the exams are written to get a professional status recognized by the federal or provincial governments or required to qualify as a licensed or certified tradesperson. The claim is based on a calendar, not an academic year, and fees must be over $100.

Foreign Studies. For the purposes of claiming the tuition, education and textbook amount, the minimum qualifying time for a course of studies for full-time students studying abroad falls from 13 to three consecutive weeks. This will also be the minimum duration for the purposes of taking Education Assistance Payments under a Registered Education Savings Plan (RESP), starting in 2011 and subsequent years.

RESP Sharing with Siblings. Tax free transfers will be allowed between individual RESPs for siblings without triggering a repayment of the Canada Education Savings Grant, so long as the receiving beneficiary is under 21 at the time of the transfer. This rule has been in effect for tax years after 2010.

Rollovers of RESPs to RDSPs. Beginning in 2014, the current RESP rollover provisions to RRSPs will be extended to rollovers to Registered Disability Savings Plans (RDSPs). RESP investments, after Canada Education Savings Grants (CESGs) and Bonds (CESBs) have been repaid may be rolled over to an RDSP so long as the plan holder has sufficient RDSP contribution room. These contributions will not generate government contributions (CDSB or CDSGs). Withdrawals of rolled over RESPs will be taxable.

Provincial Tuition Rebate Programs. In an effort to retain graduates, provinces have recently begun to reimburse tuition paid to post-secondary graduates if they remain in the province. Saskatchewan will reimburse 100% of the tuition paid if the graduate remains in the province long enough, while Manitoba will reimburse up to 60%, and New Brunswick will reimburse 50%. This reimbursement is in addition to the credits allowed to students in the year that the tuition is paid (or in a later year if carried forward). For students who continue to live and work in the same province after graduation, the result is a reimbursement of more than the amount of tuition paid (in Manitoba and Saskatchewan).

Changes for Pensioners

As a result of a significant tax reform, the way Canadians contribute to and access their public and private pensions has changed significantly.

OAS Changes. The age eligibility for the Old Age Security (OAS) and Guaranteed Income Supplement (GIS) will be increased from age 65 to age 67 between in 2023 and 2029. The age eligibility for the Spouse's Allowance and Allowance for Survivors will also increase from age 60 to age 62 in the same period.

Option to Defer OAS. Starting on July 1, 2013, Canadians will have the option to defer receiving their OAS pension for up to five years. If you elect to do so you will receive a proportionately larger pension when you do start to receive it. This may enable you to withdraw other taxable amounts first, like deposits in an RRSP, in a more tax-efficient manner.

New Clawback Zones for OAS. The income thresholds at which OAS will be clawed back has increased due to indexing. This occurs when an individual's net income exceeds $69,562 and is completely eliminated when it reaches $112,966.

Canada Pension Plan Changes. The way you contribute to the Canada Pension Plan (CPP) changed in January 2012. If you are between 60 and 64 you must continue to contribute to CPP should you continue to work in this time, even if you are drawing benefits from the plan. From age 65 to 70 you may elect to opt out by filing a new form CPT30. (The self-employed will do this on Schedule 8 of the T1 return). In either case, additional contributions made will be saved in a "*Post Retirement Benefit*" (PRB) account to bump up your monthly pension benefits beginning the following year.

Maximum CPP Pension Benefits. The maximum regular benefits payable for 2012:

Circumstances	2012
Maximum Monthly Retirement Pension (At Age 65)	$986.67
Maximum Monthly Disability Pension	$1,185.50
Monthly Disabled Contributor Child Benefit (Flat Rate)	$224.62
Monthly Survivor's Pension Under Age 65	$543.82
Monthly Survivor's Pension Over Age 65	$592.00
Monthly Orphan's Benefit	$224.62
Monthly Combined Retirement (Age 65) and Survivor	$986.67
Monthly Combined Disability and Survivor	$1,185.50
Maximum Death Benefit	$2,500.00

Pooled Retirement Pension Plans (PRPP). This new type of pension plan was passed into law by the federal government in 2012 with provincial legislation to follow. The plan provides a voluntary and affordable alternative for small employers to offer an employer-sponsored pension plan at work, and addresses calls in some circles to increase contributions to the CPP. The contribution levels will mirror those available under the Registered Pension Plan (RPP) defined contribution or money purchase rules.

Registered Pension Plans (RPP). These are employer-sponsored private pension plans, and the amounts contributed by employees are shown on the T4 slip and are tax deductible according to the type of plan in which they participate. The contribution limit for a defined contribution (money purchase) RPP is $23,820 for 2012. The maximum pension benefit for a defined benefit plan is $2,647 for 2012.

Registered Retirement Savings Plan (RRSP) Contribution Limits. The additional amount a taxpayer can contribute to an RRSP is based on 18% of last year's earned income to a dollar maximum. For 2012 the maximum additional contribution room earned is $22,970 if your 2011 earned income was $127,611 or more. If your 2012 earned income is $132,333 or more you've earned the maximum $23,820 contribution room for 2013.

Individual Pension Plan (IPP) Rules. Individual Pension Plans are established for an owner-manager who is an employee of his or her own corporation. In the past, when a commuted value of a Registered Pension Plan was transferred to an IPP, a great deal of the value of the plan became pension surplus that did not have withdrawal requirements. Starting in 2012, annual minimum amounts will be required to be withdrawn from the IPP once the plan member is 72, similar to the current rules under the Registered Retirement Income Fund (RRIF).

Also, contributions related to past years of employment will now have to come from RRSP or RPP assets or by reducing RRSP contribution room, before deductible contributions to an IPP can be made.

Changes to German Pension Filing Rules. If you receive German social security pension it's reportable in Canada, but you may qualify to claim a partial exempt portion. You also have filing obligations in Germany. A German tax return is no longer necessary but a declaration of income is. A tax will automatically be applied, unless you are a low income earner. Check this new filing requirement with a tax advisor who is well versed in the new rules.

New Registered Disability Savings Plan (RDSP) Rule Changes. There are extensive changes to the RDSP rules. In 2008 this new saving plan was introduced, designed to accumulate private pension funds for the benefit of a disabled person. RDSPs function in very much the same way as RESPs do in that contributions are not tax deductible, earnings accumulate on a tax deferred basis and the government contributes grants and bonds to enhance savings. Any person eligible to claim the Disability Amount can be the beneficiary of an RDSP and the plan can be established by them or by an authorized representative.

Anyone can contribute to an RDSP—they need not be a family member. Accumulated investment income, grants and bonds are taxable in the hands of the beneficiary as withdrawn, are reported in Box 131 of a T4A slip, and on Line 125 of the tax return. There is no annual limit on contributions but lifetime contributions cannot exceed $200,000.

New Rules on Withdrawals. Contributions are permitted until the end of the year in which the disable beneficiary turns 59. The beneficiary must start to withdraw funds from the RDSP in the year he or she turns 60. Maximum annual withdrawal amounts are to be established based on life expectancies, but where a beneficiary has a shortened life expectancy, a repayment of grants and bonds will not be required if a Disability Assistance Payment (DAP) up to a specified limit is made to the beneficiary. Only the beneficiary and/or the beneficiary's legal representatives can withdraw amounts from an RDSP.

Where it is not clear whether the disabled individual is contractually competent and they do not have a legal representative, certain family members (spouse or common-law partner or parent) will be allowed to become the plan holder for the disabled adult. If subsequently it is determined that the disabled individual is able to enter into a contract, they will replace the family member as the plan holder. Where the disabled individual is found not to be contractually competent, a legal representative of the disabled individual may replace the family member as the plan holder. This measure will be in effect until December 31, 2016.

Repayment of Grants and Bonds. For withdrawals from RDSPs after 2013, the "10-Year Replacement Rule" will be replaced with a "Proportional Repayment Rule." Under the old rule, if any amount is withdrawn from the RDSP any CDSG and CDSB amounts received in the past ten years must be repaid (except for SDSPs). Under the new rule, the repayment amount will be the lesser of

- the amount removed x 3 and
- the amount of the CDSG and CDSB amounts received in the past ten years.

Maximum Annual Limits for Withdrawals. For withdrawals made after 2013, the maximum Lifetime Disability Assistance Payment (LDAP) will be increased to no less than 10% of the fair market value of the assets in the plan at the beginning of the year. Where the maximum amount under the existing LDAP formula exceeds 10% of the asset value, then the maximum is the amount determined under the LDAP formula.

Termination of RDSPs When Beneficiary no Longer Disabled. When an RDSP beneficiary ceases to qualify for the Disability Amount, currently, the RDSP must be terminated immediately. Beginning in 2014, when this happens, the beneficiary may make an election to continue the plan for up to four calendar years after the end of the calendar year in which the beneficiary ceases to be eligible for the Disability Amount. During the election period:

- No contributions will be permitted.
- No new CDSB or CDSGs will be paid into the plan.
- Withdrawals will be permitted subject to the new Proportional Repayment Rule.

Current RDSPs which would be required to be terminated before 2014 will not be required to be terminated until the end of 2014.

Changes for Investors

There is one of note for those who invest in common and preferred shares:

Dividend Gross-Up and Tax Credit. Because of recent changes to corporate taxation rates, the treatments of dividends on the personal tax return has also changed to better integrate the corporate and personal tax systems to avoid double taxation. As a result, after 2011 the dividend gross-up on "eligible dividends" from public and large corporations is 38% and the dividend tax credit that offsets this is 15.02% of the grossed-up amount. Dividends from small business corporations on income that qualified for the small business deduction will continue to be grossed up by 25% and the dividend tax credit will be 13⅓% of the grossed-up amount.

Changes for Business Owners

The purpose of this book is to discuss changes for those who file personal tax returns, and so the reader is directed to the book *Make Sure It's Deductible* by Evelyn Jacks for a review of the tax provisions specific to the self-employed. However we'd like to include in this list of changes the following:

Hiring Credit for Small Businesses. A credit of up to $1,000 is calculated and applied by CRA as an offset to Employment Insurance premiums paid by employers if total premiums were $10,000 or less and if they increased in 2012 over 2011.

All Taxpayers

The tax return, for many, is the most important financial transaction of the year. It's important to understand how you are taxed and why you need to file: the following changes are specific to the federal T1 *Income Tax and Benefits Return*, so named because we use it to both reconcile and pay our taxes for 2012 but also to apply for social benefits like the Canada Child Tax Benefits and the Goods and Services Tax Credit as well. But remember, you will also complete the provincial tax forms depending on where you live. The provinces and the feds have a common definition of net and taxable income, but beyond this, refundable and non-refundable tax credits, tax brackets and tax rates will vary.

Tax Brackets. The Federal tax brackets have been indexed for inflation. The indexation factor for 2012 is 2.8%. (Most provincial governments have indexation adjustments as well on the provincial calculations).

2012 Brackets	2012 Rates
Up to $10,822	0%
$10,823 to $42,707	15%
$42,708 to $85,414	22%
$85,415 to $132,406	26%
Over $132,406	29%

New Federal Refundable and Non-Refundable Tax Credits. For indexed changes to these credits for 2012 see the Summary of Personal Amounts later in this appendix. In addition, note:

- **Transferring and Splitting Children's Benefits.** If you are a single parent, you can now also transfer the Universal Child Care Benefit (UCCB) to the return of the child you are claiming as the "eligible dependant." But, this tax trick only works to your advantage when you are in a higher tax bracket than the child. If you're a single parent with taxable income over the lowest tax bracket and you receive the Universal Child Care Benefit, you may be able to reduce your taxes by transferring that income to the return for the child you claim as an "eligible dependant."

  Also, if you have arranged for joint custody, each parent can apply to receive equal shares of the Canada Child Tax Benefit (CCTB), the Universal Child Care Benefit and the GST/HST Credit the month following the change in marital status. File form RC65 to inform the tax department of the change.

- **Family Caregiver Amount.** See Summary of Personal Amounts chart in this appendix. This credit adds $2,000 to five non-refundable tax credits on the return, where appropriate, if the dependant is mentally or physically infirm. If the dependant is under 18, he or she will be considered infirm only if they are likely to be dependent on others for significant assistance, for a long and continuous period of time or indefinite duration.

- **New Medical Expense Claims.** The $10,000 restriction on medical expenses claimed if you looked after a dependant adult has been waived effective the 2011 tax year. It was $10,000 previously, per dependant. There are lots of expenses that can be claimed—often missed are batteries in a hearing aid and home and driveway modifications to accommodate the newly disabled. For 2012 and subsequent years, the costs of blood coagulation monitors for use by individuals who require anti-coagulation therapy, including associated disposable peripherals such as pricking devices, lancets and test strips if prescribed by a medical practitioner may be claimed.

- **Donations to Foreign Charitable Organizations.** For gifts to foreign charitable organizations to be eligible for the donation tax credit, the organization must be a "qualified donee." Currently, the Canadian government must donate to these organizations for them to qualify. Beginning in 2013, foreign organizations that pursue activities:

  - related to disaster relief or urgent humanitarian aid or
  - in the national interest of Canada

  may apply to receive "qualified donee" status even if they do not receive a donation from the government of Canada.

Changes for Tax Credit Filers. The benefits payable as well as the income thresholds used to determine your benefits under the federal refundable and non-refundable tax credits have been indexed to inflation. A chart to summarize the amounts and their clawback zones follows. The clawback refers to the level of income at which those tax credits will be reduced.

In addition, beginning after June 30, 2011, CRA requires notification from recipients of the Canada Child Tax Benefit at the end of the month following the month in which a marital status occurs, similar to the rules under the GST/HST Credit. The amount of the credit will be adjusted immediately to take into account the new family net income. In the case of a separation, do not notify CRA until you have been separated for a continuous period of at least 90 days as the separation is deemed not to have occurred if you reconcile within 90 days.

The Benefit Year: The GST Credit and Child Tax Benefit are based on a July to June benefit year. Income levels quoted are for net income from the previous taxation year. Rates for the specified time period are indexed based on the consumer price index for the prior December.

Split Child Benefits: Note that after *June 2011*, each parent who lives with the child can receive 50% of any GST Credit and Child Tax Benefits. Each parent will want to invest these benefits in the name of the child to build up a great education fund, but also to avoid tax on resulting investment earnings.

GST Credit

	July 2012 to June 2013	July 2011 to June 2012
Adult maximum	$260	$253
Child maximum	$137	$133
Single supplement	$137	$133
Phase-in threshold for the single supplement	$8,439	$8,209
Family net income at which credit begins to phase out	$33,884	$32,961

Child Tax Benefit

	July 2012 to June 2013	July 2011 to June 2012
Base benefit	$1,405	$1,367
Additional benefit for third child	$98	$95
Family net income at which base benefit begins to phase out	$42,707	$41,544
NCB[18]: First child	$2,177	$2,118
NCB: Second child	$1,926	$1,873
NCB: Third child	$1,832	$1,782
Family income at which NCB begins to phase out	$24,863	$24,183
Family net income at which NCB supplement phase-out ends	$42,707	$41,544
CDB[19] Maximum benefit	$2,575	$2,504
Family net income at which CDB begins to phase out	$42,707	$41,544

[18] NCB—National Child Benefit supplement
[19] CDB—Child Disability Benefit

Working Income Tax Benefit

2012 Rates	Most Provinces		British Columbia		Alberta		Nunavut	
Working Income Tax Benefit	Single Taxpayer	Family (or Single Parent)	Single	Family	Single	Family	Single	Family
Minimum earned income	$3,000	$3,000	$4,750	$4,750	$2,760	$2,760	$6,000	$6,000
Credit rate	25%	25%	21%	21%	20%	20%	5%	10%
Maximum credit	$970	$1,762	$1,206	$1,914	$1,059	$1,589	$608	$1,216
Clawback of income begins at	$11,011	$15,205	$12,059	$16,254	$11,535	$15,730	$20,973	$26,740
Clawback rate	15%	15%	17%	17%	15%	15%	4%	8%
Income for maximum credit	$6,880	$10,048	$10,493	$13,864	$8,055	$10,705	$18,160	$18,160
Credit fully clawed back at this maximum income	$17,478	$26,952	$19,153	$27,513	$18,595	$26,323	$36,173	$41,940

Summary of Personal Amounts for 2010 – 2012

Personal Amounts		2010	2011	2012
Basic Personal Amount	Maximum Claim[20]	$10,382	$10,527	$10,822
Age Amount	Maximum Claim[20]	$6,446	$6,537	$6,720
	Reduced by net income over[20]	$32,506	$32,961	$33,884
Spouse or Common-Law Partner Amount	Not infirm[20]	$10,382	$10,527	$10,822
	Infirm*	$10,382	$10,527	$12.822
Eligible Child under 18	Not infirm[20]	$2,101	$2,131	$2,191
	Infirm	$2,101	$2,131	$4,191
Amount for Eligible Dependants	Not infirm[20]	$10,382	$10,527	$10,822
	Infirm*	$10,382	$10,527	$12,822
Amount for Infirm Dependants	Maximum Claim[20]	$4,223	$4,282	$6,402
	Reduced by net income over[20]	$5,992	$6,076	$6,420
Pension Income Amt.	Maximum Claim	$2,000	$2,000	$2,000
Adoption Expenses	Maximum Claim	$10,975	$11,128	$11,440
Caregiver Amount	Not infirm	$4,223	$4,282	$4,402
	Infirm	$4,223	$4,282	$6,402
	Reduced by net income over	$14,422	$14,624	$15,033
Disability Amount	Basic Amount	$7,239	$7,341	$7,546
	Supplementary Amount[20]	$4,223	$4,282	$4,402
	Base Child Care Amount[20]	$2,473	$2,508	$2,578
Tuition and Education Amounts +Textbook Tax Credit	Minimum Tuition	$100	$100	$100
	Full-time Education Amount (per month)	$400 +$65	$400 +$65	$400 +$65
	Part-time Education Amount (per month)	$120 +$20	$120 +$20	$120 +$20
Medical Expenses	3% limitation[20]	$2,024	$2,052	$2,109
	Maximum claim for other dependants	$10,000	N/A	N/A
Refundable Medical Expense Credit	Maximum[20]	$1,074	$1,089	$1,119
	Base Family Income[20]	$23,775	$24,108	$24,783
	Minimum earned income[20]	$3,116	$3,179	$3,268
Canada Employment Amount	Maximum[20]	$1,051	$1,065	$1,095
Children's Fitness Amount	Maximum	$500	$500	$500
Home Buyers' Amount	Maximum	$5,000	$5,000	$5,000
Children's Arts Amount	Maximum	N/A	$500	$500

[20] These amounts are indexed

Clawback Zones For 2012

The following table shows clawback zones for personal amounts for 2012.

Credit	2012 Reduction Begins	2012 Credit Eliminated
OAS	$69,562	$112,966
EI	$57,375	Varies with EI amount
Age Amount	$33,884	$78,684
Spouse or Common-Law Partner Amount (not infirm)	$0	$10,822
Spouse or Common-Law Partner Amount (infirm)	$0	$12,822
Amount for Eligible Dependants (not infirm)	$0	$10,822
Amount for Eligible Dependants (infirm)	$0	$12,822
Amount for Infirm Dependants	$6,402	$12,822
Caregiver Amount (not infirm)	$15,033	$19,435
Caregiver Amount (infirm)	$15,033	$21,435

Appendix 2. Tax Acronyms

Acronym	Meaning
ACB	Adjusted Cost Base: used in calculating capital gains or losses
CCA	Capital Cost Allowance: a deduction for depreciation of income-producing assets
CCTB	Canada Child Tax Benefit: a refundable credit paid monthly to parents of children under 19. The benefit may also include the National Child Benefit supplement (NCB), and the Child Disability Benefit (CDB). The amount of the benefits depends on the number and age of the children. The NCB is clawed back at a lower income level than the basic CTB and the CDB.
CDB	Child Disability Benefit: a supplement to the Child Tax Benefit for children who are eligible for the disability amount.
CESG	Canada Education Savings Grant: an amount of up to $500 given to those who contribute to Registered Education Savings Plans for their children
CLB	Canada Learning Bond: an amount allocated to low-income children than can be transferred to an RESP.
CPI	Consumer Price Index: used in the calculation of indexing of tax provisions
CPP	Canada Pension Plan: a contributions-based public pension benefit system
CRA	Canada Revenue Agency: formerly Revenue Canada
CSB	Canada Savings Bonds: a fixed rate interest-bearing investment backed by the Canadian government
EI	Employment Insurance: a premium-based public insurance program for those who lose their source of employment income through no fault of their own
GIC	Guaranteed Investment Certificate: an interest bearing investment
GIS	Guaranteed Income Supplement: a supplement paid to low-income seniors to ensure a minimum income level. The GIS is not taxable.
GST	Goods and Services Tax: a federal tax on goods and services purchased in Canada

Acronym	Meaning
GSTC	Goods and Services Tax Credit: a refundable tax credit for low income families to offset the Goods and Services Tax
HBP	Home Buyers' Plan: a plan to allow individuals to borrow from their RRSPs to assist in a home purchase
HST	Harmonized Sales Tax: a single tax which incorporates the federal GST and a provincial sales tax
LLP	Lifelong Learning Plan: a plan to allow individuals to borrow from their RRSPs to assist in full-time education
LSIF	Labour-Sponsored Investment Fund: an investment fund which is registered federally and/or with a province and qualifies for the Labour-Sponsored Funds Tax Credit
LSFTC	Labour-Sponsored Funds Tax Credit: a non-refundable tax credit for investments in a Labour-Sponsored Funds
MTR	Marginal Tax Rate: the tax rate that will be applied to the next dollar of income earned. For accuracy, we often include in this rate the federal and provincial taxes and surtaxes as well as the clawback of refundable and non-refundable credits
NCB	National Child Benefit: a supplement to the Child Tax Benefit, meant for low income Canadian families and is clawed back at a fairly low income level
NR	Non-refundable: a credit that will reduce taxes payable, but will be lost if the credit exceeds the taxes. A refundable credit, by contrast, will be paid to the taxpayer if the credit exceeds taxes payable.
OAS	Old Age Security: a universal government pension for Canadians who are 65 or older. OAS begins to be clawed back when income exceeds a certain threshold
PRPP	Pooled Retirement Pension Plans: a new retirement vehicle, introduced in November 2011 to provide a registered savings opportunity for small companies and their employees who do not have access to RPPs.
RDSP	Registered Disability Savings Plan: a registered plan within which funds can be accumulated to provide a private pension option for the disabled.
RESP	Registered Education Savings Plan: a registered plan for accumulating funds for a child's education. Contributions to such a plan may qualify for the CESG.

Acronym	Meaning
RPP	Registered Pension Plan: a private pension plan funded by the employer and/or employee which is registered and qualifies for a tax deduction.
RRIF	Registered Retirement Income Fund: a registered fund which provides for the payment of an increasing portion of the funds in the plan each year until the taxpayer turns 90.
RRSP	Registered Retirement Savings Plan: a contribution based savings plan where contribution limits are based on earned income (to a pre-defined limit). Contributions to the plan are tax deductible, income earned within the plan is not taxed until withdrawn, and funds withdrawn from the plan are taxed at the taxpayer's current marginal rate.
SDSP	Specified Disability Savings Plan: an RDSP where the beneficiary's life expectancy is less than five years. Special rules apply to allow faster withdrawal of funds.
TFSA	Tax-Free Savings Account: an account to which taxpayers over age 18 may contribute. Contribution room increases by $5,000 (indexed) each year and both earnings and withdrawals from the accounts are not taxable.
UCCB	Universal Child Care Benefit: a taxable income support program of $100 per month per child under six.
WITB	Working Income Tax Benefit: a refundable credit calculated as 20% of earned income in excess of $3,000 but reduced as income levels pass a threshold amount. Several provinces have variations.

Appendix 3. Additional Resources
Excellence in Financial Education from Knowledge Bureau Newsbooks

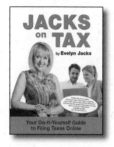

Jacks on Tax *by Evelyn Jacks*

It's back! *Jacks on Tax* is your simple, but comprehensive guide to filing your taxes online—but it's a "must have resource" for paper filers too. Learning to file your own tax return is smart and with tax software, quicker and easier than ever. It's an important life skill that will make you richer. If you want to file for the biggest possible refund, the most in refundable tax credits and the least taxes payable, get Canada's most trusted tax guide by Canada's most trusted tax educator, *so you can increase your financial freedom.* This important book is available at your favorite bookstore, or at knowledgebureau.com.

Managing the Bull: How to Detect and Deflect the Crap
by David Christianson

This is a must-read book for anyone who wants to develop the Winner's Mindset about money and is serious about financial freedom on his or her own terms. The book is inspiring, informative and impactful and, in some places, truly funny. Consumers need—more than ever—a proven path to follow. This book clears the roadblocks to smooth your financial journey. People are confronted today with confusion, noise and too much information. They want to cut through all of that bull, make the right decisions and take the right actions. *Managing the Bull* will empower you to embrace your successful financial future.

Also by Evelyn Jacks and co-authors Robert Ironside and Al Emid
Financial Recovery in a Fragile World

Better understand market volatility and its effects on your long-term goals. This is the perfect book to calm jittery nerves? You can fortify your financial decision-marking with this comprehensive guide to the new world economy and your place in it, written by three of Canada's leading authorities in tax-efficient wealth management.

Index